M is for (DATA) MONKEY

The Excel Pro's Definitive Guide to Power Query

by

Ken Puls &
Miguel Escobar

Holy Macro! Books
PO Box 541731
Merritt Island, FL 32953

M is for (Data) Monkey

Authors: Ken Puls and Miguel Escobar

Layout: Jill Bee

Copyediting: Kitty Wilson

Technical Editor: Roger Govier

Cover Design: Shannon Mattiza 6'4 Productions

Indexing: Nellie Jay

Ape Illustrations: Walter Agnew Moore

Cover Illustration: Irdan Teras

Published by: Holy Macro! Books, PO Box 541731, Merritt Island FL 32953, USA

Distributed by: Independent Publishers Group, Chicago, IL

First Printing: October, 2015

ISBN: 978-1-61547-034-1 Print, 978-1-61547-223-9 PDF, 978-1-61547-345-8 ePub, 978-1-61547-034-1 Mobi

LCCN: 2015940635

Table of Contents

Foreword How Power Query Changed Our Lives

Ken's Story: "Coffee & Power Query"

It's the name on the meeting in my Outlook calendar from back in November 2013. It was during one of the Microsoft MVP summits, the product had recently had its name changed from Data Explorer, and I was meeting with Miguel Llopis and Faisal Mohamood from the Power Query team over coffee to talk about the good and the bad of the tool from an Excel users' perspective.

In that conversation, I told them both that Power Query was great, but it was a lousy replacement for SQL Services Management Studio. I distinctly remember that part of the conversation. I'd been working with SSMS and Power Query a lot at the time, and was struggling with the fact that Power Query did some of the same tasks, but not all. I was frustrated, as I was struggling with the tool, trying to make it behave the same as SSMS, but it just wasn't doing it.

What happened after I laid out my concerns flipped my complaints on their head. I'm paraphrasing from my memory, but the response was something like this:

"Ken, this tool isn't a replacement for SSMS. We built this for Excel people... our intent is that they never need to use or learn SQL at all."

For anyone that knows me well, they know that I'm very seldom left speechless, but that was just about enough to do it. That statement upset the balance of my world.

Understand that I'm not a normal Excel pro. I know enough SQL to be dangerous, I'm extremely accomplished with VBA, and have working knowledge of VB.NET, C#, XML and a few other languages. And while I love technology and challenges, the true reason I know as many languages as I do today is that I taught myself out of necessity. Typically my needs were complicated, and that involved a painful journey of jumping into the deep end with a "sink or swim" approach.

No Excel pro should need to work with SSMS in order to get the data they need. But years of working with data and fighting issue after issue left me assuming that Power Query was an Excel focused replacement for that tool. It never occurred to me, somehow, that it was being designed to actually make the life of the Excel pro so much easier that they wouldn't even need to reach to SQL at all.

That meeting changed my view of Power Query forever. I took a step back and looked at it in a new light. And I started to use it as it was intended to be used... on its own, driving everything through the user interface, avoiding writing SQL wherever possible. And you know something... it started working better, it allowed me to go more places, it allowed me to solve things I'd never been able to do before.

I love this tool. Not because of what I can do with it, but because of how easy it makes it to get things done for a business pro without the need for coding. I love it because the people we teach pick it up rapidly and can add real value in an incredibly short amount of time. This product is truly centered around the Excel pro, allowing us to build complex solutions via one of the best user interface designs I've seen in a long time. And while we **do** teach the coding techniques in this book, the best part is that it's optional, just extending the capabilities further.

Miguel's Story: The Underdog

I truly don't remember the exact moment when I got introduced to Power Query. I believe it was early 2013 when I downloaded the tool and started playing with it. At first it just seemed like a neat tool that could help me transform data, but I still felt that Power Pivot was going to be the center of attention in the data story. Back then Power Query was called 'Data Explorer' and – like today – it focused on delivering a rich user interface, allowing you to do amazing things without ever needing to look at the code. Little did I know that this 'neat' tool would solve almost all of my data problems.

At first, Power Query might seem to you like what it seemed to me – just a guided end-user tool that can do some really cool data transformations. But then you'll realize the true power and flexibility that the Power Query engine brings to the table. Today, I feel that Power Query is as important as Power Pivot, as how you shape your data will ultimately determine how well your Power Pivot Data Model works.

Power Query is the new underdog of Business Intelligence tools. It's a major breakthrough in self-service Business Intelligence and data manipulation for the end-user or data steward. Our goal with this book is to change everyone's perspective of the tool forever.

This is the time for the underdog to rise and claim a victory – a victory for us all that work with data on a daily basis. A victory for those who want to make the data work for us and not the other way around.

Author Acknowledgements

As with any book, there are a bunch of people who are quite influential with making things happen. Without the influence of the people below, this book would never have come to fruition:

Bill Jelen – A lot of publishers would have laughed us out of the room with the title of this book, but Bill loved it. He's been incredibly enthusiastic, accommodating with the timeline, and we really appreciate his support.

Rob Collie – Rob is synonymous with Power Pivot and Power BI. He's also a friend, and the guy that suggested we (Ken & Miguel) work together and write a Power Query book. It's very likely that without Rob's prodding, this never would have happened.

Miguel Llopis – From the very first meeting over coffee, Miguel has been our go-to guy at Microsoft, even joking that his full time job is answering Ken's emails. He's been super supportive since day one, has responded to feature design requests, bugs and so much more. Viva el Atleti!

Roger Govier – A tech book isn't worth anything unless it's gone through a proper tech review. Every page of this book was reviewed by our friend Roger, and the book is so much better for it. From wording suggestions, to exposing issues, Roger's input was invaluable, even inspiring a whole new chapter in the process.

Matt Masson, Curt Hagenlocher, Gil Raviv, Faisal Mohamood, Miguel Martinez, Samuel Zhang and all the others on the Power Query/Power BI team that have answered our many questions and responded to our many emails. Your help and clarifications have been incredibly helpful in turning out the finished product.

Chris Webb and Bill Szysz for pushing the Power Query boundaries, as well as countless others that have commented on our blogs and videos in an effort to show different and better ways to accomplish solutions. Your creativity and alternate approaches have helped us explore new methods, develop techniques, and have a lot of fun with this program.

Ken would like to thank:

Over the past few months I've started my own consulting practice in addition to writing this book. None of that would have been possible without the support of my wife Deanna and my daughter Annika. Even more than being a rock in my corner, though, Deanna did the initial proof read of every page of this book, clearing up the odd wording that I sometimes write down when my brain is a paragraph further than my typing.

I don't think I could ever write a book without thanking my good friend and mentor Jim Olsen. I worked with Jim for 16 years, and the support and freedom he gave me to explore technology is the fundamental reason I am where I am today. He let me experiment with new technology, develop cutting edge solutions and test them in our work environment. Without that experience there is no way that I would have been able to develop the knowledge in order to complete this project.

I also want to thank my co-author, Miguel. It was Miguel's idea and energy that led to the creation of http://powerquery.training and the online workshop that we teach there. Without his devotion to the project, it would not have come to fruition. And without the workshop, we probably wouldn't have a book that is this well organized, this fluid, as the layout and material is based on the things we teach and have learned from that experience.

Miguel would like to thank:

I'd like to thank YOU for reading this. Yes...YOU! You're a crucial part of our main objective and our intention with this book is to provide you with the resources so you can become a Data Hero. I'd like to thank you in advance for making this world a better place – at least in the context of business decision making and the world of data. :-)

I'd also like to thank all of the Excel and BI practitioners worldwide that have shown their support towards our book and our Power Query related endeavors. It is truly an honor to be part of this worldwide community and I invite you to join us by simply using this tool.

Let's not forget about a crucial part of my life: Friends and Family. I'm not putting names in here as I'm afraid I might leave someone out of it – so I'm playing it safe here! :)

Special thanks to Ken for being extremely supportive and being able to overcome the language barrier at times with me! "Spanglish" gets me sometimes, yet Ken distinguishes what I'm trying to say and makes a better version of it.

Let's hope that Canada and Panama can go to the FIFA World Cup in 2018!

Members of the Power Query Revolution

We've received some incredible support from the Power Query community as well, including those who pre-ordered the book or attended our online workshop at http://powerquery.training/course (or both). Your support means so much to us! The following is a list of those people who jumped at the chance to be listed as part of the M is for Data Monkey supporters club:

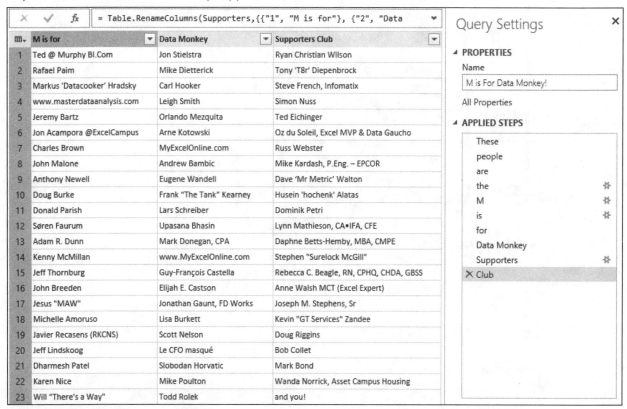

	M is for	Data Monkey	Supporters Club
1	Ted @ Murphy Bi.Com	Jon Stielstra	Ryan Christian Wilson
2	Rafael Paim	Mike Dietterick	Tony 'T8r' Diepenbrock
3	Markus 'Datacooker' Hradsky	Carl Hooker	Steve French, Infomatix
4	www.masterdataanalysis.com	Leigh Smith	Simon Nuss
5	Jeremy Bartz	Orlando Mezquita	Ted Eichinger
6	Jon Acampora @ExcelCampus	Arne Kotowski	Oz du Soleil, Excel MVP & Data Gaucho
7	Charles Brown	MyExcelOnline.com	Russ Webster
8	John Malone	Andrew Bambic	Mike Kardash, P.Eng. – EPCOR
9	Anthony Newell	Eugene Wandell	Dave 'Mr Metric' Walton
10	Doug Burke	Frank "The Tank" Kearney	Husein 'hochenk' Alatas
11	Donald Parish	Lars Schreiber	Dominik Petri
12	Søren Faurum	Upasana Bhasin	Lynn Mathieson, CA•IFA, CFE
13	Adam R. Dunn	Mark Donegan, CPA	Daphne Betts-Hemby, MBA, CMPE
14	Kenny McMillan	www.MyExcelOnline.com	Stephen "Surelock McGill"
15	Jeff Thornburg	Guy-François Castella	Rebecca C. Beagle, RN, CPHQ, CHDA, GBSS
16	John Breeden	Elijah E. Castson	Anne Walsh MCT (Excel Expert)
17	Jesus "MAW"	Jonathan Gaunt, FD Works	Joseph M. Stephens, Sr
18	Michelle Amoruso	Lisa Burkett	Kevin "GT Services" Zandee
19	Javier Recasens (RKCNS)	Scott Nelson	Doug Riggins
20	Jeff Lindskoog	Le CFO masqué	Bob Collet
21	Dharmesh Patel	Slobodan Horvatic	Mark Bond
22	Karen Nice	Mike Poulton	Wanda Norrick, Asset Campus Housing
23	Will "There's a Way"	Todd Rolek	and you!

And finally...

We'd like to thank YOU. For both buying the book, putting your trust in our teaching methods, and for becoming part of the Power Query movement.

This book was written for you, in an effort to help you master your data. We truly hope it does, and that you'll find it to be the most impactful Excel book you've ever purchased.

Chapter 0 Introduction: A New Revolution

Whether we are performing basic data entry, building simple reports, or designing full-blown business intelligence solutions using VBA, SQL, and other languages, we Excel pros all deal with data to a certain extent. Our skill sets vary greatly, but the overall jobs we are usually trying to perform include:

- Transforming data to meet our needs
- Appending one data set to another
- Merging multiple data sets together
- Enriching our data for better analysis

We may get tagged with the name "data monkey," but we are actually information workers. But no matter what we call ourselves in our formal job descriptions, our role is to clean up data and turn it into information. Our jobs may not be glorious, but they are essential, and without our work done correctly, the end results of any analysis are suspect.

While Excel has an amazing toolset to help us build business intelligence out of data, converting raw data into consumable data has been a challenge for years. In fact, it's this issue that we often spend most of our time on—prepping data for analysis and getting it into a nice tabular format to expose Excel's most powerful analytical and reporting tools.

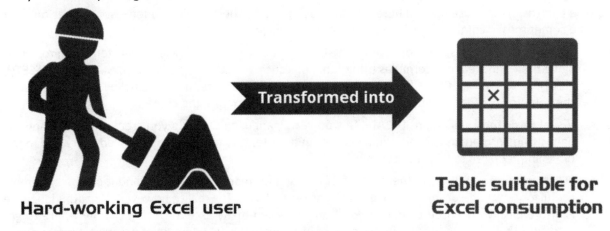

Figure 1 Behind the curtains, we are all information workers trying to reach our desired goal with data.

Despite the moniker "data monkey," we information workers are often more like data magicians. Our data seldom enters our world in a ready-to-consume format; it can take hours of cleaning, filtering, and reshaping to get things ready to go.

Once our data is prepared and ready, we can perform a vast array of powerful analytical processes with ease. Tools including conditional formatting, filters, pivot tables, charts, slicers, and more let us work magic and impress our audience.

But getting the data prepped and ready is the hard part. We're served dirty data, held in collections of text and Excel files (maybe a database, if we're *very* lucky), and we somehow have to clean it up and get it ready to use. Our end goal is simple: Get the data into an Excel table as quickly as possible, while making sure it is scoped to our needs and accurate. And every solution needs a different combination of data coming from different sources . . . which takes magic.

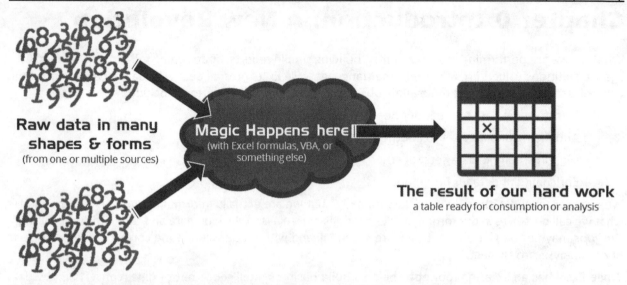

Figure 2 Black magic is what really happens to data before consumption.

The Benefits and Dangers of Black Magic

The true wizards of Excel use many different techniques to make their magic happen—sometimes on their own and sometimes in combination. These types of magic include:

- **Excel formulas**—These are some of the first techniques that the magician will often reach to, leveraging their knowledge of formulas using functions such as VLOOKUP(), INDEX(), MATCH(), OFFSET(), LEFT(), LEN(), TRIM(), CLEAN(), and many more. While formulas tend to be used by *most* Excel users, the complexity of these formulas varies by the user's experience and comfort.

- **Visual Basic for Applications (VBA)**—This powerful language can help you create powerful and dynamic transformations for your data. VBA techniques tend to be used by *advanced* users due to the discipline required to truly master them.

- **SQL statements**—SQL is another powerful language for manipulating data, and it can be extremely useful for selecting, sorting, grouping, and transforming data. The reality, however, is that this language is also typically only used by *advanced* users, and even many Excel pros don't know where to get started with it. This language is often thought of as being the sole domain of database professionals, although every Excel pro should invest some time in learning it.

All these tools have something in common: For many years, they were essentially the only tools available for cleaning and transforming data into something useful. Despite their usefulness, many of these tools also have two serious weaknesses: They require time to build a solution and time to master the techniques.

While it's true that truly savvy magicians can use these tools to build solutions to automate and import raw data in a clean format, this takes years of learning advanced languages as well as a significant amount of time scoping, developing, testing, and maintaining the solutions. Depending on the complexity of the solutions built, fixing the solutions for a minor change in the import format or extending them to embrace another source could be horrendous.

One hidden danger of having a true wizard in a company is that the person may build an incredible solution that works until long after he or she has left the company. At some point, though, others at the company realize that they don't understand the solution and don't have anyone to fix it when it eventually breaks.

On the flip side, many people tasked with this data cleanup didn't have time or opportunity to learn these advanced magic techniques. And while we could say that maybe they're better off never having a massive system collapse without anyone to fix it, instead they waste hours, days, weeks, months, and years of labor time and money performing repetitive data cleanup and imports on a regular basis.

Take a moment and think about how many hours are consumed on a monthly basis in your company simply performing repetitive data import and cleanup tasks in Excel. Multiply those hours by the average wage rate in your company . . . and by the number of companies in your industry worldwide and . . . you get the idea. The cost of productivity in this area is staggering.

Enter a product that tackles all these problems—one that is easy to learn and that others can pick up and understand with limited instruction. It's a product that lets you automate the import and cleanup of data, so you can focus on turning that data into information, adding true value to your company. That product is called *Power Query*.

The Future Transforms

Power Query solves the problems related to the toolsets just described. It is very easy to learn and has one of the most intuitive user interfaces we've ever worked with. It's easy to maintain, as it shows each step of the process, which you can review or update later. And everything done in Power Query can be refreshed with a couple of clicks.

We have spent years building solutions using black magic techniques, and we see Power Query as a game changer for many reasons. One of those is the speed with which it can be learned.

When it comes to importing, cleaning, and transforming data to get it ready for analysis, you can learn Power Query faster than you can learn Excel formulas, and it handles complex sources much more easily than VBA.

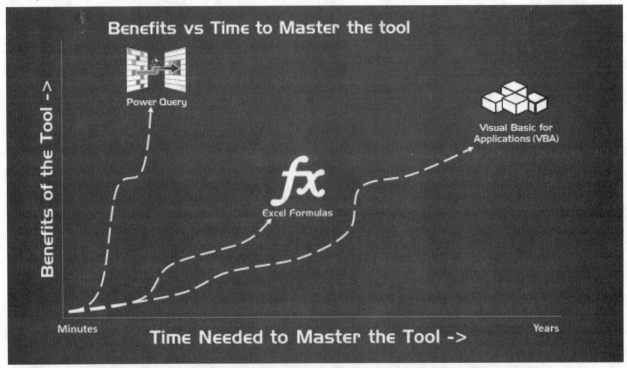

Figure 3 Power Query was designed to be an easy-to-use data transformation and manipulation tool.

Its ease of use makes Power Query the answer to the vanishing data magician problem that many businesses face. Even if a modern-day magician builds something complex in Power Query, you can have someone up to speed and able to maintain or fix the query with minimal training—we're talking hours, not weeks.

As hard as it is for true Excel pros to understand, many users actually don't *want* to master Excel formulas. They simply want to open up a tool, connect it to their data source, click a few buttons to clean it up and import it, and build the chart or report they need. It's for exactly this reason that Power Query can reach even further than formulas. With the menu-driven interface, in many cases a user can avoid ever having to learn a single formula or line of code.

TRANSFORMATION TOOLS REACH

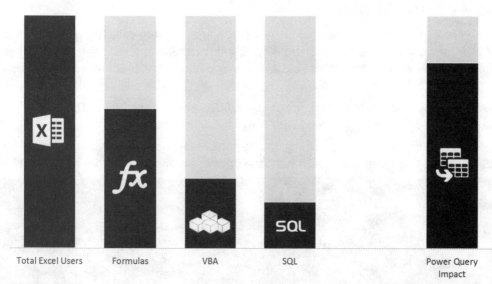

Figure 4 *Power Query's ease of use will impact more users than any of the classic methods.*

There is no doubt in our minds that Power Query will change the way Excel pros work with data forever.

We want to make it quite clear that we are not discounting the value of formulas, VBA, or SQL. In fact, we couldn't live without those tools. You can quickly knock out formulas to do many things outside the transformation context that Power Query will never do. VBA has a far greater reach in sheer capability and power, allowing you to reach to other applications, create programs to pull and push data, and so many other things. And a SQL query written by a SQL wizard will always be faster and better than one created by Power Query.

In the context of simply connecting to, cleaning, and importing data, however, Power Query offers more for less, allowing you to automate the job more quickly and in less time.

The good news for true wizards of data is that Power Query is *yet another tool* that you have access to. You can provide your own SQL queries if needed, refresh them with VBA when desired, load your Power Query–created queries directly to Power Pivot, and much more.

Why Power Query Is Magic

The number-one issue Excel pros face when building robust and stable solutions has been accessing, cleaning, and transforming the data. What we've needed, and yet many of us have never heard of, is an ETL tool—that is, a tool for extracting, transforming, and loading data.

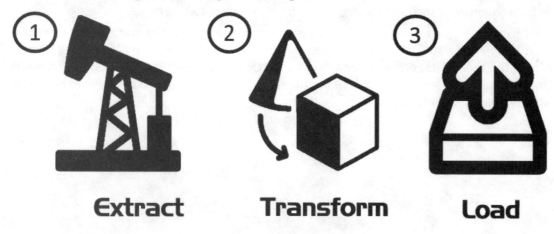

Figure 5 *ETL: extract, transform, load.*

Power Query is an ETL tool; its function is to **e**xtract data from almost any source, **t**ransform it as desired, and then **l**oad it. But what does that truly mean to us as Excel pros?

Extract

Extraction can be targeted against one or more data sources, including text files, CSV files, Excel files, databases, and web pages. In addition, the Power Query team has built many connectors to data sources that have otherwise been tough to get at—Microsoft Exchange, Facebook, Salesforce, and other Software-as-a-Service (SaaS) sources.

Transform

When we talk about transformation, we include each of the following areas:

- **Data cleaning**—Data cleaning could involve filtering out departments from a database or removing blank or garbage rows from a text file import. Other uses include changing cases from uppercase to lowercase, splitting data into multiple columns, and forcing dates to import in the correct format for a particular country. Data cleaning is anything you need to do to your data to clean it up so it can be used.

- **Data integration**—If you use VLOOKUP() or INDEX()/MATCH(), then you're probably integrating multiple data sets. Power Query can join data in either vertical or horizontal fashion, allowing you to append two tables (creating one long table) or merge tables together horizontally, without having to write a single VLOOKUP() function. You can also perform other operations, such as grouping.

- **Data enrichment**—These tasks include adding new columns or doing calculations over a data set. Power Query makes it easy to perform mathematical calculations like creating Gross Sales by multiplying Sales Quantity * Sales Price or add new formats of dates based on your transaction date column. In fact, with Power Query you can even create entire tables dynamically, based on the value in an Excel cell. Need a dynamic calendar table that runs five years back from today's date? Look no further than Power Query.

Power Query allows you to perform many transformations through menu commands rather than having to write formulas or code to do them. This tool was built for Excel pros, and with no coding experience whatsoever, you can use Power Query to perform transformations that would be incredibly complex in SQL or VBA. That's a great thing!

If you're the type of person who likes to get under the covers and tinker with formulas or code, however, you can. While there is no requirement to ever learn it, Power Query records everything in a language called M. (Languages A through L were taken.) And if you're a wizard who decides to take advantage of this language, you can build even more efficient queries and do even more amazing things than without it.

Load

With Power Query you can load data into one of four places:

- Excel tables
- The Power Pivot Data Model
- Power BI
- Connections only

The last point might seem a bit mysterious, but it simply means that you can create a query that can be used by other queries. This allows for some very interesting use cases that we'll explore more fully in the book.

While it's interesting to look at where the data loads, that really isn't the important part of the loading process in this ETL tool. It's *how* it loads or rather how to load it *again*.

Power Query is essentially a macro recorder that keeps track of every bit of the extract and transform steps. You can define a query once and determine where you'd like to load it. After you've done that, you can simply refresh your query to run it again.

Define once   Consume anytime

Figure 6 Define the transformation process once and consume anytime.

Consider this for a moment: You need a particular TXT file, and it takes you 20 minutes to import and clean it before you can use it. Power Query enables you to accomplish the same task in 10 minutes, which saves you 10 minutes the first time you use it. Then next month comes along, and you need the new version of the same TXT file. Without Power Query, you have to roll up your sleeves and relive the 20 minutes of Excel exuberance where you show Excel that you're a master at reliving the past, performing those exhilarating steps over and over again each month. Wait . . . you don't find that exhilarating? In that case, just save your new TXT file over the old one, go into Excel, and click Data → Refresh All. You're finished. *Seriously*.

This is where you see the real power of Power Query. It's easy to use, and it's also easy to *reuse*. It changes your hard work into an investment and frees up your time during the next cycle to do something worthwhile.

Power Query Versions

Before we tell you where to get Power Query, let's talk about the updates. Yes, that may seem like putting the cart before the horse, but there is a pretty solid reason for this.

The Update Cycle

The Power Query team releases monthly updates. We're not talking bug fixes (although those are certainly included); we're talking new features and performance enhancements. While some are small, others are much larger. In February 2014 the team added the ability to connect to Microsoft Exchange as a data source. In early 2015 the team released an update that cut query load time by 30%. In July 2015 the team released an update that solved some very serious issues with refreshing to Power Pivot.

Are there risks involved in installing the latest updates as soon as they become available? Sure there are. Bugs happen, particularly in complex software. But the reality is that the Power Query team works *very* hard to address serious bugs in the software. If you're particularly concerned, download the installer and save it rather than installing directly from the web. This will allow you to roll back if the need ever arises.

If you currently have Power Query installed, make sure you update it. This book was written using version 2.24, released in July 2015, and you should be on at least this update.

Where Do I Get Power Query?

The answer depends on the version of Excel that you have:

- **Excel 2010 and Excel 2013**—Download it from http://go.microsoft.com/fwlink/?LinkId=317450.
- **Excel 2016**—You already have Power Query installed, but the entry point is a bit different than in the Excel 2010 and Excel 2013 versions.
- **Power BI Desktop**—Wait, what? What does this have to do with Excel? A little and a lot, really. The short story is that Power BI Desktop is a standalone program for sourcing and modeling your data. As it happens, Power Query is the tool used to source and transform the data with Power BI Desktop, so you're going to be learning a skill in this book that is portable to other applications. The Power BI Desktop can be downloaded from www.powerbi.com.

Even though Power Query handles data sourcing for Power BI Desktop, this book is written by Excel pros *for* Excel pros. *Every solution in the pages of this book is illustrated with Excel.*

How to Use This Book

This book is intended to be your number-one resource for understanding Power Query and the M language from a practical point of view as an Excel pro. Our goal is to address Excel problems that Excel pros commonly face and show you how to use Power Query to solve them. We also cover some more advanced scenarios as well, incorporating Power Query and M best practices throughout, to help you understand not only how to build Power Query solutions but how to make them last.

The Learning Map

After working with Power Query for a long time, we've come up with a method that we believe is the optimal way to teach how to use this incredible tool. It's one that we've tested and refined in our online http://powerquery.training workshops, and it involves carefully layering techniques that build on each other. The learning map is shown below.

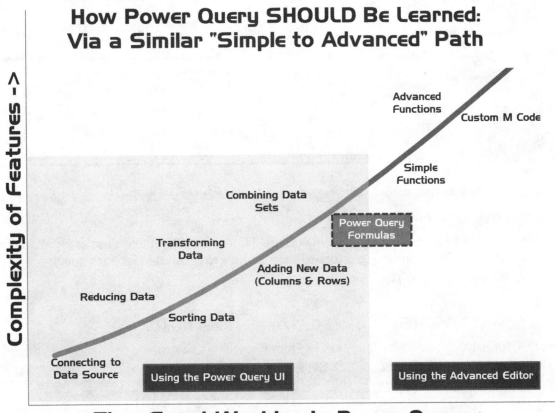

Figure 7 An optimal learning path to master Power Query and the M language.

Where to Find the Power Query Commands

Power Query was initially released after Excel 2013 as a free add-in for Excel, and it was (rather shockingly) backward compatible with Excel 2010. In both of those versions, a unique ribbon tab holds all the Power Query commands.

Because Power Query is so incredibly useful, it only made sense to integrate the tool into Excel 2016. Due to concerns about bloating the user interface, though, Power Query was not given its own ribbon tab in Excel 2016 but was instead squished down into the Get & Transform group on the Data tab. The image below shows where Power Query is accessible in each application.

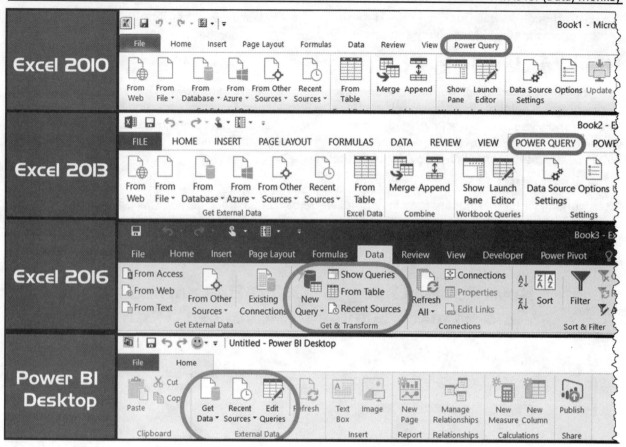

Figure 8 Locating Power Query in Excel 2010, Excel 2013, Excel 2016, and Power BI Desktop.

Creating New Queries

Since the routes to access the Power Query commands are different in different versions of Excel, we have settled on using the following command structure to describe how to get started for each query:

- Create a new query → From File → From CSV

When you see this structure, you need to interpret it as follows:

- Excel 2016:   Data tab → New Query → From File → From CSV
- Excel 2010/2013:   Power Query tab → From File → From CSV

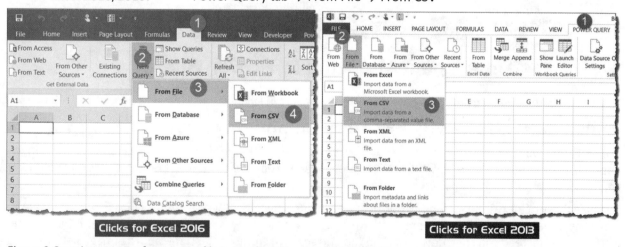

Figure 9 Creating a query from a CSV file in Excel 2016 vs Excel 2010/2013.

So let's put this to the test. If we want you to grab data from an Azure SQL Database, our directions read:

- Create a new query → From Azure → From Microsoft Azure SQL Database

The process for Excel 2016 and for Excel 2013 would look as shown below.

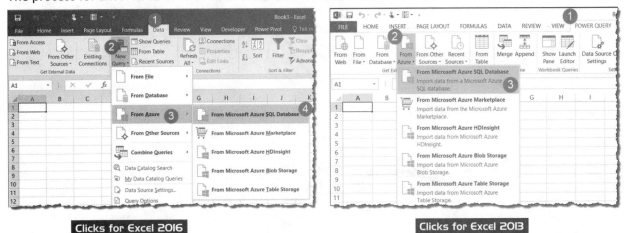

Figure 10 Creating a query from an Azure SQL database in Excel 2016 vs Excel 2010/2013.

Example Files

Before you read any further, we highly recommend that you download all the files used in this book so you can follow along with us. You can get them all at http://www.powerquery.training/book-files/.

It's time to explore this amazing tool in depth. Let's get started.

Special Elements

Notes will appear in an indented paragraph with a banana icon. These delicious paragraphs point out special features, quirks, or software tricks that will help increase your productivity with Power Query.

Warnings appear in a shaded paragraph with a banana peel icon. Pay special attention to the caution boxes as they can cause you to slip up. We want to prevent you from heading down a path that will make the query experience problems in the future.

Chapter 1 Importing Basic Data

If you're an Excel pro, it's highly likely that your life is all about importing, manipulating, and transforming data so that you can use it. Sadly, many of us don't have access to big databases with curated data. Instead, we are fed a steady diet of TXT or CSV files and have to go through the process of importing them into our Excel solutions before we can start our analysis. For us, critical business information is stored in the following formats:

- TXT files, which are delimited by characters
- CSV files, which are delimited by commas
- Excel worksheets

Fortunately, Power Query was built for us, and it allows us to import our data from any of these sources.

Importing Delimited Files

The process of importing a delimited file such as a .CSV or tab-delimited .TXT file is fairly straightforward, and follows the basic ETL (extract, transform, and load) process, as described in the following sections.

Extract (from the File)

The download package for this chapter contains two delimited files, either of which will work for this example. Both are named Ch01-Delimited, though one is a comma-delimited CSV file and the other is a tab-delimited TXT file. To import either delimited file using Power Query you can:

- Open a new (blank) workbook
- Create a new query → From File → From CSV (or From Text if you used the TXT file)
- Browse to the Ch01 Examples\Ch01-Delimited file and double-click it

 In different versions of Excel, you use slightly different methods for creating a new query. To learn how to create a new query in your version of Excel, see the section "Creating New Queries" in the Introduction.

Excel launches a new window, the Power Query editor, which looks like this:

▦▾	TranDate ▾	Account ▾	Dept ▾	Sum of Amount ▾
1	12/1/2009	61510	150	(22.07)
2	12/1/2009	61520	150	(151.82)
3	12/1/2009	61530	150	(12.4)
4	12/1/2009	61540	150	(0.92)
5	12/1/2009	61550	150	(61.87)
6	12/1/2009	61560	150	(1.6)
7	12/1/2009	61570	150	(127.03)
8	12/1/2009	62010	150	(283.84)
9	12/1/2009	62020	150	(241.45)
10	12/1/2009	62099	150	18.41
11	12/1/2009	62510	120	(70.58)

Query Settings ✕

▴ PROPERTIES

Name

Ch01-Delimited

All Properties

▴ APPLIED STEPS

Source ✳

Promoted Headers

✕ Changed Type

Figure 11 The Power Query editor with an imported delimited file.

Transform (into the Desired Output)

This Power Query editor view above shows some important pieces of information that are worth taking notice of:

- The data appears in a nice tabular format with column headers
- The query has been automatically given a name (the name of the file)
- There are three steps listed in the Applied Steps box

It's the last point that is the most salient here. If you try clicking the Source step, you see a slightly different view of your data:

⊞▾	Column1 ▾	Column2 ▾	Column3 ▾	Column4 ▾
1	TranDate	Account	Dept	Sum of Amount
2	12/1/2009	61510	150	($22.07)
3	12/1/2009	61520	150	($151.82)
4	12/1/2009	61530	150	($12.40)
5	12/1/2009	61540	150	($0.92)
6	12/1/2009	61550	150	($61.87)
7	12/1/2009	61560	150	($1.60)
8	12/1/2009	61570	150	($127.03)
9	12/1/2009	62010	150	($283.84)
10	12/1/2009	62020	150	($241.45)
11	12/1/2009	62099	150	$18.41

Query Settings   ✕

▲ PROPERTIES

Name

Ch01-Delimited

All Properties

▲ APPLIED STEPS

  Source   ⚙

  Promoted Headers

  Changed Type

Figure 12 The data as Power Query originally imported it, shown by clicking the Source step.

The impact of this is fairly important. Power Query imported your data, analyzed it, and noticed some trends. What you don't see is that Power Query determined that your data is columnar (based on the fact that CSV files have their columns separated by commas), so it (correctly) split it into columns. That data landed in the Source step.

Power Query then analyzed your data further and identified that the first row had text headers that were inconsistent with the values in the columns. It therefore added the step Promoted Headers to promote the first row to be the column headers for your table.

Next, Power Query attempted to identify and set the data types in the columns. It made the assumption that the TranDate column is dates, the Account and Dept columns are numbers, and the Sum of Amount column is values. It then applied those data types in the Changed Type step you see in the Applied Steps box.

The great thing here is that you can step backward and forward through these steps to see what Power Query did to the data.

You can make some modifications to clean up the data . . . like fixing the terms in the column headers to be more readable. To do this, follow these steps:

- Select Changed Type in the Applied Steps box
- Right-click the header of the TranDate column → Rename → Date
- Right-click Sum of Amount → Rename → Amount

The Power Query editor now looks like this:

⊞▾	Date ▾	Account ▾	Dept ▾	Amount ▾
1	12/1/2009	61510	150	(22.07)
2	12/1/2009	61520	150	(151.82)
3	12/1/2009	61530	150	(12.4)
4	12/1/2009	61540	150	(0.92)
5	12/1/2009	61550	150	(61.87)
6	12/1/2009	61560	150	(1.6)
7	12/1/2009	61570	150	(127.03)
8	12/1/2009	62010	150	(283.84)
9	12/1/2009	62020	150	(241.45)
10	12/1/2009	62099	150	18.41
11	12/1/2009	62510	120	(70.58)

Query Settings   ✕

▲ PROPERTIES

Name

Ch01-Delimited

All Properties

▲ APPLIED STEPS

  Source   ⚙

  Promoted Headers

  Changed Type

✕ Renamed Columns

Figure 13 The data set with renamed columns.

Take another look at the Applied Steps box right now. If you were watching closely as you did this, you'd have noticed that a new step was created when you renamed the Date column. But another step was *not* created when you renamed the Amount column. Instead, the two steps were merged together. Power Query tries to keep things efficient by merging like operations as you are building a query.

The query is looking pretty nice, but what if you don't agree with Power Query's data type choices? For example, the Account and Dept column values should be formatted as text, not numbers. Fixing this is no problem:

- Select the Account column

- Hold down the Ctrl key and select the Dept column

- Right-click either column header → Change Type → Text

The Account and Dept fields are now aligned to the left of the column, which indicates that they are formatted as text, not values, consistent with Excel. You can also see a new step in the Applied Steps box, called Changed Type1:

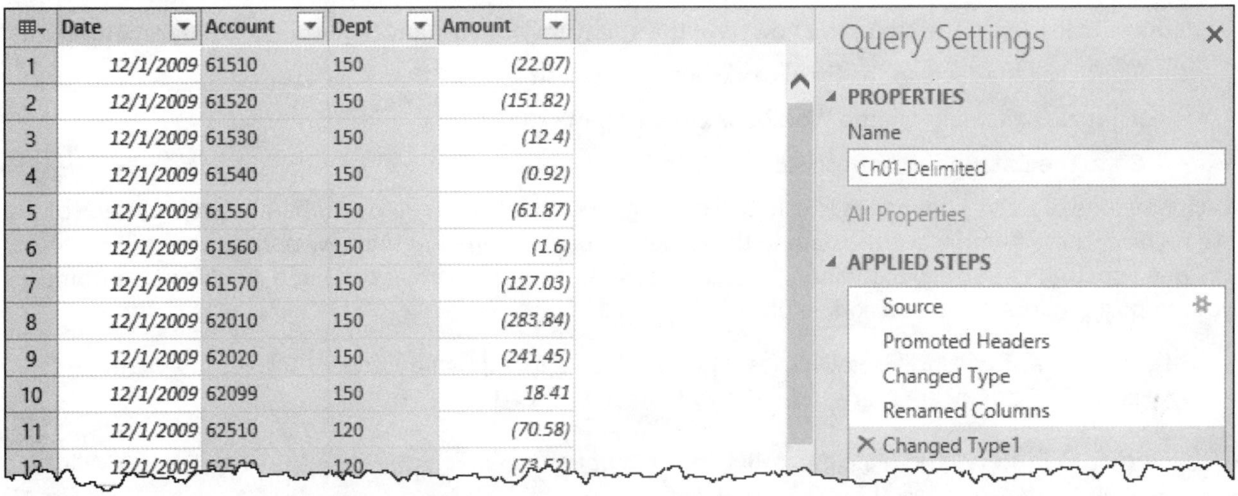

⊞▾	Date	▾	Account	▾	Dept	▾	Amount	▾
1	12/1/2009		61510		150		(22.07)	
2	12/1/2009		61520		150		(151.82)	
3	12/1/2009		61530		150		(12.4)	
4	12/1/2009		61540		150		(0.92)	
5	12/1/2009		61550		150		(61.87)	
6	12/1/2009		61560		150		(1.6)	
7	12/1/2009		61570		150		(127.03)	
8	12/1/2009		62010		150		(283.84)	
9	12/1/2009		62020		150		(241.45)	
10	12/1/2009		62099		150		18.41	
11	12/1/2009		62510		120		(70.58)	
12	12/1/2009		62520		120		(73.52)	

Query Settings ×

PROPERTIES

Name

Ch01-Delimited

All Properties

APPLIED STEPS

Source

Promoted Headers

Changed Type

Renamed Columns

✕ Changed Type1

Figure 14 The data set, looking all pretty and ready for loading.

So why didn't the type changes merge back into the original Changed Type step? The answer is that Power Query doesn't know if you did something important in the preceding step, so it reacts the safe way and creates a new step.

Power Query essentially works as a sequential macro recorder: It will execute exactly these steps, in exactly this order, each time you refresh the data.

Load

It's now time to finalize the query, with the load step. Before you commit your query, you should give it a more descriptive name than the default. Excel will use the name you provide here as the name of your output table or query. Follow these steps:

- Change the name from Ch01-Delimited to Transactions

- Go to the File menu → Close & Load

By default, the data is loaded into an Excel table bearing the name of the query. You can actually see the table get created in a gray color scheme and then turn green. Each table query goes through this process whenever it is refreshed—first turning gray and then turning green when it is good to go.

You'll also notice a new task pane, the Workbook Queries pane, pop up on the right side of your Excel window. This useful interface provides you with key information about your queries (such as number of rows loaded and errors encountered), and it also allows you to locate and manage your queries in the future.

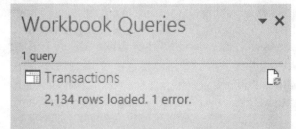

Figure 15 The Workbook Queries task pane, showing the results of the query.

> If you're working along with the book and your query shows a significant number of errors, don't panic. This simply means that your regional settings are not set to a U.S. format. Right now we are focused on how to use the Power Query interface to import data, but rest assured that we will show you how to address this specific issue (among others) in Chapter 2.

With the data loaded in the table, you now have the ability to refresh it any time via a few different methods:

- Right-click the table in the Excel worksheet → Refresh
- Right-click the query in the Workbook Queries pane → Refresh
- Go to the Data tab → Refresh All

Each time one of these commands is issued, Excel triggers Power Query to open the file, process each of the steps you recorded, and place the data in the table. As long as you save the new transactions file on top of the one you used to build your solution, and as long as the data structure is the same, you've just automated your import process down to a couple of clicks!

> If you dismiss the Workbook Queries pane, you can show it again via Data tab → Show Queries in Excel 2016 or Power Query tab → Show Pane in Excel 2010/2013.

> In order to preserve the table and other features of Power Query, this file must be saved in a valid Excel file format, such as XLSX, XLSB, or XLSM.

Importing Excel Data

You can import three general formats of Excel data from a workbook. You can import data held in:

- Excel tables
- Named ranges
- Dynamic named ranges

> Chapter 5 covers importing data from worksheets without tables and data contained in other workbooks.

Connecting to Excel Tables

Rather than connect to an official Excel table, in this case you will connect to data that is in a tabular format but with no table style yet applied. The data to use for this is located in the Ch01 Examples\Excel Data.xlsx file on the Table worksheet, and it looks like this:

	A	B	C	D	E	F
1			Fred's Pet Store			
2			Sales Listing For Month of:			
3			6/30/2014			
4						
5	Date	Inventory Item	Sold By	Cost	Price	Commission
6	6/26/2014	Tubby Turtle	Fred	8.00	30.00	0.90
7	6/26/2014	Talkative Parrot	Jane	17.00	32.00	0.96
8	6/20/2014	Rambunctious Puppy	Fred	9.00	30.00	0.90
9	6/21/2014	Lovable Kitten	John	12.00	45.00	1.35

Figure 16 Raw data in an Excel worksheet.

To pull this data into Power Query, follow these steps:

- Click any cell inside the data range
- Create a new query → From Table

At this point, Excel kicks off the process of creating an official Excel table for you, prompting you to confirm the table boundaries and whether the data set includes headers. Once you confirm the details, you are launched into the Power Query interface.

 If you started with an official Excel table, you would just be launched directly into the Power Query editor, without being prompted to confirm the range.

As shown below, this interface has some differences from when you pulled in data from a delimited file.

	Date	Inventory Item	Sold By	Cost	Price	Query Settings ✕
1	6/26/2014 12:00:00 AM	Tubby Turtle	Fred	8		
2	6/26/2014 12:00:00 AM	Talkative Parrot	Jane	17		▲ PROPERTIES
3	6/20/2014 12:00:00 AM	Rambunctious Puppy	Fred	9		Name
4	6/21/2014 12:00:00 AM	Lovable Kitten	John	12		Table1
5	6/28/2014 12:00:00 AM	Cranky Crocodile	Fred	10		
6	6/14/2014 12:00:00 AM	Slithering Snake	Fred	13		All Properties
7	6/2/2014 12:00:00 AM	Talkative Parrot	Fred	17		▲ APPLIED STEPS
8	6/23/2014 12:00:00 AM	Cranky Crocodile	Mary	10		Source
9	6/9/2014 12:00:00 AM	Rambunctious Puppy	Mary	9		✕ Changed Type

Figure 17 Data loaded from an Excel table.

Note the differences:

- The table headers were imported from the table, so there is no Promoted Headers step.
- The query name is inherited based on the newly created table name.

 When you click Close & Load, Excel attempts to create a new table, using the name of the query shown in the Power Query editor. If the name conflicts with the name of an existing table, Excel appends an underscore and a number to the newly created table name to ensure that there are no duplicated names.

Finalize this query with these steps:

- Change the name from Table1 to FromTable
- Go to Home → Close & Load

A new worksheet is created, and it contains a duplicate of the original table. The only differences at this point are the table name and that Power Query now has a connection to the data.

There is very little reason to create a duplicate of your table without performing any transformations in the process. We show this process merely to illustrate how to connect and load from an Excel table.

Connecting to Named Ranges

Pulling data from Excel tables is by far the easiest way to pull Excel data into Power Query, but it isn't the only method.

The challenge with applying a table style in Excel is that it locks column headers in place (breaking dynamic table headers driven by formulas), applies color banding, and makes other stylistic changes to your worksheet that you may not want. This might be a problem if you've spent a large amount of time building an analysis, and you don't want a table style applied to the data range.

The good news is that you can also connect to Excel ranges, not just to tables. To do this, you can use the NamedRange worksheet in the Ch01-Excel Data.xlsx sample file. The data in it is identical to the data in the previous example, but it's still in raw form, with no table style applied.

Pulling data into Power Query from a named range involves three distinct steps:

- Defining a named range that covers the data,
- Selecting the named range, and then
- Creating a new query.

Follow these steps with the NamedRange worksheet:

- Select cells A5:F42
- Go to the Name box → enter the name Data → press Enter

Data						Date
	A	B	C	D	E	F
4						
5	Date	Inventory Item	Sold By	Cost	Price	Commission
6	6/26/2014	Tubby Turtle	Fred	8.00	30.00	0.90
7	6/26/2014	Talkative Parrot	Jane	17.00	32.00	0.96
8	6/20/2014	Rambunctious Puppy	Fred	9.00	30.00	0.90
9	6/21/2014	Lovable Kitten	John	12.00	45.00	1.35
10	6/28/2014	Cranky Crocodile	Fred	10.00	35.00	1.05

Figure 18 Creating a named range.

After you've created this name, you can select it by using the drop-down arrow on the left. No matter where you are in your workbook, you will then jump to this worksheet, and the data in the named range will be selected.

- Ensure that the entire named range is selected and that its name is showing in the Name box
- Create a new query → From Table

If the named range is selected when you use the From Table command, Power Query does not force a table style on your data and instead refers directly to the data in the named range.

As you can see below, now the Power Query interface looks the way it looks when you import delimited files rather than how it looks when you connect to an Excel table:

📊	Date		Inventory Item		Sold By		Cost		Price
1	6/26/2014 12:00:00 AM		Tubby Turtle		Fred		8		
2	6/26/2014 12:00:00 AM		Talkative Parrot		Jane		17		
3	6/20/2014 12:00:00 AM		Rambunctious Puppy		Fred		9		
4	6/21/2014 12:00:00 AM		Lovable Kitten		John		12		
5	6/28/2014 12:00:00 AM		Cranky Crocodile		Fred		10		
6	6/14/2014 12:00:00 AM		Slithering Snake		Fred		13		
7	6/2/2014 12:00:00 AM		Talkative Parrot		Fred		17		
8	6/23/2014 12:00:00 AM		Cranky Crocodile		Mary		10		
9	6/9/2014 12:00:00 AM		Rambunctious Puppy		Mary		9		
10	6/12/2014 12:00:00 AM		Hilarious Hamster		Mary		31		

Query Settings ✕

◢ PROPERTIES

Name

Data

All Properties

◢ APPLIED STEPS

   Source

   Promoted Headers

✕ Changed Type

Figure 19 Data imported via a named range.

One of the features of Excel tables is that they have a predefined header row. Since that doesn't exist with a named range, Power Query has to connect to the raw data source and run its analysis to figure out how to treat the data. Much like with delimited text files, it identifies a row that appears to be headers, promotes the headers, and attempts to apply data types to the columns.

Notice that the default name of the query is the name of the named range. Again, it's a good idea to change this, as Excel will append a number to the table's name when it is created because a table's name cannot be identical to any other table or named range. Follow these steps:

- Change the query name to FromNamedRange
- Go to Home → Close & Load

Dynamic Named Ranges

Excel tables automatically expand both vertically and horizontally as new data is added. This is one of the great features of Excel tables. But again, the challenge is that they carry a bunch of formatting with them. Named ranges don't carry all that formatting, but they lack the automatic expansion ability that is so fantastic with Excel tables. As a workaround, you can create a dynamic named range that automatically expands as the data grows.

On the DynamicRange worksheet of the Ch01-Excel Data.xlsx file you'll find another copy of the original data. Follow these steps to set up a dynamic named range that expands as new records are added:

- Go to the Formulas tab → Name Manager → New
- Change the name to DynamicRange
- Enter the following formula in the formula bar:

      =Dynamic!$A$5:INDEX(Dynamic!$F:$F,MATCH(99^99,Dynamic!$A:$A))

- Click OK

The challenge now is that you can refer to this named range in Power Query, but because it is a dynamic name, you cannot select it from the Name box in Excel. So if you can't select it, how can you attach to it with Power Query in the first place? The secret is to create a blank query and then tell Power Query which range you want to connect to. Here's how:

- Create a new query → From Other Sources → Blank Query

> If you don't see the formula bar in the Query Editor between the ribbon and the data area, go to the View tab and click the Formula Bar checkbox.

- In the formula bar, type the following:

      =Excel.CurrentWorkbook()

- Press Enter

As shown below, you see a table that lists all the Excel objects in this workbook that you can connect to.

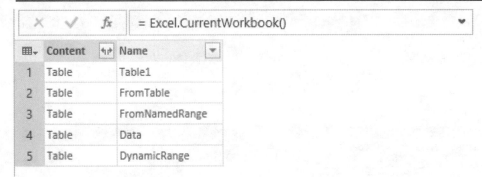

Figure 20 *A list of all the objects Power Query sees in the current Excel workbook.*

There at the bottom is the DynamicRange object you just created. Click the green word Table in the Content column to the left of DynamicRange. Power Query drills into the range, as shown below.

Figure 21 *The contents of the DynamicRange named range.*

By looking at the Applied Steps box, you can see that you took these steps:

- Connected to the source of the data (the Excel workbook)
- Navigated in to the DynamicRange table

In addition, Power Query made some assumptions about the data for you, and it took the liberty of applying a few more steps, such as promoting column headers and setting the data types. All you have to do now is follow these steps:

- Rename the query FromDynamicRange
- Go to Home → Close & Load

Considerations

Where possible, it is preferable to build your solutions against Excel tables. They are easier to set up than the alternatives, easier to maintain, and quite transparent about where the data is stored.

In specific situations, you might have reasons to avoid tables, however, and you can do that where needed. We recommend that you should generally reach to these techniques only when you have good reasons to do so.

Chapter 2 Overriding Power Query Defaults

Your job is tough when everyone follows the rules. But every now and then when you're trying to import a data file into Excel, you're likely to discover that the report programmer didn't follow the proper report standards. The file may have a particular file extension that implies it should follow a certain standard, but it is actually just masquerading as that type of file. Yet when you open it up, you find something that is not compliant with the standard, and it doesn't work correctly.

Malformed File Example

Say that you're working with a CSV data set that looks like this when viewed in Notepad:

```
Downloaded from MarSys: 2008-02-13T10:13:29
TranDate,Account,Dept,Amount
1/2/2008,61510,150,($26.03)
1/2/2008,61520,150,($55.07)
1/2/2008,61530,150,($10.60)
1/2/2008,61540,150,($0.29)
1/2/2008,61550,150,($48.02)
```

Figure 22 A raw look at a malformed CSV file, which has an extra header row.

So what's wrong with this data set? Starting on row 2, it has a nice consistent list of data showing in a proper comma-separated format, with one a header row and four columns of data, separated by commas. The issue here is that there is an extra row at the top of the page, with no commas in it. In a normal CSV setup, this should not occur, as most programs work out the column count based on the first row.

Interestingly, when Excel opens this file, it handles it without issue:

▲	A	B	C	D	E
1	Downloaded from MarSys: 2008-02-13T10:13:29				
2	TranDate	Account	Dept	Amount	
3	1/2/2008	61510	150	($26.03)	
4	1/2/2008	61520	150	($55.07)	
5	1/2/2008	61530	150	($10.60)	
6	1/2/2008	61540	150	($0.29)	
7	1/2/2008	61550	150	($48.02)	

Figure 23 Malformed CSV file loaded into Excel.

Power Query, unfortunately, doesn't handle this quite as gracefully, as you can see if you follow these steps:

- Open a blank workbook
- Create a new query → From File → From CSV
- Browse to Ch02 Examples\MalformedCSV.csv

When Power Query launches, the data is imported as follows:

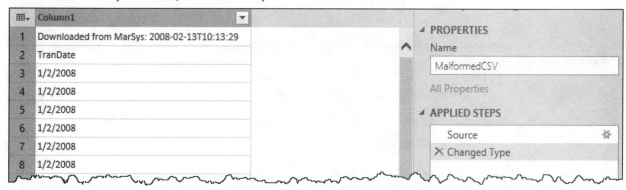

Figure 24 Malformed CSV file loaded into Power Query.

This is obviously not good. You're looking at a single column of data. Worse, it appears that Power Query recognized the column as delimited, and it failed to import the last three columns!

The challenge here is that Power Query relies on the CSV file being a proper CSV file because it wants to split the data based on the commas. It then reads the first row to determine how many columns exist. Since there are no commas in that line, Power Query figures that it must be a single column. It then starts to read each row and stops at the first comma.

Normally this process works just fine. But in the case of this file, Power Query ignores a large part of the data you need. The good news is that you can fix this by telling Power Query how the file needs to be treated.

Overriding Power Query's Default Choices

Power Query loves to be helpful by trying to make assumptions about data. While it's often right, it can occasionally be wrong and needs some manipulation.

There are two main ways these issues manifest in the user interface: Power Query sometimes inserts extra steps that are incorrect/irrelevant, and sometimes it misconfigures steps. You deal with these two problems differently, as discussed in the following sections.

Removing Power Query Steps

Of the two Power Query problems just mentioned, removing extra added steps is by far the easier.

In the case of the import shown earlier in this chapter, Power Query did two things. First, it imported the file, and then it set the data type on Column1. The challenge here is that you need to change the import format, and you may not be sure if you'll even have a Column1 after this is done. For that reason, you need to delete the Changed Type step. This is very easy to do—simply mouse over the step in the Applied Steps box and click the little x on the left side of the step to delete it from the Power Query sequence:

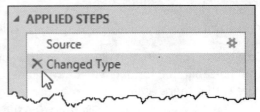

Figure 25 Removing a step in Power Query.

> Be aware that if you delete steps in the middle of a query that are important to the end result, you may cause the query to throw an error by the end. In addition, there is no undo functionality in this area of the user interface!

In this case, deleting the Changed Type step doesn't appear to change anything in the query view at this point. (After all, Power Query just forced the text to be treated as text.) It does, however, help you avoid potential errors as you fix the true problem, described next.

Reconfiguring Steps

Now you need to change the way Power Query handles the file at import. To do that, you need to click the little gear icon on the right side of the Source step. When you do that, you're launched into a configuration window:

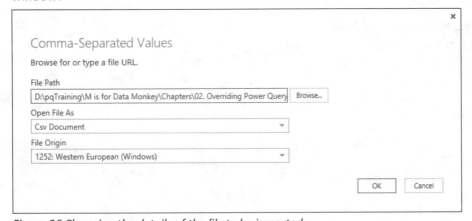

Figure 26 Changing the details of the file to be imported.

This dialog allows you to change a few important things about the file, including the file path and what type of file Power Query should assume this is when trying to import it. Because the file in this case carries the CSV file type extension, Power Query chose the Csv Document type.

Each of the example files for this book has a "Completed" version. In order to get them to refresh, you need to click the gear icon on the Source step and change the folder location to the location on your PC.

At this point you need to tell Power Query that CSV is not the correct format for this document, even though it is masquerading under a CSV extension. To do this, click the dropdown next to Open File As → select Text File → OK.

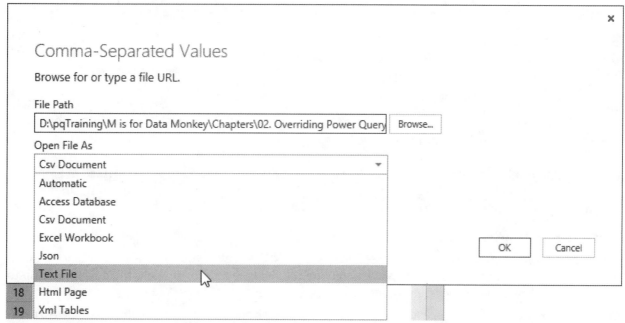

Figure 27 The different options available for data imports.

The results are much more comforting, although there is definitely a bit more work to do now:

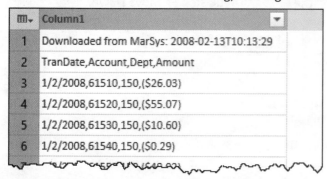

Figure 28 All of the data is showing again!

It looks like you'll need to manually split this data up into columns, but that's not a huge deal. At least it is comma delimited, and that will make things a bit easier. Now you need to go through the steps that you probably wish Power Query had done for you:

- On the Home tab → Remove Rows → Remove Top Rows → 1
- Go to the Transform tab → Split Column → By Delimiter
- Choose to split by Comma → At Each Occurrence of the Delimiter → OK
- Go to the Transform tab → Use First Row as Headers → OK

The import now looks much better:

⊞▾	TranDate ▾	Account ▾	Dept ▾	Amount ▾
1	1/2/2008	61510	150	($26.03)
2	1/2/2008	61520	150	($55.07)
3	1/2/2008	61530	150	($10.60)
4	1/2/2008	61540	150	($0.29)
5	1/2/2008	61550	150	($48.02)
6	1/2/2008	61560	150	($1.35)
7	1/2/2008	61570	150	($77.04)
8	1/2/2008	62010	150	($305.95)
9	1/2/2008	62020	150	($95.15)
10	1/2/2008	62099	150	$8.79
11	1/2/2008	62510	120	($57.74)

PROPERTIES

Name

MalformedCSV

All Properties

APPLIED STEPS

Source

Removed Top Rows

Split Column by Delimiter

Changed Type

✕ Promoted Headers

Figure 29 The data the way you wanted it imported.

You might think that you could skip this process by choosing to import From Text instead of From CSV. Unfortunately, because Power Query is so helpful, it will override your choice and still import the file as a CSV anyway.

Reordering Steps

When you review the steps in the Applied Steps box, you can see that after you split the columns by delimiter, Power Query automatically inserts a step to change the column types. Unfortunately, the data is lined up to the left, so you know that Power Query configured everything as text.

You need to fix that, but if you step back to the Changed Type step and start converting the data types to dates and values, you'll cause errors across row 1. (They are all text values and haven't been promoted to headers yet.) So it really makes sense to change the column types after you've promoted headers, not before. Try moving that Changed Type step down by right-clicking the Changed Type step → Move Down.

The step moves, but it causes an error when doing so:

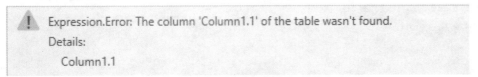

⚠ Expression.Error: The column 'Column1.1' of the table wasn't found.

Details:

Column1.1

Figure 30 Power Query tells you it can't find a specific column anymore.

The reason this error shows up is that the Changed Type step was setting the data types on Column1.1. But since you promoted the column headers, there is no Column1.1 anymore; it's now TranDate.

Moving steps in Power Query can be a very handy feature, but you have to watch out for errors like the one just shown.

As you become more comfortable with Power Query, you may decide to just fix a problem like this by editing the formula step directly, but for now the easiest way to fix this specific issue is simply to delete the step and re-create it:

- Remove the Changed Type step by deleting it in the Applied Steps box
- Right-click Amount → Change Type → Decimal Number

If you get an error in the column when you do this, you can fix it by doing the following: Select the Promoted Headers step → right-click the Amount column → Replace Values. Replace the $ sign with nothing. At this point, things will work when you select the Changed Type step. The root cause of the issue is that your regional settings use a − sign for negative numbers as opposed to putting negative numbers in parentheses.

You're almost done. You just have the date column left to go. For now, go to Home → Close & Load to finalize the query.

Forcing Date Types

A huge issue for Excel pros, particularly those outside the United States, is importing dates and getting them correct.

Once data is in Excel, dates are no big issue. No matter where the workbook goes, the dates will render correctly and can easily be switched to display in the format the reader needs, wherever in the world they are or whichever standard they wish to follow. The difficulty is in importing data representing dates in the first place.

The problem is that Excel and Power Query need to interpret the date from the external data source, determine what date it is, and return the correct date serial number. What makes the job difficult is the fact that not all of the software we use in our daily jobs is written using the same date standards that our country uses as a standard. In fact, if there is a mismatch between the data source and the regional settings on your PC, you'll have issues.

The examples and illustrations in this chapter have been constructed using a PC with a U.S. date standard format. If your system settings are in a different format, the results may be different from what is shown here.

Demonstrating Date Issues

The see this problem, follow these steps:

- Start a new query → From File → From Text
- Browse to and open Ch02 Examples\Dates.txt

The view you get depends on the Windows regional settings in your PC. If you have your settings configured to use the U.S. date standard MM/DD/YYYY, your import will appear as shown below. If your system uses a DD/MM/YYYY setting, however, you'll find that the first column will be left aligned, and the second column will be right aligned.

⊞▾	MM/DD/YYYY ▾	DD/MM/YYYY ▾	Text Date ▾
1	3/5/2015	5/3/2015	March 5th 2015
2	6/9/2015	9/6/2015	June 9th 2015
3	6/12/2015	12/6/2015	June 12th 2015
4	6/17/2015	17/6/2015	June 17th 2015
5	12/13/2015	13/12/2015	December 13th 2015

Figure 31 Dates imported and formatted using U.S. standards.

Change the format of the left-aligned column to Date by right-clicking it and choosing Change Type → Date. The result should look similar to that shown below (although the column you selected may vary):

⊞▾	MM/DD/YYYY ▾	DD/MM/YYYY ▾	Text Date ▾
1	3/5/2015	5/3/2015	March 5th 2015
2	6/9/2015	9/6/2015	June 9th 2015
3	6/12/2015	12/6/2015	June 12th 2015
4	6/17/2015	Error	June 17th 2015
5	12/13/2015	Error	December 13th 2015

Figure 32 Applying a Date format to data sourced from a different region.

Notice that a couple of issues present themselves immediately. First, the days and months appear flipped, and second, you get errors in the column.

With the Windows regional settings set to MM/DD/YYYY, Power Query tries to interpret all dates in that format. And when it hits a date like 17/6/2015, it throws an error because there are only 12 months in the year.

Fixing Date Issues

The secret to avoiding the problems just discussed is explicitly telling Power Query the format of the data being imported. And while it's easy to do this once you know how, the terminology used to label this feature wasn't put in terms that Excel pros recognize.

To force Power Query to read the dates using the correct setup for each column, follow these steps:

- Remove the existing Changed Type step
- Right-click the MM/DD/YYYY column → Change Type → Using Locale
- Change the Data Type to Date
- Change the Locale to English (United States), as shown below
- Right-click the DD/MM/YYYY column → Change Type → Using Locale
- Change the Data Type to Date
- Change the Locale to English (United Kingdom)

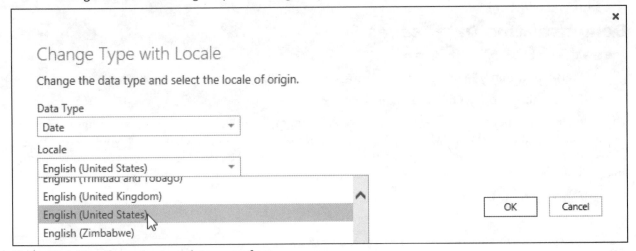

Figure 33 Setting the region your data comes from.

As shown below, now the dates all render consistently according to the format declared in the regional settings of your Windows Control Panel. This is because the dates—no matter their original format—have been converted to the date settings on your system.

⊞▾	MM/DD/YY... ▾	DD/MM/YY... ▾	Text Date ▾
1	3/5/2015	3/5/2015	March 5th 2015
2	6/9/2015	6/9/2015	June 9th 2015
3	6/12/2015	6/12/2015	June 12th 2015
4	6/17/2015	6/17/2015	June 17th 2015
5	12/13/2015	12/13/2015	December 13th 2015

Figure 34 A consistent view of dates originally contained in two different formats.

> If you don't know which date standard your country uses, experiment and choose one that returns the correct results.

If there is any chance that your data may be shipped to someone using different regional settings, it is highly advisable that you force the date input formats. This will eliminate the chance of surprising errors occurring and is a practice that we follow throughout this book.

You can now finalize this query by going to Home → Close & Load, and you can edit the MalformedCSV query to force the dates to load correctly:

- In the Workbook Queries pane, right-click the MalformedCSV query → Edit
- Right-click the TranDate column → Change Type → Using Locale
- Set to Date → English (United States) → OK

The query now looks as follows and is ready to be loaded to the worksheet.

▦▾	TranDate ▼	Account ▼	Dept ▼	Amount ▼
1	1/2/2008	61510	150	(26.03)
2	1/2/2008	61520	150	(55.07)
3	1/2/2008	61530	150	(10.6)
4	1/2/2008	61540	150	(0.29)
5	1/2/2008	61550	150	(48.02)
6	1/2/2008	61560	150	(1.35)
7	1/2/2008	61570	150	(77.04)
8	1/2/2008	62010	150	(305.95)
9	1/2/2008	62020	150	(95.15)
10	1/2/2008	62099	150	8.79
11	1/2/2008	62510	120	(56.74)

PROPERTIES

Name

MalformedCSV

All Properties

APPLIED STEPS

Source

Removed Top Rows

Split Column by Delimiter

Promoted Headers

Changed Type

✕ Changed Type with Locale

Figure 35 The query is ready to be loaded to the worksheet.

Changed Type with Locale steps will not merge with Changed Type steps. If a Changed Type step includes a date conversion, you must remove that step. The reason the query above worked is that the Changed Type step did not set the data type for the TranDate column.

©2014 WALTER MOORE
28 MAY 14

Chapter 3 Basic Append Operations

One of the jobs that Excel pros do on a regular basis is appending one file to another one. Particularly in organizations where data is shared by CSV, TXT, or Excel files, the process usually boils down to the following:

- Import and transform file #1
- Import and transform file #2
- Copy file #1's data and paste it at the end of file #2
- Save the file as Consolidated

The user then builds a business intelligence solution in the Consolidated file. When the next month comes along, the data from the next monthly file is copied into the Consolidated file, the solution is updated, and all is good.

But the process is plainly not all sunshine and rainbows, and there are some very obvious issues here. This chapter does not solve the issue of a user making a mistake in the transformations (although future chapters do), but it does show you how Power Query can consolidate two or more data sets without ever worrying about a user pasting over the last few rows of data.

Importing Data Files

The Ch03 Examples folder contains three CSV files: Jan 2008.csv, Feb 2008.csv, and Mar 2008.csv. This section walks through the process of importing and appending each file.

Importing the files is fairly straightforward:

- Create a new query → From File → From CSV
- Browse to the Ch03 Examples\Jan 2008.csv → Open

Power Query opens the file and executes the following steps automatically for this data source:

- Promotes the first row to headers, showing TranDate, Account, Dept, and Sum of Amount.
- Sets the data types to Date, Whole Number, Whole Number, and Decimal Value.

To be safe, you should remove the Changed Type step and re-create it to force the dates to import based on the U.S. standard that they came from:

- Remove the Changed Type step
- Right-click TranDate → Change Type → Using Locale → Date → English (United States) → OK
- Right-click Account → Change Type → Whole Number
- Right-click Dept → Change Type → Whole Number
- Right-click Amount → Change Type → Decimal Number

Remember, if your number format is set to display negative numbers with a – sign instead of using parentheses, you may have to also have to remove the $ signs from the Sum of Amount column before changing that column to a decimal number in order to avoid errors. To do this, select the Changed Type with Locale step → right-click the Sum of Amount column → Replace Values → Replace $ with nothing. After you've performed these steps, select the Changed Type step again to make sure you're at the end of the query before continuing.

In addition, you should also make the following transformations:

- Select the TranDate column → Home → Reduce Rows → Remove Errors
- Right-click the TranDate column header → Rename → Date
- Right-click the Sum of Amount column header → Rename → Amount

Errors are explored in detail in Chapter 7.

At this point, the query should look as shown below.

⊞▾	Date	▾	Account	▾	Dept	▾	Amount	▾
1	1/2/2008		61510		150		(26.03)	
2	1/2/2008		61520		150		(55.07)	
3	1/2/2008		61530		150		(10.6)	
4	1/2/2008		61540		150		(0.29)	
5	1/2/2008		61550		150		(48.02)	
6	1/2/2008		61560		150		(1.35)	
7	1/2/2008		61570		150		(77.04)	
8	1/2/2008		62010		150		(305.95)	
9	1/2/2008		62020		150		(95.15)	
10	1/2/2008		62099		150		8.79	

PROPERTIES
Name
Jan2008
All Properties

APPLIED STEPS
Source   ⚙
First Row as Header
Changed Type with Locale   ⚙
Changed Type
✕ Renamed Columns

Figure 36 The Jan2008 query before loading to the worksheet.

Go to Home and click Close & Load to load the Jan2008 query to the worksheet.

You now need to replicate the process with both the Feb 2008.csv and Mar 2008.csv files. The import process uses exactly the same steps, and when you're done, you should have three new tables in your Excel workbook in all:

- Jan_2008
- Feb_2008
- Mar_2008

Appending One Table to Another

Next, you need to append the Jan_2008 and Feb_2008 tables. To do this you need to create a new query, but this time you want an append query. To create one, follow these steps:

- Excel 2016:   Go to New Query → Combine Queries → Append
- Excel 2010/2013:   Go to the Combine group → Append

The Append dialog appears, and in it you can choose the queries you'd like to append:

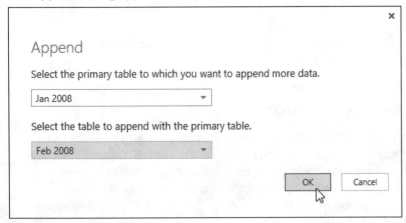

Figure 37 The Append dialog.

You need to understand a couple of tricks here:

- This dialog only allows you to combine Power Query queries, not Excel tables.
- The query you choose in the top drop-down appears first in the query output.

Clicking OK opens the Power Query editor with a new query called Append1, which has a single Source step.

At this point you may be tempted to scroll down the query to see if all of your records are actually there. Unfortunately, this won't really work. Power Query doesn't actually load all your data in the initial window; rather, it shows a preview of your data. The number of rows it shows you varies with the number of columns you add, but you can see this in the bottom-left corner of the Power Query editor:

4 COLUMNS, 999+ ROWS

Figure 38 Power Query shows you how many preview rows it can handle right now.

The reason for this behavior is that Power Query can be used to handle large data sets. Imagine for a second that you want to connect to a data set that has 5 million rows, but you only want to pull in the records for department 150. The Power Query team describes the preview as "looking at the first inch of water in the fire hose," under the assumption that the preview should give you enough information to determine the key structure of the data. You then make your transformations on the preview data and create a pattern. At load time, Power Query processes this pattern against the data, pulling in only the records it needs to give you your output. This is much more efficient than loading all the data to the workbook and then processing every row and column. But if you can't see all the data, how do you know it worked?

The answer is to finalize the query. Here's how:

- Change the name of the query to Transactions
- Go to Home → Close & Load

A new table is created in the worksheet, and you see some key information in the Workbook Queries pane:

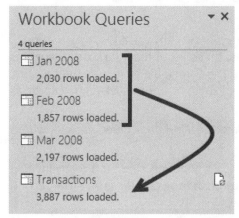

Figure 39 The Workbook Queries pane show that the record counts match.

Still, you shouldn't just believe that everything has worked. You can create a PivotTable to make sure Excel isn't lying to you:

- Select any cell in the Transactions table → Insert → PivotTable
- Place the PivotTable in cell F2 of the current worksheet
- Drag Amount to the Values area
- Drag Date to the Rows area

If you're using Excel 2010 or 2013, you also need to take these steps:

- Right-click cell F3 → Group → by Days and Months → OK
- Right-click cell F3 → Expand Collapse → Collapse Entire Field

You end up with a PivotTable that shows that both tables were indeed consolidated into one:

	A	B	C	D	E	F	G
1	Date	Account	Dept	Amount			
2	1/2/2008	61510	150	-26.03		Row Labels	Sum of Amount
3	1/2/2008	61520	150	-55.07		⊞ Jan	89790.94
4	1/2/2008	61530	150	-10.6		⊞ Feb	56211.14
5	1/2/2008	61540	150	-0.29		Grand Total	146002.08
6	1/2/2008	61550	150	-48.02			
7	1/2/2008	61560	150	-1.35			

Figure 40 January and February transactions are now in one PivotTable.

Appending Additional Tables

Say that you want to add the March records to the query as well. You might be tempted to head back to the same spot to append the March records:

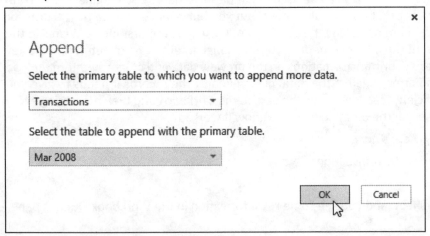

Figure 41 Setting up to merge March's records.

But wait! Will this actually work? Won't this create a new query? Yes, that's absolutely the case. Doing this will kick off a *new* append query, which won't make any sense at all. The PivotTable is already built against the Transactions table, so you really need to go back and modify that table to append March's records as well. But how do you do that?

The answer is to cancel the Append dialog shown above and go back to the Workbook Queries pane, where you right-click the Transactions query → Edit.

In the Power Query editor, you can modify your existing query. And, as it happens, there is a really inviting button on the Home tab that looks promising: the Append Queries button in the Combine group (the second group from the right).

Unlike the Append button in the Excel user interface, the button in the Power Query user interface asks for only a single table, as it already knows which query to append it to (the one you're currently in).

Interestingly, the options include not only the other Power Queries you have set up but also the query you are currently building:

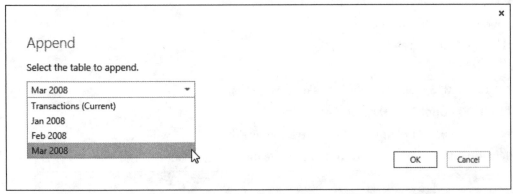

Figure 42 Options to append include the table you are working with.

Selecting the table listed as current would append a copy of the query to that point, essentially duplicating the data set. While this is certainly not something that most users would use on a frequent basis, it's nice to know that the capability exists.

At this point, you should choose the Mar 2008 query, and it will be appended to the Transactions query that already holds Jan and Feb records:

- Select Mar 2008 → OK
- Go to Home → Close & Load

Now you see an unfortunate issue with Power Query queries. When you look at the worksheet that holds your PivotTable, you can see that the Transactions query (and, therefore, the Excel table) does hold all 6,084 rows—the combined totals of the three previous data sets. Yet the PivotTable has not changed:

	A	B	C	D	E	F	G
1	Date	Account	Dept	Amount		Row Labels	Sum of Amount
2	1/2/2008	61510	150	-26.03		⊞ Jan	89790.94
3	1/2/2008	61520	150	-55.07		⊞ Feb	56211.14
4	1/2/2008	61530	150	-10.6		Grand Total	146002.08
5	1/2/2008	61540	150	-0.29			
6	1/2/2008	61550	150	-48.02			
7	1/2/2008	61560	150	-1.35			
8	1/2/2008	61570	150	-77.04			
9	1/2/2008	62010	150	-305.95			
10	1/2/2008	62020	150	-95.15			
11	1/2/2008	62099	150	8.79			
12	1/2/2008	62510	120	-56.74			

Workbook Q...
4 queries
Jan 2008 — 2,030 rows loaded.
Feb 2008 — 1,857 rows loaded.
Mar 2008 — 2,197 rows loaded.
Transactions — 6,084 rows loaded.

Figure 43 The Transactions actions table has updated, yet the PivotTable has not.

This is a minor inconvenience, but you'll need to refresh the PivotTable as well in order to have the updated values flow through. To do that, right-click the PivotTable → Refresh. And it does, indeed, update:

	A	B	C	D	E	F	G
1	Date	Account	Dept	Amount		Row Labels	Sum of Amount
2	1/2/2008	61510	150	-26.03		⊞ Jan	89790.94
3	1/2/2008	61520	150	-55.07		⊞ Feb	56211.14
4	1/2/2008	61530	150	-10.6		⊞ Mar	23820.33
5	1/2/2008	61540	150	-0.29		Grand Total	169822.41
6	1/2/2008	61550	150	-48.02			
7	1/2/2008	61560	150	-1.35			
8	1/2/2008	61570	150	-77.04			
9	1/2/2008	62010	150	-305.95			
10	1/2/2008	62020	150	-95.15			
11	1/2/2008	62099	150	8.79			
12	1/2/2008	62510	120	-56.74			

Workbook Q...
4 queries
Jan 2008 — 2,030 rows loaded.
Feb 2008 — 1,857 rows loaded.
Mar 2008 — 2,197 rows loaded.
Transactions — 6,084 rows loaded.

Figure 44 The January through March records are now showing in a single PivotTable.

Combining Queries with Different Headers

When you're appending queries, as long as the headers of the queries being combined are identical, the second query will just be appended to the first one, as you'd expect. But what if the columns don't have the same column headers?

In the case of the image below, the user forgot to rename the TranDate column in the Mar 2008 query. Everything was fine as the user merged the Jan 2008 and Feb 2008 records together. But when the user appended the Mar 2008 records to the table, things broke down:

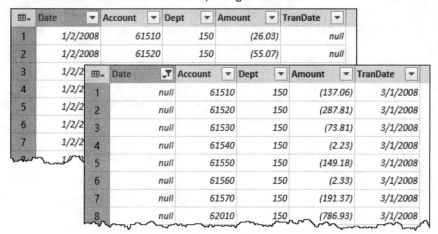

Figure 45 The TranDate column full of null values in January and the Date column full of null values in March.

When you append one table to another, Power Query loads the data from the first query. It then scans the header row of the second query and all subsequent queries. If any of the headers are not present in the results retrieved to date, Power Query adds the new column(s). It then fills the appropriate record into each column for each data set, filling any gaps with *null* values.

In the scenario above, this means that the TranDate column is filled with *null* values in January, since the Jan 2008 query doesn't have a TranDate column.

On the flip side, because the user forgot to rename the TranDate column, the Mar 2008 query has no Date column. For this reason, the Date column is filled with *null* values for each March record, while the TranDate column holds the values that were intended to be in the Date column.

The fix for this is to do the following:

- Go to the Workbook Queries pane → right-click the Mar 2008 query → Edit
- Right-click the TranDate column → Rename → Date
- Save the Mar 2008 query
- Go to the Workbook Queries pane → right-click the Transactions query → Edit

As soon as you open the Transactions query, you see that it has already fixed itself.

Implications of Append Queries

The implications of the ability to append queries are numerous. Consider for a second that you have just reached out to three separate files, imported them, combined them into a single table, and built a PivotTable from them. That is one PivotTable from three separate files.

And when you want to refresh the solution, you simply need to go to Data → Refresh All to refresh it. Power Query kicks off the refresh of the Transactions table, which kicks off the refresh of the three individual data tables to feed it.

Assume now that this solution was built on files that weren't date specific but were instead Product 1, Product 2, and Product 3. Say that you've built a solution by loading in the CSV files that hold the pertinent data, and you've built a PivotTable against them. And then the next month comes along . . . and the IT department sends you replacement files with new transactions for each product.

You save the new Product 1 file over the old one, and you do the same for Product 2 and Product 3. Then you click Refresh All, and you're done.

Seriously, let that sink in for a moment: You're done.

You've cut your work time to a fraction of what was required in the previous process, and there is no risk of having users accidentally paste over existing data, as Power Query doesn't work using cut and paste. It simply appends one set to the other and removes the duplicated headers. You get the best of both speed and consistency in a single solution.

Note, however, that the process of appending queries is not specific to working with external CSV or TXT files. Say that you have tables of transactions such as the promotional gift certificates your company has issued this year. The author of the workbook set up 12 tables, one for each month of the year, stored on separate worksheets. You can see that in this case, you could easily consolidate those individual tables into one master list for analysis.

Chapter 4 Importing All Files in a Folder

The classic way that Excel pros deal with importing all files in a folder is incredibly tedious and error prone. Each file needs to be imported, transformed, copied, and pasted into the master table. Depending on how big and complex the transformations are, how many files there are, and how long the solutions have been running, this process can be terrifying.

You've already seen that Power Query can eliminate the copying/pasting dangers involved with importing and appending files on a one-by-one basis, but what about these pretty serious issues:

- Importing multiple files is tedious.
- Repeating complex transformation steps is error prone.

The good news is that Power Query has a way to deal with both of these issues as well.

 This chapter focuses on importing binary files, such as TXT and CSV files. Chapter 5 covers importing data from multiple workbooks.

Sourcing All Files in a Folder

The example files for this chapter are broken down into four subfolders:

- Begin
- 2008 – More
- 2009
- 2010

Each folder contains a variety of text files that you will combine.

Extracting the Files Listing

To get started, open a blank workbook:

- Start a new query → From File → From Folder
- Click Browse

You are presented with the dialog that Power Query uses to select folders.

- Locate the Ch04 Examples\Begin folder → select it → OK (to close the folder picker dialog)
- Click OK (to load the folder to Power Query)

You now see a new Power Query window. This time, things look quite different than what you've seen so far. Instead of transactions, you see a list of files and their properties:

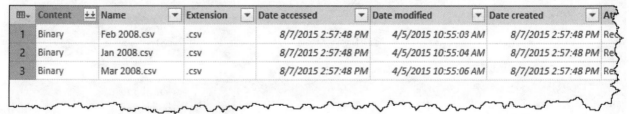

	Content	Name	Extension	Date accessed	Date modified	Date created	At
1	Binary	Feb 2008.csv	.csv	8/7/2015 2:57:48 PM	4/5/2015 10:55:03 AM	8/7/2015 2:57:48 PM	Re
2	Binary	Jan 2008.csv	.csv	8/7/2015 2:57:48 PM	4/5/2015 10:55:04 AM	8/7/2015 2:57:48 PM	Re
3	Binary	Mar 2008.csv	.csv	8/7/2015 2:57:48 PM	4/5/2015 10:55:06 AM	8/7/2015 2:57:48 PM	Re

Figure 46 The list of files in the Begin folder.

Future-Proofing File Selection

In this chapter, you will be combining all the CSV files from the four folders. Before you go any further, you should filter this list to ensure that only CSV files are present. Even though you see only CSV files in the screen above, you just never know when someone else will decide to store an Excel workbook in this folder. If that happens, it's sure to break your solution right when you're at your busiest. For the amount of effort it takes, a little future-proofing is well worth the time.

To filter to just CSV files, you'd normally click the filter arrow on the Extension column, uncheck the (Select All) option, and then check CSV. Unfortunately, because you only have CSV files in the list right now, doing that rechecks the (Select All) option, which is not going to help. You're going to need to go a bit deeper to protect yourself here and force your filter to CSV.

Before you do that, however, you also need to guard against accidentally filtering out "CSV" files when you filter for "csv" (as text filters are case sensitive). To deal with this, follow these steps:

- Right-click the Extension column → Transform → Lowercase
- Select the Extension column's filter arrow → Text Filters → Equals
- Set the filter to Equals .csv

  Don't forget the period in front of the csv! If you forget it, you won't get any files, as csv is not the same as .csv.

- Click OK

Even though things don't look any different after you take these steps, you've now forced the system to only accept CSV files for your operations, reducing the chance of contaminated data blowing apart your solution.

Combining Files

Now the time has come to combine files. Provided that you are working with binary files such as TXT or CSV files, this is incredibly easy once you know the trick.

Combining the Initial File Set

Take a careful look at the icons in the first three columns of the current query:

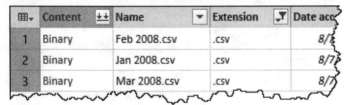

Figure 47 The first three columns of the current query.

The Name column shows an unfiltered filter icon, and the Extension column shows a filter that is currently being used. But what about the Content column? What is that icon?

It's *incredible*, that's what it is. That tiny little button appears on columns containing binary files, and when you click it, magic happens:

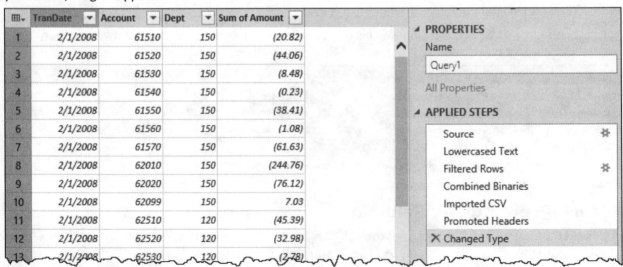

Figure 48 Magic in action (combining binaries).

A *lot* of stuff happens when you clicked that magic button, and looking at the Applied Steps box lets you retrace all of it.

In this example, we were on the Filtered Rows step when we clicked. From there Power Query combined all the individual files into one massive CSV, imported it, scanned it, promoted the first row to headers, and made a guess about the data types. All this happened with the click of one tiny button!

That seems too good to be true, and naturally the preview window is saying that you've got 999+ rows, so you can't even verify that it worked. You need to finalize this query and pivot it so that you can reassure yourself that this is working. Follow these steps:

- Remove the Changed Type step
- Right-click TranDate → Change Type → Using Locale → Date → English (United States) → OK
- Right-click Account → Change Type → Whole Number
- Right-click Dept → Change Type → Whole Number
- Right-click Amount → Change Type → Decimal Number
- Rename the query from Query1 (or Begin in 2013) to Transactions
- Select TranDate → Home → Reduce Rows → Remove Errors
- Right-click TranDate → Rename → Date
- Right-click Sum of Amount → Rename → Amount
- Home → Close & Load

The data lands 6,084 rows in an Excel worksheet, which looks promising. Now you can pivot it:

- Select a cell in the table → Insert → PivotTable
- Create the PivotTable on the same worksheet in cell F2
- Drag Amount to Values
- Drag Date to Rows
- Right-click F3 → Group → Select Months & Years → OK

You can see below that you are indeed looking at the data from all three files—and you didn't have to pre-import each file and then append them manually!

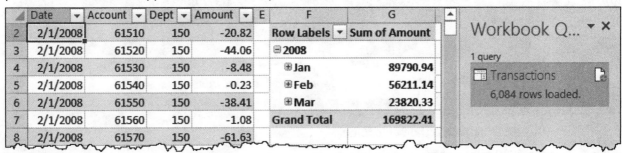

Figure 49 Data representing all files imported from a single folder.

Adding More Files

One of the things that makes Power Query so great is the ability to refresh a solution at will and see it work. So far in this book the examples have been targeted at specific files and, without changing the details of the files, it's hard to see that a refresh has any effect. That changes now.

Go back to the Ch04 Example Files folder. Remember that there were four folders in there, and you targeted a solution against the Begin folder. Now you're going to simulate the process of adding new files to the solution:

- Drag the 2008 – More folder into the Begin folder
- Return to Excel → Data → Refresh All

Power Query kicks off the refresh process and updates the Transactions table, showing that it has loaded 25,700 rows. However, once again, the PivotTable doesn't update:

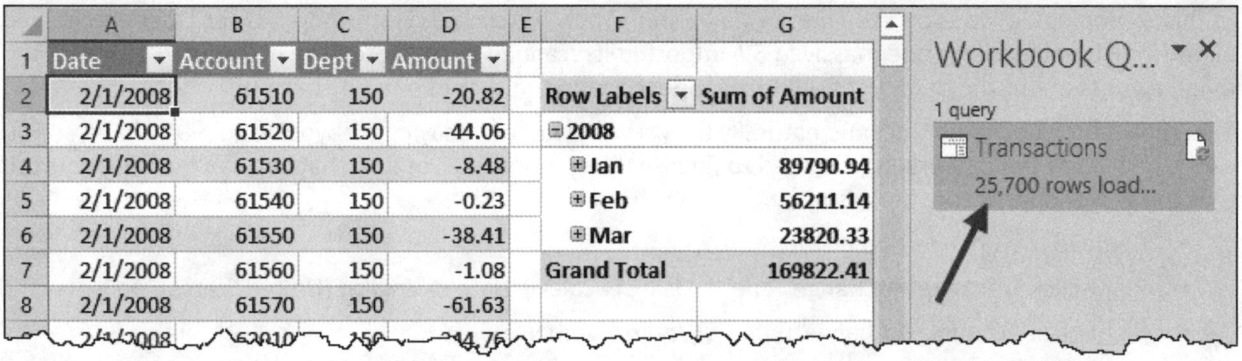

	A	B	C	D	E	F	G	
1	Date ▼	Account ▼	Dept ▼	Amount ▼				
2	2/1/2008	61510	150	-20.82		Row Labels ▼	Sum of Amount	
3	2/1/2008	61520	150	-44.06		⊟ 2008		
4	2/1/2008	61530	150	-8.48		⊞ Jan	89790.94	
5	2/1/2008	61540	150	-0.23		⊞ Feb	56211.14	
6	2/1/2008	61550	150	-38.41		⊞ Mar	23820.33	
7	2/1/2008	61560	150	-1.08		Grand Total	169822.41	
8	2/1/2008	61570	150	-61.63				
	2/1/2008	62010	150	-44.76				

Workbook Q... ▾ ✕

1 query

▦ Transactions

25,700 rows load...

Figure 50 Plainly you've got more files, but why aren't they in the PivotTable?

It's an easy fix. Either right-click the PivotTable → Refresh, or just use Data → Refresh All again. Here's what you end up with:

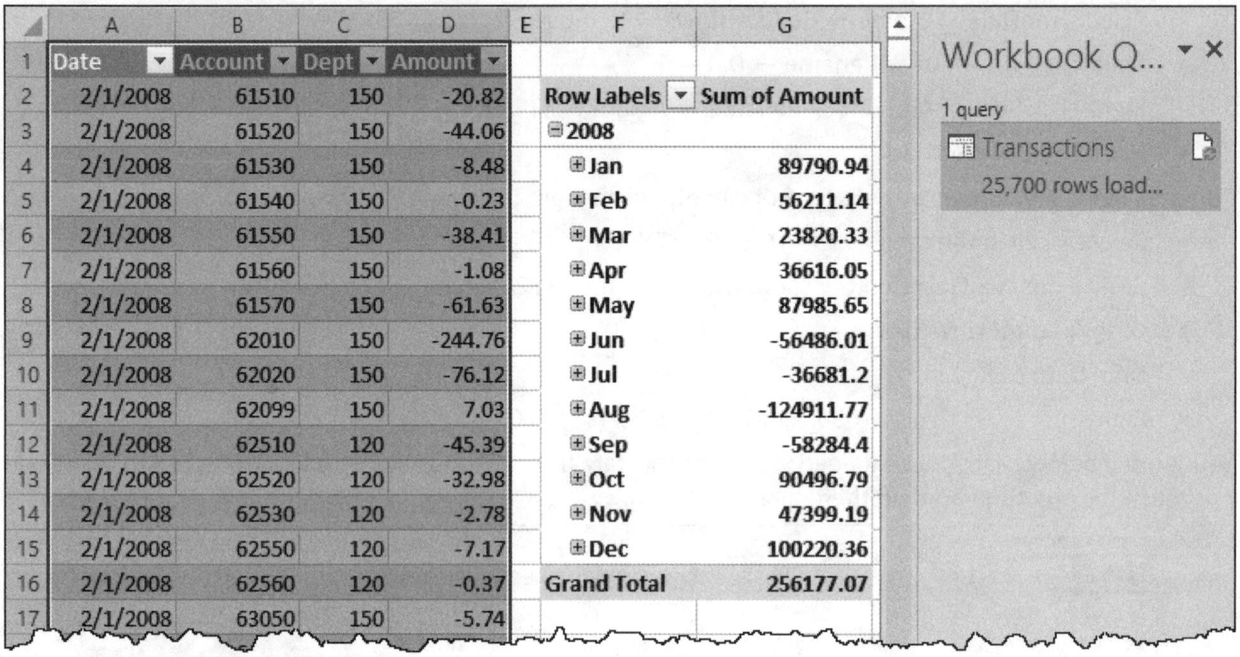

	A	B	C	D	E	F	G	
1	Date ▼	Account ▼	Dept ▼	Amount ▼				
2	2/1/2008	61510	150	-20.82		Row Labels ▼	Sum of Amount	
3	2/1/2008	61520	150	-44.06		⊟ 2008		
4	2/1/2008	61530	150	-8.48		⊞ Jan	89790.94	
5	2/1/2008	61540	150	-0.23		⊞ Feb	56211.14	
6	2/1/2008	61550	150	-38.41		⊞ Mar	23820.33	
7	2/1/2008	61560	150	-1.08		⊞ Apr	36616.05	
8	2/1/2008	61570	150	-61.63		⊞ May	87985.65	
9	2/1/2008	62010	150	-244.76		⊞ Jun	-56486.01	
10	2/1/2008	62020	150	-76.12		⊞ Jul	-36681.2	
11	2/1/2008	62099	150	7.03		⊞ Aug	-124911.77	
12	2/1/2008	62510	120	-45.39		⊞ Sep	-58284.4	
13	2/1/2008	62520	120	-32.98		⊞ Oct	90496.79	
14	2/1/2008	62530	120	-2.78		⊞ Nov	47399.19	
15	2/1/2008	62550	120	-7.17		⊞ Dec	100220.36	
16	2/1/2008	62560	120	-0.37		Grand Total	256177.07	
17	2/1/2008	63050	150	-5.74				

Workbook Q... ▾ ✕

1 query

▦ Transactions

25,700 rows load...

Figure 51 The PivotTable properly updates, proving that you pulled in the records.

How about you add even more files?

- Drag the 2009 folder into the Begin folder
- Drag the 2010 folder into the Begin folder
- Return to Excel → Data → Refresh All → Refresh All

Using a double Refresh All approach works fine for small data sets. When they get large, however, you might want to use VBA to automate the process of refreshing the queries first and the Pivot Tables second, as that avoids duplicate calls to the data source. This topic is covered in Chapter 16.

Absolute magic!

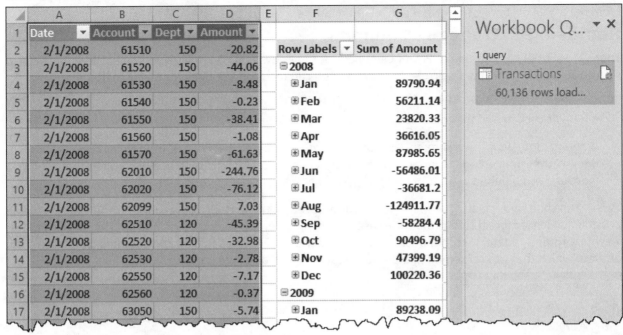

	A	B	C	D	E	F	G
1	Date	Account	Dept	Amount		Row Labels	Sum of Amount
2	2/1/2008	61510	150	-20.82		⊟2008	
3	2/1/2008	61520	150	-44.06		⊞Jan	89790.94
4	2/1/2008	61530	150	-8.48		⊞Feb	56211.14
5	2/1/2008	61540	150	-0.23		⊞Mar	23820.33
6	2/1/2008	61550	150	-38.41		⊞Apr	36616.05
7	2/1/2008	61560	150	-1.08		⊞May	87985.65
8	2/1/2008	61570	150	-61.63		⊞Jun	-56486.01
9	2/1/2008	62010	150	-244.76		⊞Jul	-36681.2
10	2/1/2008	62020	150	-76.12		⊞Aug	-124911.77
11	2/1/2008	62099	150	7.03		⊞Sep	-58284.4
12	2/1/2008	62510	120	-45.39		⊞Oct	90496.79
13	2/1/2008	62520	120	-32.98		⊞Nov	47399.19
14	2/1/2008	62530	120	-2.78		⊞Dec	100220.36
15	2/1/2008	62550	120	-7.17		⊟2009	
16	2/1/2008	62560	120	-0.37		⊞Jan	89238.09
17	2/1/2008	63050	150	-5.74			

Workbook Q... ▾ ✕

1 query

▦ Transactions

60,136 rows load...

Figure 52 60,136 records at the click of a button (or two).

With a solution built in this manner, all you have to do each month is add your data files to the subfolder as you receive them and then refresh the solution.

Recursion

One of the really interesting factors in this solution is that you didn't need to drop the files directly into the root of the Begin folder in order to have them pulled into the Power Query solution. Power Query practices recursion by default, meaning that it examines the folder and all its subfolders for files. This allows you to keep your data files subclassified by year, if desired, and the solution will still work.

If you go back and edit the query, refresh the preview and then returning to the Source step, you see that the folder path for each file is also listed in the Folder Path column. Using this, you could filter to include only the root folder or exclude certain subfolders should that need arise.

Preserving File Properties on Import

Being able to import all files in one shot is a huge time saver, but consider the following real-world scenario.

A system was set up to export a list of transactions to a file and name it based on the last month and the year (for example, Feb 2008.csv). The issue in this particular case is that the system was not set up to include a transaction date inside the file, as all transactions were assumed to be the month-end date. The user who imported these files was expected to import all transactions and place the appropriate month-end date on each row, and he had two years' worth of files to process. Unfortunately, when combining files using the method outlined earlier in this chapter for combining binaries, you lose access to the filenames, which were a key component in solving this solution.

Does this mean you can't use Power Query to do the job? Not at all. You just need to use some different tricks, described next.

Setting Up the Import

The initial steps in setting up the import are the same as outlined earlier in the chapter, with the only difference being that you'll now get a large list of files (since you moved the extra folders into the Begin folder). Start by following these steps, which are the same ones you took earlier:

- New Query → From File → From Folder
- Select the Begin Folder
- Right-click the Extension column → Transform → Lowercase
- Select the Extension column's filter arrow → Text Filters → Equals → Equals .csv

From here, things change from what you've done before

Removing Extraneous Columns

There are a lot of columns in the Power Query editor right now, and you really don't need them for the next steps. You should get rid of the irrelevant ones so you can focus on the ones that truly matter:

- Select the Name column → hold down Ctrl → select the Content column
- Right-click one of the columns → Remove Other Columns

> Power Query works as a sequential macro recorder, processing each step before moving on. This means that unlike Excel, it doesn't require precedent columns to stick around. Given that, and because you've already filtered CSV files, you can remove that column as well.

These steps had two effects. The first is that you removed all the extraneous columns in the easiest fashion possible (which is more future-proofing in case the Power Query team decides to add another column to this view in a future update). Second, because of the order in which you selected the columns, you flipped the order in which they are presented in the Power Query editor, as shown below:

⊞▾	Name	▾	Content	↓↓
1	Feb 2008.csv		Binary	
2	Jan 2008.csv		Binary	
3	Mar 2008.csv		Binary	
4	Apr 2008.csv		Binary	
5	Aug 2008.csv		Binary	

Figure 53 Columns thinned down and reordered in the Power Query editor.

Converting Text to Dates

The next task is to convert the filenames into valid dates for the month end. Power Query actually has some very good facilities for this, but in order for them to work, the data needs to look like a date, which takes a couple of tricks:

- Right-click the Name column → Replace Values
- Set Value to Find to .csv → leave Replace With blank → OK
- Right-click the Name column → Replace Values
- Set Value to Find to a single space → set Replace With to " 1, " (space number one comma space—but without the quotation marks) → OK

The data should now look as follows:

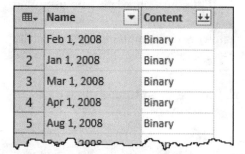

⊞▾	Name	▾	Content	↓↓
1	Feb 1, 2008		Binary	
2	Jan 1, 2008		Binary	
3	Mar 1, 2008		Binary	
4	Apr 1, 2008		Binary	
5	Aug 1, 2008		Binary	

Figure 54 Data that looks like a date but is still text.

At this point you can force the data to be a valid date and increment it to the last day of the month:

- Right-click the Name column → Change Type → Date
- Go to the Transform tab → Date → Month → End of Month
- Right-click the Name column → Rename → Date

You now have the month-end dates prepared to merge with your transactional records:

	Date	▼	Content	±±
1	2/29/2008		Binary	
2	1/31/2008		Binary	
3	3/31/2008		Binary	
4	4/30/2008		Binary	
5	8/31/2008		Binary	

Figure 55 Proper dates in the Date column.

 There is no need to force this set of dates to import using the locale settings, as Power Query will correctly recognize a full text date.

Merging File Properties with Binary Content

At this point you are ready to merge the month-end dates with all the rows inside the binary files. The big challenge is that clicking the Combine Binaries button just throws away the Date column you worked so hard on. So you need to extract the contents of each binary file. Here's what you do:

- Go to the Add Column tab → Add Custom Column
- Enter the following formula:

```
=Csv.Document([Content])
```

- Click OK

 Power Query formulas are case sensitive, so make sure that everything is cased correctly, or it won't work.

 If you don't want to type a long field name, you can just double-click it in the field list when you are building your custom column formula. This will place the field list in your formula, surrounded by square braces.

The result is a new column called Custom, which is filled with a bunch of tables:

	Date	▼	Content	±±	Custom	�).↑↓
1	2/29/2008		Binary		Table	
2	1/31/2008		Binary		Table	
3	3/31/2008		Binary		Table	
4	4/30/2008		Binary		Table	
5	8/31/2008		Binary		Table	
6	12/...		Binary		Table	

Figure 56 A column of tables.

Stop and think about that formula for a second. The Csv.Document() function is the function you can use to turn the contents of a binary file into a table. [Content] simply refers to the column name.

 Although you might expect one, there is no Txt.Document() function. If you want to convert the contents of a text file into a table, you use the Csv.Document() function.

To see what is inside one of those files, click in the whitespace beside the word Table. (If you actually click the word Table, Power Query will drill into the table, but if you click to the right side, you see a preview at the bottom of the screen, as shown below.)

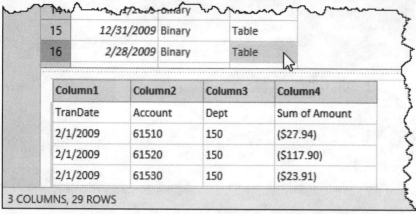

| 15 | 12/31/2009 | Binary | Table |
| 16 | 2/28/2009 | Binary | Table |

Column1	Column2	Column3	Column4
TranDate	Account	Dept	Sum of Amount
2/1/2009	61510	150	($27.94)
2/1/2009	61520	150	($117.90)
2/1/2009	61530	150	($23.91)

3 COLUMNS, 29 ROWS

Figure 57 A preview of the Feb 2009 binary files contents in table format.

With that content now available to you, how do you get to it? First, clear out the noise by right-clicking the Content column → Remove.

It's finally time. There is a new little double-headed arrow symbol at the top right of the Custom column. Click it, and you get this:

Search Columns to Expand

⦿ Expand   ◯ Aggregate

☑ (Select All Columns)
☑ Column1
☑ Column2
☑ Column3
☑ Column4

☐ Use original column name as prefix

[OK]   [Cancel]

Figure 58 Expanding tables into columns.

This dialog allows you to choose which columns to expand. If there were columns you didn't want, you would simply uncheck them. You've already seen via the preview that each of these four columns contains useful information, so in this case, you can keep them all.

The only change that you'll want to make here is to uncheck the Use Original Column Name as Prefix checkbox. If you leave this set, Power Query will prefix each column with Custom, so you get Custom.Column1, Custom.Column2, and so on.

When you click OK, your columns all expand, but this time Power Query preserves the Date column (unlike the Combine Binaries feature, which removed it):

⊞▾	Date ▾	Column1 ▾	Column2 ▾	Column3 ▾	Column4 ▾
1	2/29/2008	TranDate	Account	Dept	Sum of Amount
2	2/29/2008	2/1/2008	61510	150	($20.82)
3	2/29/2008	2/1/2008	61520	150	($44.06)
4	2/29/2008	2/1/2008	61530	150	($8.48)
5	2/29/2008	2/1/2008	61540	150	($0.23)
6	2/29/2008	2/1/2008	61550	150	($38.41)
7	2/29/2008	2/1/2008	61560	150	($1.08)
8	2/29/2008	2/1/2008	61570	150	($61.63)

⊿ PROPERTIES

Name

Query1

All Properties

⊿ APPLIED STEPS

Source   ⚙
Removed Other Columns   ⚙
⌐ played Value   ⚙

Figure 59 The dates stick around when the column is expanded.

It's unfortunate that Power Query doesn't try to take any liberties and help you out with data types and such here. You have to do that manual cleanup yourself, but at least this is a one-time thing, as it will just refresh in future. Here's what you need to do:

- Go to the Transform tab → Use First Row as Headers
- Right-click Column 1 → Rename → Month End
- Right-click TranDate → Change Type → Using Locale → Date → English (US)
- Select TranDate → Home → Reduce Rows → Remove Errors
- Right-click TranDate → Rename → Date
- Right-click Sum of Amount → Rename → Amount
- Right-click Account → Change Type → Whole Number
- Right-click Dept → Change Type → Whole Number
- Right-click Amount → Change Type → Decimal Number

The query is now shaped up to be consistent with the previous output:

▦▾	Month End ▾	Date ▾	Account ▾	Dept ▾	Amount ▾
1	2/29/2008	2/1/2008	61510	150	(20.82)
2	2/29/2008	2/1/2008	61520	150	(44.06)
3	2/29/2008	2/1/2008	61530	150	(8.48)
4	2/29/2008	2/1/2008	61540	150	(0.23)
5	2/29/2008	2/1/2008	61550	150	(38.41)
6	2/29/2008	2/1/2008	61560	150	(1.08)
7	2/29/2008	2/1/2008	61570	150	(61.63)
8	2/29/2008	2/1/2008	61010		

Figure 60 All files imported from a folder, preserving data based on the file properties.

Finally, you can complete the query:

- Change the query name to ManualCombine
- Home → Close & Load
- And at this point you can build a PivotTable and prove that it matches the results you got in the previous section, with the only difference being that you've included a new field that was derived from the properties—something that is impossible using the easy Combine Binaries method.

Implications of the From Folder Feature

Importing files on an individual basis as described in Chapter 2 is generally the way people start building Power Query solutions. That approach can work well in any of the following scenarios:

- Where the data set will grow slowly over time
- Where the transformation requirements are different for each file in the folder
- Where you didn't realize the solution would expand over multiple files

If, however, you suspect that a solution may grow to be bigger than one file, and the data setup will be consistent, there is nothing to stop you from using the approach in this chapter as follows:

- Set up a subfolder
- Move your single file into that folder
- Leverage the Import From Folder functionality against the subfolder

Yes, there is only one file in there today, but so what? As you get new files that pertain to the solution, you just throw them in the subfolder, and they are instantly part of your solution!

Sometimes a little foresight can go a long way in building solutions that stand the test of time.

Chapter 5 Aggregating Excel Worksheets

So far, each of the techniques demonstrated for appending data has been based on pulling data from external CSV or TXT files. As any Excel pro knows, however, the world of data is much bigger than just these types of files. There is a huge amount of data stored inside Excel files as well, and you need the ability to combine those data sources together. For example, you might want to be able to append all tables in a workbook. Or you might want to be able to append all worksheets in a workbook (where tables haven't been set up). And, naturally, you need to be able to accomplish these goals from within the active workbook or from an external one.

While the good news is that these feats can all be accomplished, the bad news is that there is no easy way to accomplish these tasks via the standard user interface. Each of them requires some minor manipulation of the Power Query formula bar—although nothing more serious than what you've seen so far.

It's important to understand here that the methods for dealing with data in your active workbook are quite different from those for pulling data from an external file.

Aggregating Tables and Ranges in the Current File

Pulling data from within the current file works like this:

- Start with a blank query
- Enter the following function in the Power Query formula bar:
  ```
  =Excel.CurrentWorkbook()
  ```
- Filter and expand the tables or ranges you need

This process gives you access to the following objects:

- Excel tables
- Named ranges
- Workbook connections

Unfortunately, this process doesn't allow you to enumerate all worksheets in the file.

Consolidating Tables

Let's look at some specific examples, starting with the Ch05 Example Files\Consolidate Tables-Start.xlsx.

In this file you'll find three worksheets that list gift certificates issued by a spa for the current month. The clerk who created the workbook never added any issue dates to the certificates, although she did dutifully create table names in the format Jan_2008, Feb_2008, and so on.

In order to analyze these transactions, the data obviously needs to be consolidated, and Power Query is the perfect tool for doing that. Let's get started:

- Create a new query → From Other Sources → Blank Query
- Type the following into the formula bar:
  ```
  =Excel.CurrentWorkbook()
  ```

You now see your list of tables:

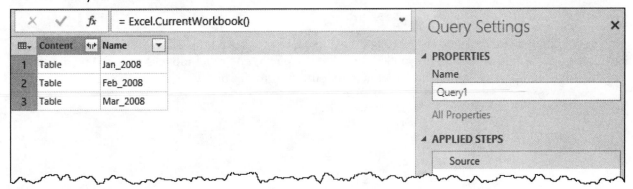

Figure 61 The list of tables in the current workbook.

As you learned in Chapter 4, you can click in the whitespace beside the dark green words in the Content column to preview the data. You also know that if you click the double-headed arrow at the top of that column, you'll be able to expand the columns of the tables without losing the Name column's details. Here's what you do:

- Click the double-headed arrow to expand the Content column
- Uncheck Use Original Column Name as Prefix → OK

The data expands nicely, keeping the name column in place, allowing you to continue on and convert the table names into dates:

- Right-click the Name column → Replace Values
- Replace the _ character with " 1, " (space number one comma space—but without the quotation marks)
- Right-click the Name column → Change Type → Date
- Go to the Transform tab → Date → Month → End of Month
- Right-click the Name column → Rename → Month End
- Change the name of the query to Gift Certificates

The completed query now looks as follows:

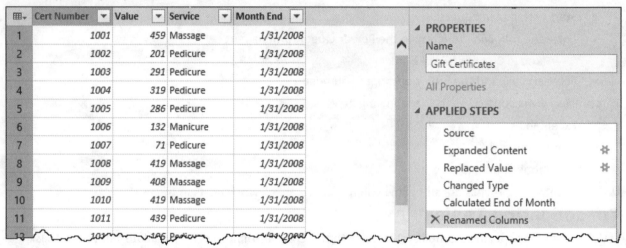

Figure 62 Completed query, ready to go.

Everything looks good here, but when you choose Close & Load, you trigger a bunch of errors:

Figure 63 It looked so good! How can there be 62 errors?

So what happened? Go back and step through the query by right-clicking the Gift Certificate query → Edit → Select the Source step. At this point, you'll notice that you've got one more table listed than you did earlier. It's the Gift Certificates table that was created as an output from this query!

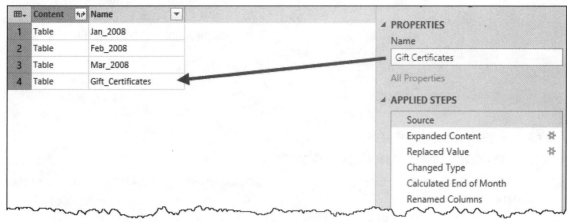

⊞ ▾	Content	↕↔	Name	▼
1	Table		Jan_2008	
2	Table		Feb_2008	
3	Table		Mar_2008	
4	Table		Gift_Certificates	

◢ PROPERTIES
Name
Gift Certificates

All Properties

◢ APPLIED STEPS
Source
Expanded Content   ✿
Replaced Value   ✿
Changed Type
Calculated End of Month
Renamed Columns

Figure 64 The finalized query appears in the list of tables.

 When using =Excel.CurrentWorkbook() to enumerate tables or ranges, remember that the output query will also be recognized upon refresh. To deal with this, some future-proofing steps may be required, depending on how you built your query. These steps could include filtering to avoid potential duplication or errors, changing data types, or changing anything else that you set up in advance to guard against the possibilities of your query breaking.

You should now step through each step of the query, paying attention to what happens.

When you get to the Replaced Value step, scroll down to row 63. Do you notice anything dangerous unfolding here?

⊞ ▾	Cert Number	▼	Value	▼	Service	▼	Name	▼
61	3025		280		Manicure		Mar 1, 2008	
62	3026		106		Pedicure		Mar 1, 2008	
63	1001		459		Massage		Gift 1, Certificates	
64	1002		201		Pedicure		Gift 1, Certificates	
65	1003				dicure		Gift 1	

Figure 65 Problems arising in the values to be converted to dates.

When the Changed Types step is evaluated next, it tries to convert all data in the Name column to dates, which it obviously can't do for Gift 1, Certificates. Instead, it places an error value in the column for each cell that contained that text:

⊞ ▾	Cert Number	▼	Value	▼	Service	▼	Name	▼
61	3025		280		Manicure		3/1/2008	
62	3026		106		Pedicure		3/1/2008	
63	1001		459		Massage		Error	
64	1002		201		Pedicure		Error	
65	1003		291		Pedicure		Error	

Figure 66 Invalid dates converted into errors.

This issue actually works in your favor, as everything from the Gift Certificates table is a duplication of the data. With those rows throwing errors, you can simply filter them out:

- Make sure the Changed Type step is selected
- Select the Name column → Home → Reduce Rows → Remove Errors
- Confirm that you'd like to insert a new step into the middle of your query
- Go to Home → Close & Load

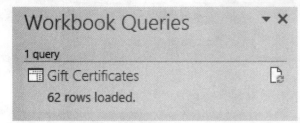

With the filtering done, you get a positive result from Power Query loading only 62 rows of data—with no errors.

Figure 67 There are 62 rows loaded from 3 tables.

Consolidating Ranges and Worksheets

Now what if the worksheets didn't have tables, but the clerk named the worksheets instead? In that case, could you consolidate all the worksheets? Yes, but as mentioned before, there is no built-in facility to do this. Instead, you have to make use of the ability to talk to named ranges by calling a specific named range.

The trick is to define a print area. Why? Because the print area's name is, in fact, a dynamic range name. So to pull a print range into Power Query, you need to follow the steps to connect to a dynamic named range, as explained in Chapter 1:

- Select the Jan 2008 worksheet → go to the Page Layout tab → Print Titles
- In the Print area box enter A:D → OK
- Repeat this process for the Feb 2008 and Mar 2008 worksheets
- Create a new query → From Other Sources → Blank Query
- Enter the following in the formula bar:

```
=Excel.CurrentWorkbook()
```

You now see a list of all the tables and named ranges, including the print areas!

⊞▾	Content ⁴ᵣ⁺	Name ▾
1	Table	Jan_2008
2	Table	Feb_2008
3	Table	Mar_2008
4	Table	'Feb 2008'!Print_Area
5	Table	'Jan 2008'!Print_Area
6	Table	'Mar 2008'!Print_Area

Figure 68 Excel.CurrentWorkbook() showing the print areas.

You currently have both tables and the print areas, but you can filter this down and expand it to see what you get:

- Filter the Name column → Text Filters → Ends With → Print_Area → OK
- Click the Expand button at the top of the Content column
- Leave all columns selected → uncheck the Use Original Column Name as Prefix → OK

Notice that things are different here. You have the entire worksheet, including each column in your print range:

⊞▾	Column1 ▾	Column2 ▾	Column3 ▾	Column4 ▾	Name ▾
1	Gift Certificates Issued - Feb 2008	null	null	null	'Feb 2008'!Print_Area
2		null	null	null	null	'Feb 2008'!Print_Area
3	Cert Number	Value	Service	null	'Feb 2008'!Print_Area
4		2001	498	Massage	null	'Feb 2008'!Print_Area
5		2002	448	Massage	null	'Feb 2008'!Print_Area
6		2003	249	Manicure	null	'Feb 2008'!Print_Area
7		2004	284	Manicure	null	'Feb 2008'!Print_Area

Figure 69 A raw look at the worksheet.

This obviously means that more data cleanup needs to be done in order to aggregate these ranges and turn them into clean tables, but the good news is that it can be done. To clean up this particular data set, follow these steps:

- Go to Home → Remove Rows → Remove Top Rows → 2 → OK
- Transform → Use First Row as Headers
- Filter the Cert Number column → uncheck *null*
- Right-click the Cert Number column → Change Type → Whole Number
- Select the Cert Number column
- Go to Home → Reduce Rows → Remove Errors → OK
- Select the Cert Number column → hold down Shift → select the Service column
- Right-click one of the selected column headers → Remove Other Columns
- Change the query name to AllSheets → OK
- Go to Home → Close & Load

When working with print areas, it is a good idea to try to restrict a print area to only the rows and columns you need—for two reasons. The first reason is that it takes Power Query longer to process more data points. The second reason is that each column is just referred to as Column# in the expansion window, which makes it very easy to pull in extraneous columns that just need to be removed later.

Aggregating Data from Other Workbooks

Say that you are building a solution that relies on data stored in other Excel workbooks. In this case, the user is storing data in worksheets named with the month and year, but only one quarter per workbook. Those workbooks are stored in a folder on the network, and you need to consolidate the data within them.

The methods used earlier in this chapter have been targeted at the objects inside the current workbook, and they don't work when you're talking to external workbooks. Instead, you actually need to generate a list of Excel workbooks and extract their contents, similar to what you did in Chapter 4 when you extracted the contents of CSV files.

Sourcing the Data

You start the data sourcing process from a blank workbook:

- Create a new query → From File → From Folder
- Select the Ch05 Examples\Source Files folder

When Power Query lists the files, you can see that you already have several files in here that are non-Excel files:

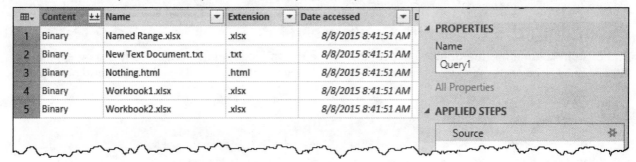

Figure 70 Non-Excel files mixed in with the files you actually want.

You need to filter those files out of the list, as you only want Excel workbooks:

- Right-click the Extension column → Transform → Lowercase
- Filter the Extension column → Text filters → Begins with → .xls
- Select the Content and Name columns → right-click → Remove Other Columns

At this point you might be tempted to click the Combine Binaries button, and unfortunately Power Query will let you do it. If you do, though, you'll find that Power Query combines the files but can't import them:

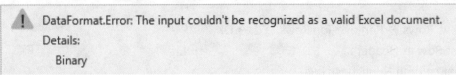

DataFormat.Error: The input couldn't be recognized as a valid Excel document.
Details:
    Binary

Figure 71 Power Query says it can't combine Excel binaries.

> If you actually clicked the Combine Binaries button, you now need to go to the Applied Steps box and remove both the Imported Excel and Combined Binaries steps.

So if you can't combine and import the files using the easy method, you have to do it the hard way:

- Go to the Add Column tab → Add Custom Column
- Enter the following formula:

```
=Excel.Workbook([Content])
```

- Click OK
- Right-click the Content column → Remove

Your new custom column now contains a column of tables, which contain each of the objects you can connect to—including all Excel tables, named ranges, and even worksheets in the Excel file:

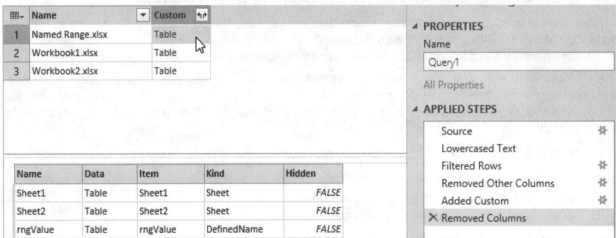

Figure 72 Previewing the parts of the Named Range.xlsx file.

Expanding the Excel File Contents

The Custom column has the double-headed arrow (the expand icon) in its header, so it can be expanded. When you click on the expand icon on the Custom column, you get a list of all the different workbook parts:

	Name	Name.1	Data	Item	Kind
1	Named Range.xlsx	Sheet1	Table	Sheet1	Sheet
2	Named Range.xlsx	Sheet2	Table	Sheet2	Sheet
3	Named Range.xlsx	rngValue	Table	rngValue	DefinedName
4	Workbook1.xlsx	Jan 2008	Table	Jan 2008	Sheet
5	Workbook1.xlsx	Feb 2008	Table	Feb 2008	Sheet
6	Workbook1.xlsx	Mar 2008	Table	Mar 2008	Sheet
7	Workbook1.xlsx	Jan_2008	Table	Jan_2008	Table
8	Workbook1.xlsx	Feb_2008	Table	Feb_2008	Table

Figure 73 All workbook parts expanded.

At this point, it is critical that you recognize what you have here. The Kind column shows that you have Sheet, DefinedName, and Table objects. Remember, however, that you can define names over specific cells in a table and/or worksheet and that tables exist in worksheets. It is very easy to duplicate data in your import if you don't filter this area appropriately.

Importing objects of different types as listed in the Kind column could lead to duplication of data!

You want to extract the worksheet data only, so follow these steps:

- Filter the Kind column to show only Sheet data types
- Filter the Name column to remove the Named Range.xlsx file
- Select the Name, Name.1 and Data columns → right-click → Remove Other Columns
- Expand all three columns contained in the Data column (and clear the prefix setting)

The query now looks as follows:

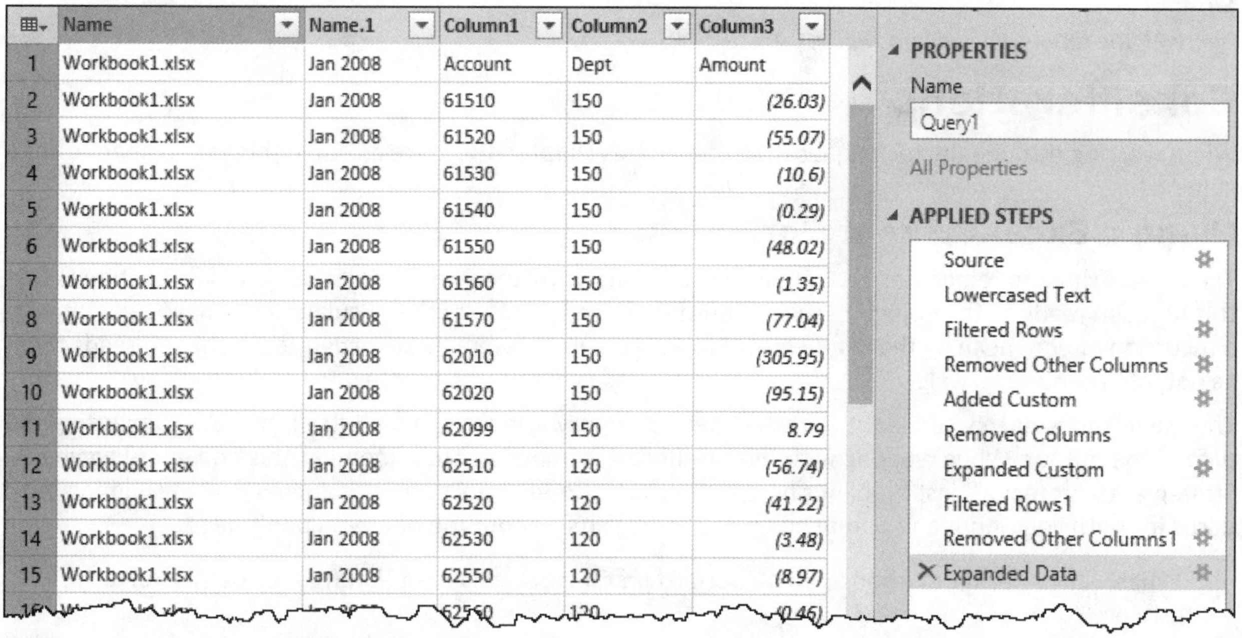

#	Name	Name.1	Column1	Column2	Column3
1	Workbook1.xlsx	Jan 2008	Account	Dept	Amount
2	Workbook1.xlsx	Jan 2008	61510	150	(26.03)
3	Workbook1.xlsx	Jan 2008	61520	150	(55.07)
4	Workbook1.xlsx	Jan 2008	61530	150	(10.6)
5	Workbook1.xlsx	Jan 2008	61540	150	(0.29)
6	Workbook1.xlsx	Jan 2008	61550	150	(48.02)
7	Workbook1.xlsx	Jan 2008	61560	150	(1.35)
8	Workbook1.xlsx	Jan 2008	61570	150	(77.04)
9	Workbook1.xlsx	Jan 2008	62010	150	(305.95)
10	Workbook1.xlsx	Jan 2008	62020	150	(95.15)
11	Workbook1.xlsx	Jan 2008	62099	150	8.79
12	Workbook1.xlsx	Jan 2008	62510	120	(56.74)
13	Workbook1.xlsx	Jan 2008	62520	120	(41.22)
14	Workbook1.xlsx	Jan 2008	62530	120	(3.48)
15	Workbook1.xlsx	Jan 2008	62550	120	(8.97)
16			62560	120	(0.46)

PROPERTIES

Name

Query1

All Properties

APPLIED STEPS

Source

Lowercased Text

Filtered Rows

Removed Other Columns

Added Custom

Removed Columns

Expanded Custom

Filtered Rows1

Removed Other Columns1

✕ Expanded Data

Figure 74 Excel data imported from an External workbook.

Transforming the Data

Obviously, the data in this example still needs some cleanup. You should do that now and finalize the query:

- Go to Transform → Use First Row as Headers
- Right-click the Workbook1.xlsx column → Rename → Source File
- Right-click the Jan 2008 column → Rename → Month
- Right-click the Amount column → Change Type → Decimal Number
- Select the Amount column → Home → Reduce Rows → Remove Errors
- Change the name of the query to FromExcelFiles
- Go to Home → Close & Load

The data is loaded into a table, so you can create a PivotTable configured as follows in order to see what you pulled in. Use these settings:

- Source File and Month on Rows
- Month and Amount on Values

Here you can see that you've successfully pulled data from two different files and three worksheets within each, for a total of more than 12,000 records:

Row Labels ▼	Count of Month	Sum of Amount
⊟ **Workbook1.xlsx**	**6084**	**169822.41**
Feb 2008	1857	56211.14
Jan 2008	2030	89790.94
Mar 2008	2197	23820.33
⊟ **Workbook2.xlsx**	**6084**	**169822.41**
Apr 2008	2030	89790.94
Jun 2008	2197	23820.33
May 2008	1857	56211.14
Grand Total	**12168**	**339644.82**

Figure 75 The results of your hard work.

Considerations

When working through the techniques described in this chapter, there are a couple things you need to keep in mind.

Using =Excel.CurrentWorkbook()

The biggest thing to remember about building solutions using the Excel.CurrentWorkbook() function is that this function reads all the objects in the current file. Since this affects the calculation chain, you get hit with a recursion effect, meaning that as the new tables are built, Power Query recognizes them and reads them as potential content as well.

The implications of this appear at refresh, when the query attempts to load itself, thereby duplicating the data in the output. When working with this method, it is important to remember this and guard against it. Strategies to protect against problems here range from filtering errors on key columns to using naming standards for both your input and output columns so you can filter out the ones you don't need.

> Whatever method you choose, make sure to test it through a couple refreshes before releasing it to production!

Using =Excel.Workbook([Content])

Unlike with Excel.CurrentWorkbook(), using the Excel.Workbook() function doesn't cause any recursion issues. The reason is that Excel.Workbook() reads from *the most recently saved copy* of an external Excel workbook. This can obviously have implications if a user is in the process of updating the file but hasn't saved it, as you won't get the most current data that you might expect.

The other key concern when using the Excel.Workbook() function to extract the contents of a workbook is that it pulls worksheets in addition to ranges and tables. This makes it very easy to duplicate data if you are not careful, as all named ranges and tables exist in worksheets. Pay careful attention to filtering the Kind column to avoid this issue.

> Even if there is only one kind of data in the workbook when you build the solution, it's not a bad idea to future-proof your solution by forcing a filter to accept only the desired kind. This will prevent issues when a user adds a table to a data file that never had one.

It should also be recognized that it is entirely possible to use Excel.Workbook() to read from the current workbook, thereby exposing the ability to read worksheet content. (This is useful if you can't define print ranges or other ranges over your data.) Remember, however, that the query will read from the most recently saved copy of the workbook, not the live copy. This has the unfortunate side effect of still facing the recursion issues from the Excel.CurrentWorkbook() function, but you may not see them until the next time you open the file.

Chapter 6 Unpivoting Data

One of the big issues we Excel pros face is that no matter where we get our data, it doesn't always arrive in a useful state. So not only do we waste time getting the data into a workbook to begin with, we then have to spend even more time cleaning it up and changing its layout in order to work with it.

The Curse of Pivoted Data

Say that a user has started tracking his sales on a daily basis, and he sends his data to you in the format shown below:

Sales in Units								
Sales Category	1/1/2014	1/2/2014	1/3/2014	1/4/2014	1/5/2014	1/6/2014	1/7/2014	Total
Beer	103	243	101	137	103	185	111	983
Wine	175	223	138	57	66	199	83	941
Liquor	162	207	103	179	150	147	180	1,128
Total	440	673	342	373	319	531	374	3,052

Figure 76 The dreaded pivoted data set.

Naturally, after tracking his sales in this way for days or weeks, he brings it to you and asks you to build a variety of different reports from it. The answer to this dilemma is, of course, to build PivotTables against the data source. But the issue is that this data set is already pivoted.

This problem comes up for Excel pros all the time. PivotTables were built to quickly turn tables of data into reports that users can more easily consume. The challenge is that users think in this kind of output format, not in tabular format, so they tend to build their data in the format that a PivotTable produces, not in a format that a PivotTable consumes.

Many users think that a simple transposing of the data set will work, but you know that this only changes the look of the data—it doesn't truly convert it into a format that PivotTables are ready to consume.

Category	Beer	Wine	Liquor
1/1/2014	103	175	162
1/2/2014	243	223	207
1/3/2014	101	138	103
1/4/2014	137	57	179
1/5/2014	103	66	150
1/6/2014	185	199	147
1/7/2014	111	83	180

Category	Date	Units
Beer	1/1/2014	103
Beer	1/2/2014	243
Beer	1/3/2014	101
Beer	1/4/2014	137
Beer	1/5/2014	103
Beer	1/6/2014	185
Beer	1/7/2014	111

Figure 77 Transposed data (on the left) vs properly unpivoted data (on the right).

The worst part about this issue is that in the past, there was no tool to easily convert the data back from pivoted to unpivoted, which meant a huge amount of labor was needed to pull this off. But here's another place where Power Query comes to the rescue.

Unpivoting with Ease

This example shows how your life truly changes with Power Query. Open the Ch06 Examples\UnPivot.xlsx file and get ready to unpivot the data set within:

Sales in Units								
Sales Category	1/1/2014	1/2/2014	1/3/2014	1/4/2014	1/5/2014	1/6/2014	1/7/2014	Total
Beer	103	243	101	137	103	185	111	983
Wine	175	223	138	57	66	199	83	941
Liquor	162	207	103	179	150	147	180	1,128
Total	440	673	342	373	319	531	374	3,052

Figure 78 Raw data build in a pivoted format.

Preparing the Data

As you can see, the data is contained in a worksheet, but it has no table associated with it. You already know that you can fix that, so click somewhere in the data and create a new query:

- Create a new query → From Table → OK (to confirm the table boundaries)
- In Excel 2010/2013 adjust the range to $A$4:$I$7 (removing the last row)

The data lands in Power Query, and you now have the ability to make any transformations or manipulations you need. The overall goal here is to unpivot the data, but there is a column you really don't need. The Total column can be removed because you can simply rebuild it with a PivotTable. So right-click the Total column → Remove. You're now left with just the key data: the Sales Category column and a column for each day.

Unpivoting Columns

To unpivot the data set in UnPivot.xlsx, follow these steps:

- Select the 1/1/2014 column → hold down Shift → select the 1/7/2014 column
- Right-click one of the columns → Unpivot Columns

The results are simply astounding: You're already done.

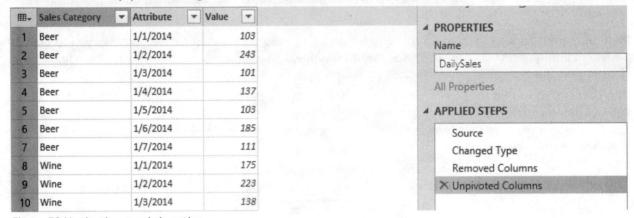

Figure 79 Unpivoting magic in action.

You have only a couple more changes to make here before you finalize your data set:

- Right-click the Attribute column → Change Type → Date
- Right-click the Attribute column → Rename → Date
- Right-click the Value column → Rename → Units
- Rename the query to DailySales
- Go to Home → Close & Load

Can you believe how easy this is?

> Notice that there is no need to use Change Type Using Locale in this instance. Since the data already resides inside Excel, Power Query will recognize this data correctly no matter what your regional settings are.

Repivoting

Next you can build a couple of PivotTables from this data. First, you rebuild the user's existing data:

- Select a cell in the table → Insert PivotTable
- Insert the PivotTable in F1 of the same worksheet
- Place Sales Category on Rows, Date on Columns, and Units on Values

Now you can build an alternate view from the same data set:

- Select a cell in the table → Insert PivotTable
- Insert the PivotTable in F11 of the same worksheet

- Place Sales Category on Rows, Date on Rows (below Category), and Units on Values
- Right-click F12 → Expand/Collapse → Collapse Entire Field

Now you have two completely different sets created very easily from a set of unpivoted data:

	A	B	C	D	E	F	G	H	I
1	Sales Category ▼	Date ▼	Units ▼			Sum of Units	Column Labels ▼		
2	Beer	1/1/2014	103			Row Labels ▼	1/1/2014	1/2/2014	1/3/201
3	Beer	1/2/2014	243			Beer	103	243	10
4	Beer	1/3/2014	101			Liquor	162	207	10
5	Beer	1/4/2014	137			Wine	175	223	13
6	Beer	1/5/2014	103			Grand Total	440	673	3
7	Beer	1/6/2014	185						
8	Beer	1/7/2014	111						
9	Wine	1/1/2014	175						
10	Wine	1/2/2014	223						
11	Wine	1/3/2014	138			Row Labels ▼	Sum of Units		
12	Wine	1/4/2014	57			⊞ Beer	983		
13	Wine	1/5/2014	66			⊞ Liquor	1128		
14	Wine	1/6/2014	199			⊞ Wine	941		
15	Wine	1/7/2014	83			Grand Total	3052		

Figure 80 Two PivotTables built from an unpivoted data set.

Surviving an Update

At this point, you'd probably be fairly comfortable saving the file, returning it to the user, and letting him continue to update it. After all, Power Query solutions can be refreshed at any time.

But say that you do so and the user makes updates and sends it back to you. Upon opening the file, you see that the user has done things that only an end user could think of as acceptable:

Sales Category ▼	1/1/2014 ▼	1/2/2014 ▼	1/3/2014 ▼	1/4/2014 ▼	1/5/2014 ▼	1/6/2014 ▼	1/7/2014 ▼	Total ▼	1/8/20 ▼
Beer	103	243	101	137	103	185	111	983	34
Wine	175	223	138	57	66	199	83	941	86
Cider						78	92	170	47
Liquor	162	207	103	179	150	147	180	1,128	23
Total	440	673	342	373	319	609	466	3,222	

Figure 81 The table, as returned by the end user.

Looking through the changes, you're astounded to see the following issues:

- The new day is added *after* the total column.
- A new sales category has been injected with retroactive data.
- The user didn't complete the total on the new column.

How will the refresh fare, given these changes? To find out, go to the Data tab and click Refresh All two times (once for the Power Query and once for the PivotTables).

The results are nothing short of amazing, as you can see below:

Sum of Units	Column Labels ▼								
Row Labels ▼	1/1/2014	1/2/2014	1/3/2014	1/4/2014	1/5/2014	1/6/2014	1/7/2014	1/8/2014	Grand Total
Beer	103	243	101	137	103	185	111	34	1017
Liquor	162	207	103	179	150	147	180	23	1151
Wine	175	223	138	57	66	199	83	86	1027
Cider						78	92	47	217
Grand Total	440	673	342	373	319	609	466	190	3412

Row Labels ▼	Sum of Units
⊞ Beer	1017
⊞ Liquor	1151
⊞ Wine	1027
⊟ Cider	217
1/6/2014	78
1/7/2014	92
1/8/2014	47
Grand Total	3412

Figure 82 Your PivotTables still work, despite your end user's actions.

Every issue that your user threw at you was handled. The totals are there, the data is in the right order, and the historical values have been updated.

Understanding the Unpivot Functions

There are actually two unpivot functions on the right-click menu in Power Query: Unpivot Columns and Unpivot Other Columns.

How Unpivot Other Columns Works

To be fair, we had you make some unnecessary steps in the example above. Instead of selecting the 1/1/2014 through 1/7/2014 columns, you could have just right-clicked the Sales Category column and chosen the Unpivot Other Columns command. What this command does is unpivot every column other than the one(s) you selected. From a logical point of view, it would have made complete sense when the solution was updated that it just worked as well.

Having said this, the demo was set up this way for a reason—to explain what really happens when you use the Unpivot Columns command.

How Unpivot Columns Actually Works

Based on the terminology of the user interface, you would have expected that when you recorded the step above to unpivot the 1/1/2014 through 1/7/2014 columns, Power Query would hard code those specific columns. It should be plainly obvious now that this is not the case.

Here's what Power Query actually did: It looked at all the columns in the data set and determined that there was one column you did not select. Rather than build you a specific "unpivot these columns" command, it actually recorded code that says "unpivot everything except the column(s) that weren't selected." In this case, that was "unpivot everything except Sales Category."

While this change seems subtle, it actually has some fairly large impacts, both good and bad.

The good news is that it is very difficult to make a mistake and build a scenario that blows up when new daily data columns are added. Essentially, it future-proofs your solution for new dates, as they will always be pulled in.

The bad news is that there is no way through the user interface to lock in a specific "unpivot this column only" command. This means that if you have an Unpivot Columns command in your query, and you add a new column to the data table, it will be unpivoted as well.

Locking Columns to Unpivot

While this need should be unusual, there may come a time when you need the ability to lock in a specific column or columns that you want to unpivot and ensure that new columns added to your source data are not unpivoted by default. Doing so takes some manipulation of the formula in the formula bar.

Assume that you only want to unpivot the Total column, for example. You would take the following steps:

- Create a new query → From Table
- Right-click the Total column → Unpivot Column
- The query at this point would look similar to this, with the final two columns being the unpivoted totals:

	Sales Category	1/1/2014	1/7/2014	1/8/2014	Attribute	Value
1	Beer	103	111	34	Total	983
2	Wine	179	83	86	Total	941
3	Cider	nu	92	47	Total	170
4	Liquor	162	180	23	Total	1128

Figure 83 The Total column has been unpivoted.

- Use the V icon at the right of the formula bar to expand the formula bar
- At this point the formula in the formula bar would read as follows:

```
= Table.UnpivotOtherColumns(#"Changed Type", {"Sales Category",
"1/1/2014", "1/2/2014", "1/3/2014", "1/4/2014", "1/5/2014", "1/6/2014",
"1/7/2014", "1/8/2014"}, "Attribute", "Value")
```

Here's how this code breaks down:

- Table.UnpivotOtherColumns() is the function to be executed
- #"Changed Type" is the name of the previous step from the Applied Steps box
- { . . . } is a list of all the columns, separated by commas
- "Attribute" is the name of the new column that will hold the unpivoted text
- "Value" is the name of the column that will hold the unpivoted values

If you wanted to lock your code to make sure that no other columns were ever unpivoted, you would need to change this from the Table.UnpivotOtherColumns function to use the Table.Unpivot function.

Like Table.UnpivotOtherColumns, the Table.Unpivot function takes four parameters:

- The step name you want to unpivot: #"Changed Type"
- A list of the columns you want to unpivot: {"Total"}
- The name of the column to hold the unpivoted text: "Attribute"
- The name of the column to hold the unpivoted values: "Value"

So the overall formula would read as follows:

```
=Table.Unpivot(#"Changed Type",{"Total"},"Attribute","Value")
```

And the effect would look exactly the same as the version that was produced above with the original code. The difference is that any other column added to the source data table after the fact would not also get unpivoted upon refresh.

In order to lock the unpivot of multiple columns, you just provide the full list of the columns to unpivot between the {} characters, with each column header surrounded in quotes and separated by commas.

Chapter 7 Importing Nondelimited Text Files

One of the biggest challenges for many Excel pros is importing and cleaning nondelimited text files. If you've ever dealt with one of these, you know how painful it can be. They typically arrive with some default name like ASCII.TXT and are essentially character-by-character representations of what the output should look like when printed. This means that they're subject to all kinds of crazy issues, including the following:

- Characters aligned by position instead of delimited by a character
- Inconsistent alignment
- Nonprinting characters (such as control codes)
- Repeating header rows

A major part of the job for many Excel pros is importing this type of information into Excel and cleaning it. And all this has to happen *before* they can get to the analysis that actually adds business value.

If you've been there, you know the process follows this general flow:

1. Import the file into Excel via Data → From Text.
2. Work in a postage stamp–sized Import Wizard window, trying to determine how the columns are delimited and which to skip.
3. Dump the results of the Import Wizard into a worksheet.
4. Turn the data into a proper Excel table.
5. Sort and filter the table to remove garbage rows.
6. Clean and trim the text in the columns.

And the best part is that next month, when you get the updated data file, you get to relive this exciting process *all over again*. Wouldn't it be nice if there were a better way? Great news! There is, and you've found it.

Connecting to the File

You connect to a nondelimited text file the same way you connect to any other text file:

- Create a New Query → From File → From Text
- Browse to Ch07 Examples → GL Jan-Mar.TXT

Power Query puts the data in a single column:

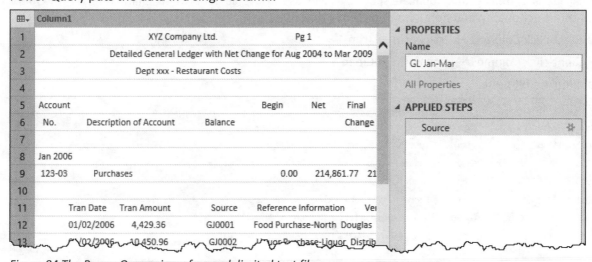

Figure 84 The Power Query view of a nondelimited text file.

The first benefit you'll notice over the standard Excel import process is that you get to work in a full-sized window. That's a massive improvement all on its own, as you can actually see what is going on.

 If your column is too narrow, just mouse over the right side of the column header, hold down the left mouse button, and drag it wider.

You'll also notice that, since the file is not delimited with any consistent delimiters, Power Query has not made any guesses about your data. Instead, it has left the entire process to you. Given the state of this file, that is probably not a bad thing.

> Before we dig any further into this topic, note that there are *many* ways to import nondelimited text files, and none of them are right or wrong. The example in this chapter has been architected to show a great deal of transformations via the user interface, as well as the typical way an Excel pro might approach this task. With more experience, you'll find that quicker routes to the end goal are almost certainly possible.

Cleaning Nondelimited Files

The general goal when starting to clean up a nondelimited file is to try to get the data into a semblance of columnar data as quickly as possible. In this case, the top 10 rows don't seem to add much value, while the 11th row looks like it may be column headers. Therefore, go to Home → Reduce Rows → Remove Rows → Remove top Rows → 10 → OK.

The rows disappear and will not be imported into the end solution:

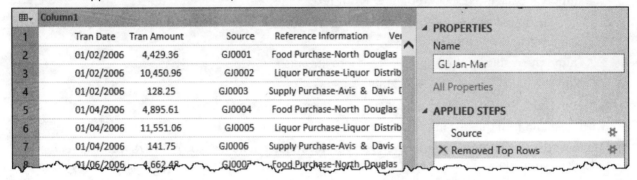

Figure 85 The top rows are removed, bringing the headers closer to the top.

Next, you need to choose a direction to break into this data. You could try breaking in from the left or right, but currently there are a ton of extra leading spaces, and there are duplicated spaces in the middle. It would be nice to get rid of those.

In Excel it is a standard practice to run textual data through the TRIM() and CLEAN() functions in order to remove all leading, trailing, and duplicate spaces, as well as remove all nonprinting characters. Power Query also has this functionality, and here's how you apply that now:

- Right-click Column1 → Transform → Trim
- Right-click Column1 → Transform → Clean

The data looks a bit better:

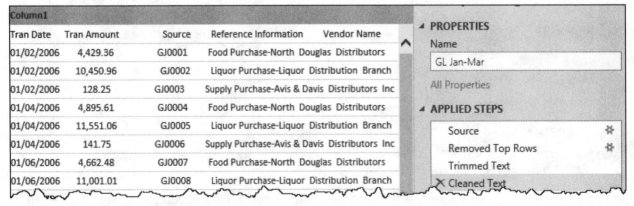

Figure 86 Data trimmed and cleaned.

At this point, you may notice that Power Query's trim functionality doesn't work quite the same as Excel's. While Excel's TRIM() function removes all leading and trailing spaces and replaces any duplicate spaces in the middle of the data with a single space, Power Query's doesn't do that last part. Instead, it only trims off the leading and trailing spaces.

The CLEAN() function in Power Query does line up with Excel's, although it's more difficult to see. Nonprinting characters are rendered as a little question mark in a box within the Excel user interface. In Power Query they show as a space. Regardless, if you step back and forth between the Trimmed Text and Cleaned Text steps in the Applied Steps box, you'll see that the spaces around the & in Avis & Davis have been cleaned away by the Cleaned Text step.

Splitting Columns by Position

The next step is to start splitting apart the columns. The basic approach at this point is to split by the number of characters, making an educated guess about how many you need and then refining that guess. Since the number of characters in the date is 10 characters, you can try 12 for a first go:

- Go to Home → Split Column → By Number of Characters → 12 → Repeatedly → OK

That plainly didn't work out! As you can see below, the date column may be fine, but the others sure aren't:

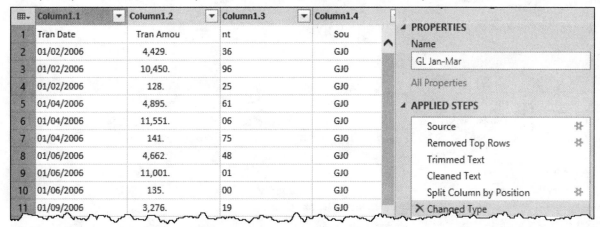

Figure 87 The data didn't split as well as you'd intended.

This is not a big deal, as you can just try again by refining your original efforts:

- Remove the Changed Type step
- Click the gear beside the Split Column by Position step
- Change it to 15 → OK

The result is much better:

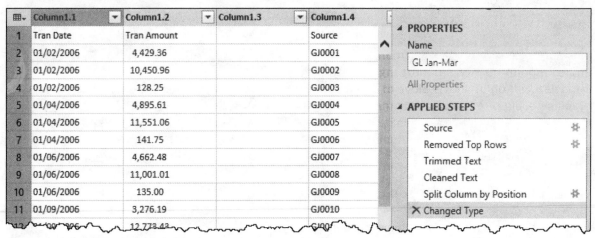

Figure 88 A much more inspiring view of the data.

It is also worth mentioning that there is nothing forcing you to choose the Repeatedly setting in the options when splitting columns. If the document is inconsistent, you can choose to split once from the left/right side. This allows you very granular control, on a column-by-column basis.

You can now make two more changes. Since the Changed Type step just declares all the columns as text (which they won't be when you're done), you can remove the Changed Type step because it's irrelevant. You can then promote the first row to column headers. Follow these steps:

- Remove the Changed Type step
- Go to the Transform tab → Use First Row as Headers

The Beauty of Errors in Power Query

The data is now starting to look somewhat cleaned, even if you'd like to change some of the column headers as you go along. At this point, it's typically recommended that you work from left to right, cleaning up as much of the columnar data as you can and making sure it's all valid.

If you scroll down at this point, you'll find that there are a lot of garbage rows in this data, mostly from the repeating page headers and section breaks that were included in the document. The first block of these issues occurs at row 40 and introduces a bunch of ugliness:

▦▾	Tran Date	▾	Tran Amount	▾	▾	Source
38	01/30/2006		11,612.20			GJ0038
39	01/30/2006		122.14			GJ0039
40		null		null	null	
41	Feb 2006			null	null	
42	123-03		Purchases			
43		null		null	null	
44	Tran Date		Tran Amount			Source
45	02/01/2006		4,395.03			GJ0040
46		null		null	null	
47	March 20,2009		2:08pm			
48	XYZ Company Ltd		.			Pg 2
49	Detailed Genera		l Ledger with N		et Change for A	ug 2004 to Mar

Figure 89 Irrelevant rows mixed in with real data.

The question is how to deal with these. Some are dates, some are text, some are nulls. Try this:

- Right-click the Tran Date column → Change Type → Using Locale → Date → English (US) → OK

The result is a bunch of errors in the Tran Date column:

▦▾	Tran Date	▾	Tran Amount	▾	▾	Source
38	1/30/2006		11,612.20			GJ0038
39	1/30/2006		122.14			GJ0039
40		null		null	null	
41	2/1/2006			null	null	
42	3/1/0123		Purchases			
43		null		null	null	
44	Error		Tran Amount			Source
45	2/1/2006		4,395.03			GJ0040
46		null		null	null	
47	3/20/2009		2:08pm			
48	Error		.			Pg 2
49	Error		I Ledger with N		et Change for A	ug 2004 to Mar

Figure 90 Errors that result from trying to convert to dates.

Unlike in any other program, errors are truly exciting in Power Query. They are exciting because you can control them and react to them. If you look carefully at this data, you'll see that errors were caused only in rows that happen to be part of the rows that you want to filter out anyway. In addition, every row that has a null in the Tran Date column holds values in the subsequent columns that are also not part of the transactional data that you want to keep. So you can get rid of both of those:

- Select the Tran Date column → Home tab → Reduce Rows → Remove Errors
- Filter the Tran Date column → uncheck *null*

The results are quite encouraging, and you now have a TranDate column with valid dates from top to bottom:

⊞▾	Tran Date	🔽	Tran Amount	▼		▼	Source
39	1/30/2006		122.14				GJ0039
40	2/1/2006			null		null	
41	3/1/0123		Purchases				
42	2/1/2006		4,395.03				GJ0040
43	3/20/2009		2:08pm				
44	2/1/2006		12,834.54				GJ0041

Figure 91 The TranDate column showing valid dates from top to bottom.

Now, you should recognize that there are a few rows that still appear but don't belong in this data set. The challenge is that you don't really want to filter out those dates as some of them might be valid one day (maybe on 3/1/0123). So you can move on to the next column and see if you can fix these issues there:

- Right-click the Tran Date column → Rename → Date → OK
- Right-click the Tran Amount column → Rename → Amount
- Right-click the Amount column → Change Type → Decimal Number

Power Query attempts to set all the entries to values with decimals, which triggers some errors. Remove those and the nulls out of the data set:

- Select the Amount column → Home → Reduce Rows → Remove Errors
- Filter the Amount column → uncheck *null*

If you now check the data set around row 40 (and further), you'll see that all the garbage rows are completely gone.

Removing Garbage Columns

Removing extra columns is very simple: You just need to follow a process when doing so. That process is simply this:

- Filter the column
- Ensure that the values in the column are all blank or *null*
- Right-click and remove the column

Checking each of the columns in the data set, you can see that the third column (with a blank header) appears to hold only blank values. That column can be removed.

Likewise, if you scroll all the way over to column9, you see that this column holds only *null* values. That column can also be removed.

Aggregating Columns

At this point, it is fairly clear that your initial splitting of the columns was a bit aggressive. It seems that you have four columns that were broken apart incorrectly, as shown below.

Reference Infor	▼	mation	▼	Vendor Name	▼	Column8	▼
Supply Purchase		-Avis & Davis		Distributors I		nc	
Food Purchase-N		orth Douglas		Distributors			null
Liquor Purchase		-Liquor Distri		bution Branch			null
Supply Purchase		-Avis & Davis		Distributors I		nc	
Food Purchase-N		orth Douglas		Distributors			null

Figure 92 Columns split apart in error.

Fortunately, all is not lost here, and you certainly don't need to go back and start over. You just need to put the columns back together again. Here's how:

- Select the Reference Infor column → hold down Shift → select Column8
- Right-click one of the column headers → Merge Columns

You're then given the option of using a separator and providing a new name for the (new) column. In this case you don't need a separator of any kind. And since you're going to split this column up differently in a second anyway, the name really isn't important. Click OK, and your columns are put back together:

▼ Source	▼ Merged
4429.36 GJ0001	Food Purchase-North Douglas Distributors
10450.96 GJ0002	Liquor Purchase-Liquor Distribution Branch
128.25 GJ0003	Supply Purchase-Avis & Davis Distributors Inc
4895.61 GJ0004	Food Purchase-North Douglas Distributors
11551.06 GJ0005	Liquor Purchase-Liquor Distribution Branch
141.75 GJ0006	Supply Purchase-Avis & Davis Distributors Inc
4662.48 GJ0007	Food Purchase-North Douglas Distributors

Figure 93 Humpty Dumpty wishes he had Power Query!

Splitting Columns by Delimiter

The re-aggregated data makes it very clear that the new Merged column is delimited by the - character. This means you have something you can use to break it apart into its components. One thing to take into consideration is that you don't know if there is a vendor who uses a hyphen in its company name, so you don't want to go too aggressive with a split based on the - character. Follow these steps:

- Right-click the Merged column → Split Column → By Delimiter
- Choose --Custom-- from the list of delimiters and enter a - (minus sign)
- Choose to split At the Left-most Delimiter

> You are not limited to delimiters of a single character when splitting by delimiter. In fact, if you want to split by an entire word, you can enter that word as your delimiter.

The data is then split into two separate columns: Merged.1 and Merged.2. These should be renamed to something more sensible:

- Right-click Merged.1 → Rename → Category
- Right-click Merged.2 → Rename → Vendor

The result is a data set that is almost perfect:

▼ Source	▼ Category	▼ Vendor
429.36 GJ0001	Food Purchase	North Douglas Distributors
450.96 GJ0002	Liquor Purchase	Liquor Distribution Branch
128.25 GJ0003	Supply Purchase	Avis & Davis Distributors Inc
895.61 GJ0004	Food Purchase	North Douglas Distributors
551.06 GJ0005	Liquor Purchase	Liquor Distribution Branch
141.75 GJ0006	Supply Purchase	Avis & Davis Distributors Inc
662.48 GJ0007	Food Purchase	North Douglas Distributors

Figure 94 The data set is now almost perfect.

Trimming Duplicate Spaces

The last thing you need to deal with in this data set is the duplicate spaces that have been left between words in the Vendor column. Since you can't rely on Power Query's trim function, you need to take care of this yourself:

- Right-click Vendor → Replace Values
- Set Value to Find to 2 spaces
- Set Replace With to 1 space

You now have a completely clean data set that can be loaded into a table.

 Unfortunately, there is no function that easily removes internal "whitespace" from a text string. If you suspect that you have some instances of two spaces, you may have to run this trim process a couple times in order to completely clean the data.

At this point, you can finalize your query and actually build a report from it. Naturally, you'll do that by creating a PivotTable. Before you can do that, follow these steps:

- Change the query name to Transactions
- Go to Home → Close & Load

Power Query's Moment to Shine

At this point, you should pause and recognize something important: Your data is clean. Unlike when you load data using Excel's standard method to import from a text file, no further cleanup is necessary. You were able to load, clean, and transform the data in one user interface dedicated to the process. You're now sitting in a position where the data can actually be used.

Click anywhere in the table and choose to insert a new PivotTable. Place it in G2 of the current worksheet and configure it as follows:

- Date on Rows, grouped by Month
- Vendor on Rows, under Group
- Category on Columns
- Amount on Values

Your PivotTable should look as follows:

Sum of Amount	Column Labels			
Row Labels	Food Purchase	Liquor Purchase	Supply Purchase	Grand Total
Jan				
Avis & Davis Distributors Inc			1664.94	1664.94
Liquor Distribution Branch		158292.64		158292.64
North Douglas Distributors	54904.19			54904.19
Feb				
Avis & Davis Distributors Inc			1848.72	1848.72
Liquor Distribution Branch		186132.13		186132.13
North Douglas Distributors	67719.29			67719.29
Mar				
Avis & Davis Distributors Inc			3383.58	3383.58
Liquor Distribution Branch		242315.79		242315.79
North Douglas Distributors	104769.36			104769.36
Grand Total	227392.84	586740.56	6897.24	821030.64

Figure 95 A PivotTable built from this chapter's text file.

This PivotTable is certainly handy, but face it: Everything accomplished in this chapter so far is entirely possible with just standard Excel. So why do you need Power Query? Is it the full-sized window? That's cool, but it's not critical.

You see why Power Query is so critical when you deal with the next part of the equation. Next quarter comes along, and you get a new data file. In an Excel pro's world, that means another tedious afternoon of importing, cleaning, and reformatting. But armed with Power Query, all that changes. Thanks to Power Query, this is all you do:

- Locate your query in the Workbook Queries pane

- Right-click the query → Edit
- Go back to the Source step and click the gear icon
- Update the file path to Ch07 Examples\GL Apr-Jun.TXT
- Go to Home → Close & Load

The query's output updates the table, but you have to force the PivotTable to update. So do that by right-clicking the PivotTable → Refresh.

Now you see the benefit of using Power Query:

Sum of Amount	Column Labels ▾			
Row Labels ▾	Food Purchase	Liquor Purchase	Supply Purchase	Grand Total
⊟ Apr				
Avis & Davis Distributors Inc			1660.94	1660.94
Liquor Distribution Branch		191992.54		191992.54
North Douglas Distributors	55196.09			55196.09
⊟ May				
Avis & Davis Distributors Inc			261.07	261.07
Liquor Distribution Branch		177125.03		177125.03
North Douglas Distributors	62668.47			62668.47
ACME&Co Supply Haus LLC			1580.15	1580.15
Sysco	5847.82			5847.82
⊟ Jun				
Liquor Distribution Branch		226607.59		226607.59
ACME&Co Supply Haus LLC			3376.48	3376.48
Sysco	102759.26			102759.26
Grand Total	226471.64	595725.16	6878.64	829075.44

Figure 96 The same PivotTable, now updated for the next quarter.

There are new vendors, new transactions, and new dates, and they're all working with no issues. It's revolutionary, and you're going to wonder how you ever did your job without this help from Power Query.

> If you just save the new file over the old one, you don't even have to edit the Source step to update the file path. Instead, you simply go to Data → Refresh All (twice) to update the solution.

You should also recognize that this isn't the end of the journey. In this case, you still had to manually edit the Source step to update the path to the new file. Consider the impact if you'd sourced the data file via the From File → From Folder method described in Chapter 4. If you did, you'd be able to take the list of files in the folder and:

- Sort the Date Modified column in descending order
- Filter to Keep Top Rows → 1
- Drill into the single remaining binary file in the Content column
- Perform the rest of the steps listed in this chapter

What would you have at this point? You'd have a solution that pulled in the data from the most recently modified file in the subfolder. The need to manually change the file path in the query each quarter would be a thing of the past. As each new quarter's file got added to the folder, you'd be able to just refresh your solution and bring in the most current data automatically.

> If you decide to use the route listed above, be aware that the Date Modified property is changed each time the file is saved. While Power Query won't change this property by reading from the file, any modifications made and saved by a user will force the Date Modified property to update. If this is a concern, the Date Accessed and Date Created properties may provide better options for you to use as filters, depending on your end goals.

Chapter 8 Importing from Databases

Your organization may grant you direct access to the company databases, and if that's the case, you're lucky: Such a database is by far the best source from which to get your data. Not only are you guaranteed to get access to the most up-to-date data, but loading from databases is generally more efficient than loading from files.

It doesn't matter much what type of database you're connecting to, as the experience of collecting, filtering, and summarizing database data is virtually identical no matter which database is connected to. The connection experience does have some very minor differences, but the interface for connecting to each type of database will guide you through the process, which essentially boils down to the following three steps:

1. Provide the location of the database.
2. Enter your authentication credentials.
3. Select the table(s) you wish to work with.

The goal of this book is to show you situations that you will most likely encounter in the real world. For this reason, it's important that you experience how Power Query works with the most common SQL database on the planet: Microsoft's SQL Server.

As SQL Server databases aren't easily portable, we are hosting an SQL Azure database on Microsoft's Azure web service in order for you to practice these techniques. This is essentially an SQL Server database that is hosted in the cloud and is available for you to freely access and explore. This means that no matter where in the world you are, you can connect and explore the data within this database.

Loading Data from a Database

Power Query supports connecting to a large variety of databases without the need to install any additional drivers. The connections available can be found in three separate areas in the Excel user interface:

*   New query → From Database
*   New query → From Azure
*   New query → From Other Sources

If you can't find the one you need, don't lose hope. If you install the vendor's ODBC driver, you should be able to connect to your database via the From Other Sources → ODBC Connector.

Connecting to the Database

For this example, you'll connect to the AdventureWorks database contained in our SQL Server and analyze the total sales by year by region for the AdventureWorks company.

 In an effort to make sure you don't cause yourself issues when making your initial database connection, we highly recommend that you read the steps below (up to the "Managing Connections" section) before attempting to actually make a connection.

To get started, you need to go through the following steps:

*   Create a new query → From Azure → From Microsoft Azure SQL Database
*   Connect to the following database:
*   Server: azuredb.powerqueryworkshop.com
*   Database: AdventureWorks2012

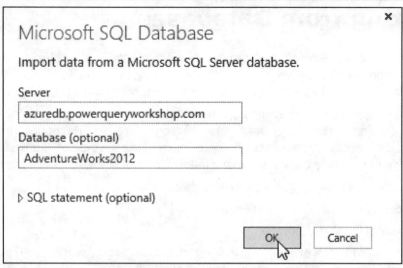

Figure 97 Connecting to the Azure database.

> When you're connecting to databases, there is an option to provide a custom SQL statement. (This can be accessed by clicking the triangle shown in the image above.) Avoid using this option unless you are an SQL ninja and can write deadly efficient code. If you can't, using this feature will actually hurt the performance of your queries.

At this point, you are prompted to enter the credentials needed to connect to the database. You have a few options here:

- The default option is to use the Windows credentials that you use to log on to your computer. If you are working on a database that is within your organization and the IT department has allowed Windows authentication, this will most likely work for you.

- You are also able, on the same tab, to provide an alternate set of Windows credentials. This is useful if you need to connect to the database using a different set of user credentials.

- To connect to the database in this case, however, you need to flip to the Database tab of the dialog, as we've used database security, not Windows security, when creating our user IDs. On that tab you need to enter the following credentials:

- Username: DataMonkey@ptypanama

- Password: D4t4M0nk3y!

Once you have the credentials correct, click the Connect button:

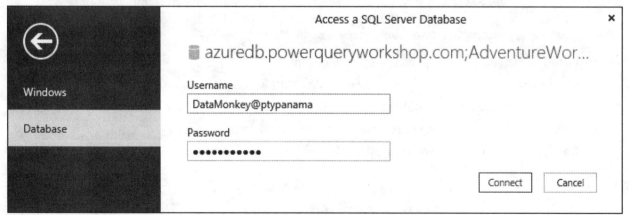

Figure 98 Connecting to the database using database security credentials.

When you are prompted about Encryption support, just click OK.

The user credentials you used are cached in a file that resides within your local user settings. This means that the username and password do not (and cannot currently be set to) travel with the solution when it is emailed or even opened by another user. This security feature ensures that each user actually has the proper credentials to access and refresh the data.

Managing Connections

If you mistype the name of your connection, database, user ID, or password and need to modify anything, you can do so by going through the following steps:

- Excel 2016:   Data → New Query → Data Source Settings
- Excel 2010/2013:   Power Query → Settings → Data Source Settings

This will launch you into the Data Source Settings box:

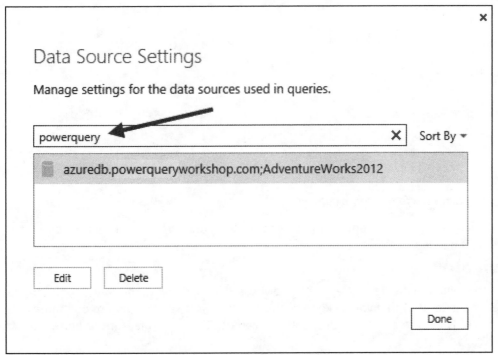

Figure 99 The Data Source Settings interface, filtered for the term powerquery.

This dialog can become *very* crowded over time, so it's very handy that you can filter it by using the search pane. In the image above, we've filtered to find the term powerquery because we know that it was part of the URL to the Azure database.

From here you have two options:

- **Delete the connection**—This is a good option if you want to remove the data source from the cached connections, forcing you to re-authenticate the next time you connect to it. This is also a great option if you have messed up the initial connection and want to start over.
- **Edit the connection**—This is a good option if you just need to update the username and password or if you want to change the connection privacy levels for some reason.

You can click the Edit button to see the connection type:

Figure 100 The Data Source Settings box for the Azure database.

You can also trigger the window to update/replace the username and password by clicking the Edit button in the Credentials section, if needed.

Using the Navigator

Once Power Query has connected to the database, you'll find yourself launched into the Navigator interface, which allows you to select the table(s) that you'd like to connect to. In this case, you want to pull some data from the SalesOrders table. There are a lot of tables, and you can use the search feature to narrow down the list:

- Enter salesorder into the search area
- Click on the Sales.SalesOrderHeader table

The preview pane reaches out to the database and gives you a glimpse into the data that is stored within that table:

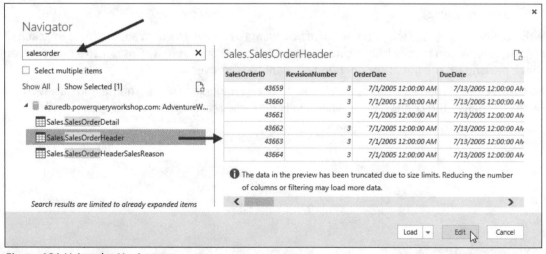

Figure 101 Using the Navigator.

The data in here looks fairly useful. Click Edit and see what useful information you can glean from it.

Exploring the Data

After you click Edit in the Navigator, the first thing you'll notice is that there are two steps in the Applied Steps window: Source and Navigation. If you select the Source step, you see that it goes back to the raw schema of the database, allowing you to see what other tables, views, and objects exist in the database. The Navigation step then drills into the table you selected.

The second thing you'll notice is that there is a *lot* of data here. You can thin it down a bit:

- Select the columns OrderDate, SalesOrderNumber, SubTotal, TaxAmt, Freight, and Sales.SalesTerritory
- Right-click one of the headers → Remove Other Columns
- Right-click the OrderDate column → Transform → Year
- Right-click the OrderDate column → Rename → Year
- Right-click the SalesOrderNumber column → Rename → Order#

The query is now a lot more compact and focused.

▦▾	Year ▾	Order# ▾	SubTotal ▾	TaxAmt ▾	Freight ▾	Sales.SalesTerritory ᵗⁱᵖ
1	2005	SO43659	20565.6206	1971.5149	616.0984	Value
2	2005	SO43660	1294.2529	124.2483	38.8276	Value
3	2005	SO43661	32726.4786	3153.7696	985.553	Value
4	2005	SO43662	28832.5289	2775.1646	867.2389	Value
5	2005	SO43663	419.4589	40.2681	12.5838	Value
6	2005	SO43664	24432.6088	2344.9921	732.81	Value
7	2005	SO43665	14352.7713	1375.9427	429.9821	Value
8	2005	SO43666	5056.4896	486.3747	151.9921	Value
9	2005	SO43667	6107.082	586.1203	183.1626	Value
10	2005	SO43668	35944.1562	3461.7654	1081.8017	Value

▲ PROPERTIES

Name

Sales SalesOrderHeader

All Properties

▲ APPLIED STEPS

Source ⚙
Navigation ⚙
Removed Other C... ⚙
Extracted Year
✕ Renamed Columns

Figure 102 Trimming down the SalesOrderHeader table.

Most of the column headers make perfect sense, but there is something significant about the Sales.SalesTerritory column. That column isn't showing values from the SalesOrderHeader table; it's showing the related values from the SalesTerritory table!

This is one of the great things about connecting to databases: Most databases support automatic relationship detection, so you can browse through the related records without even having to set up a relationship yourself or perform any merges at all. Even better, when you go to expand that column, you see that there are even more fields coming from other tables. To see how this works:

- Click the double-headed arrow at the top right of the Sales.SaleTerritory column

Power Query asks which columns you want to expand as shown in Figure 103.

Figure 103 Every record containing a period shows a related table.

While it's incredible that you *can* keep drilling in to related tables, you really only need the Group field from the SalesTerritory table, so expand that column to pull only that record:

- Uncheck (Select All Columns)

- Check Group
- Remove the check from Use Original Column Name as Prefix
- Click OK
- Rename the query RegionByYear

The data set is now ready to be loaded for analysis:

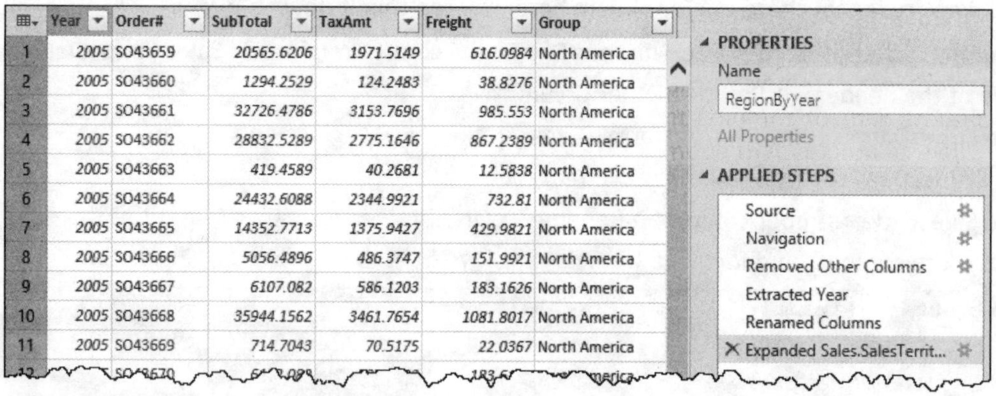

▦▾	Year ▾	Order# ▾	SubTotal ▾	TaxAmt ▾	Freight ▾	Group ▾
1	2005	SO43659	20565.6206	1971.5149	616.0984	North America
2	2005	SO43660	1294.2529	124.2483	38.8276	North America
3	2005	SO43661	32726.4786	3153.7696	985.553	North America
4	2005	SO43662	28832.5289	2775.1646	867.2389	North America
5	2005	SO43663	419.4589	40.2681	12.5838	North America
6	2005	SO43664	24432.6088	2344.9921	732.81	North America
7	2005	SO43665	14352.7713	1375.9427	429.9821	North America
8	2005	SO43666	5056.4896	486.3747	151.9921	North America
9	2005	SO43667	6107.082	586.1203	183.1626	North America
10	2005	SO43668	35944.1562	3461.7654	1081.8017	North America
11	2005	SO43669	714.7043	70.5175	22.0367	North America

PROPERTIES
Name
RegionByYear
All Properties

APPLIED STEPS
Source
Navigation
Removed Other Columns
Extracted Year
Renamed Columns
✕ Expanded Sales.SalesTerrit...

Figure 104 The data is now ready to be loaded and analyzed.

You can now go to the Home tab and click Close & Load to load the data into an Excel worksheet. After a short wait, the table turns green, and you're ready to build a PivotTable. Then follow these steps:

- Select a cell in the table → Insert → PivotTable
- Place the table on the same worksheet, starting in cell H2
- Configure the PivotTable as follows:
- Put Year and Group on Rows
- Put SubTotal, Tax Amt, and Freight on Values
- Set each column to show in an accounting style, with no decimals or symbols.

The result is a nice PivotTable that you can update at any time:

Row Labels ▾	Sum of SubTotal	Sum of TaxAmt	Sum of Freight
⊟2005	11,331,809	1,037,289	324,153
Europe	709,947	56,796	17,749
North America	9,312,815	875,769	273,678
Pacific	1,309,047	104,724	32,726
⊟2006	30,674,773	2,886,914	902,161
Europe	3,326,641	294,799	92,125
North America	25,193,848	2,419,773	756,179
Pacific	2,154,285	172,343	53,857
⊟2007	42,011,037	3,931,773	1,228,679
Europe	9,033,103	828,726	258,977
North America	29,096,719	2,773,843	866,826
Pacific	3,881,215	329,204	102,876
⊟2008	25,828,762	2,330,998	728,437
Europe	6,767,993	599,437	187,324
North America	15,749,980	1,454,753	454,610
Pacific	3,310,789	276,808	86,503
Grand Total	**109,846,381**	**10,186,974**	**3,183,430**

Figure 105 The PivotTable created from a Windows Azure SQL database.

The beauty of this solution is that you could also add slicers, PivotCharts, and other items to the worksheet to display the data as you want to see it. But the best part is that with a simple Data → Refresh All, you can refresh the data from the online database at any time to update the solution as needed.

Using SSAS as a Source

SQL Server Analysis Services (SSAS) is one of the many sources that you might find in a corporate environment. SSAS can be divided into the tabular models and multidimensional models, both of which can easily be pulled into Power Query.

 Please note that all numbers used in the following data set are completely fictitious and were randomly seeded in the database.

Connecting to SSAS Sources

In order to connect to SSAS you'll need to create a new query → From Database → From SQL Server Analysis Services Database. Power Query launches a new window where you need to enter the name (or address) of your server.

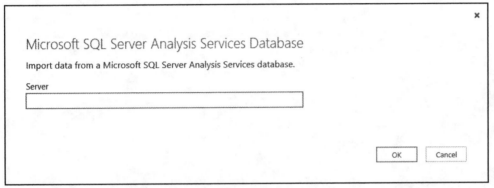

Figure 106 Enter your server address in order to connect to it.

The example in this section is built against a summary of box office results, housed on a local SSAS instance. After authenticating to the SSAS instance, you're immediately presented with the Navigator, just as you are when you connect to any other database:

Figure 107 This new window gives you a tree view to navigate through the SSAS server.

From here, you can select the dimensions, measures, and KPIs that you want from your model by simply checking the boxes beside them. For this example, assume that you select the FILM_NAME dimension from the TAB_FILMS table, as well as a few measures like Screens, Locations, Sum of BORTot, and Sum of ADM. (These measures give the numerical values related to the overall information of the box office performance for each film.)

Building queries against an SSAS source is quite different from a normal SQL connection. In a normal SQL instance, you connect to the entire table and filter out the columns you do *not* want to include. With an SSAS instance, you approach the job the other way around, checking the columns you *do* want to include, building the output table column-by-column as you go.

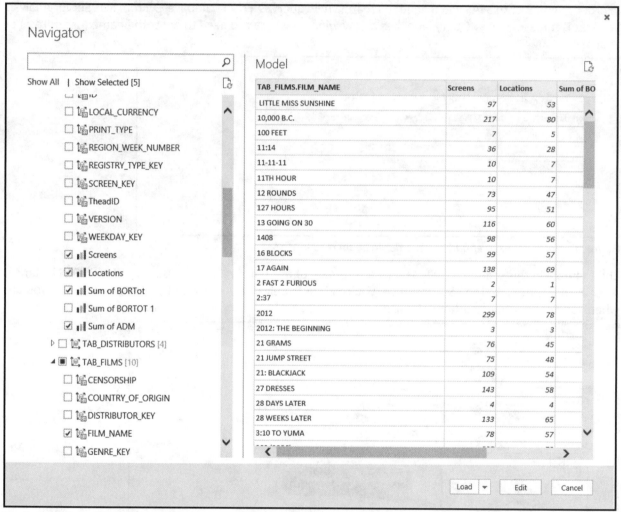

Figure 108 The preview window creates your table as you select items on the left.

When the table preview meets your expectations, you can go ahead and click the Edit button to be launched into the Power Query editor.

This window looks a bit different than the one you've seen before. Unlike previous instances, where you are given commands related to table operations, this time you find that the Cube Tools contextual ribbon is active, giving you the options Add Items and Collapse Columns:

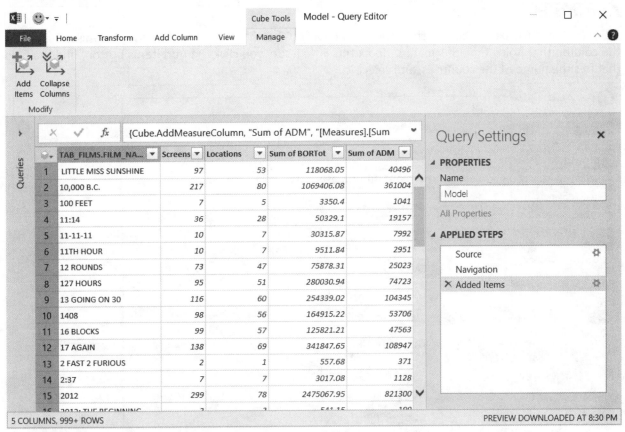

Figure 109 Three applied steps, one table, and two mysterious new buttons.

This particular model has information for the entire Central Americas region, but say that you want to focus in on one specific film: *Titanic*. In this case, you need to filter the TAB_FILMS_FILM_NAME column down to just that one movie.

Adding Fields Missed

Now say that you'd like to know the breakdown by country. The only problem here is that you missed selecting the column that holds that information. To fix this little issue, you click the Add Items button, find the field that has the name of the countries, and select it:

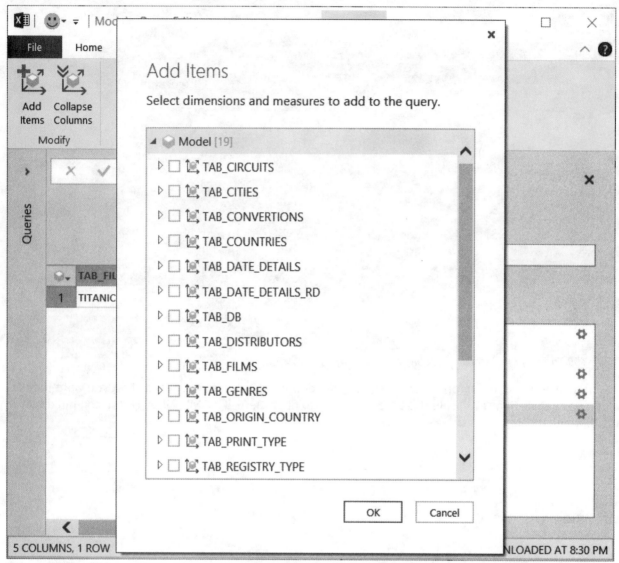

Figure 110 The Add Items button lets you select more fields.

The new column is immediately added to the table output on the far right side of the table:

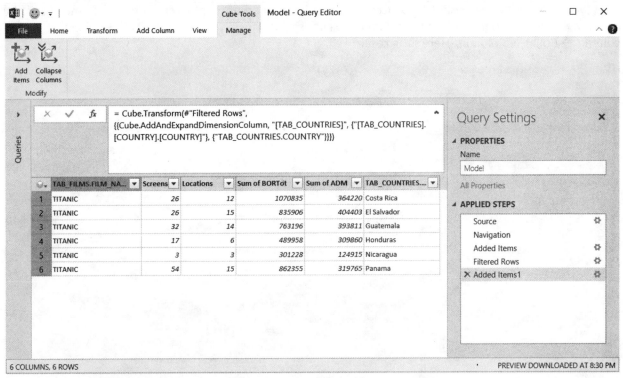

Figure 111 The newly added item is added to the far right of the table.

 Although the Cube Tools contextual ribbon is still enabled, that doesn't mean you can't use the other ribbons you've used before. The Cube Tools ribbon simply offers you new features when you connect to this special type of data source.

Collapsing Fields

You've seen how to add new fields, but what does the Collapse Columns button do?

After looking at the results for *Titanic*, say that you decide that you really want to see a different view of the data. You therefore go back and remove the Filtered Rows step. As a result, all the films are listed, with a breakdown by each country as well:

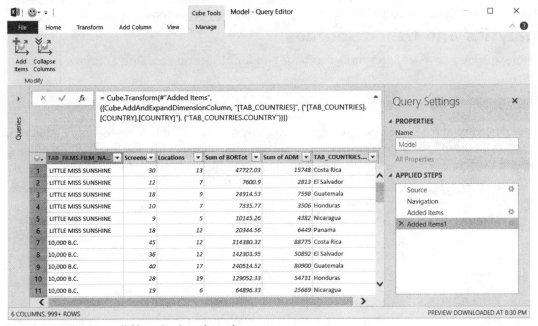

Figure 112 Showing all films, broken down by country.

Next, you can remove the TAB_FILMS.FILM_NAME column in an attempt to show the box office totals by country. Rather than right-clicking the column and choosing Remove, you select the TAB_FILMS.FILM_NAME column → Collapse Columns. Here's the result:

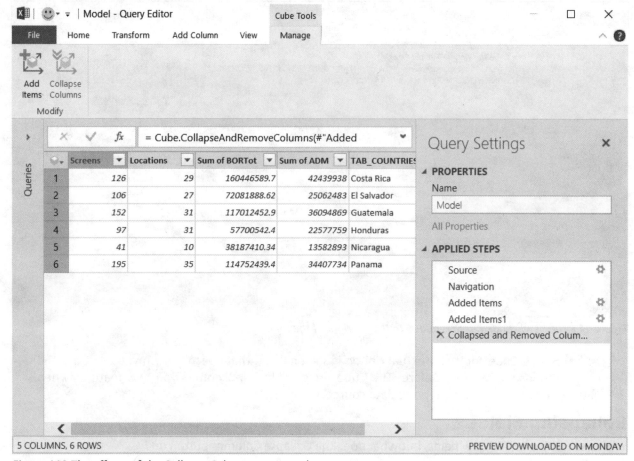

Figure 113 The effects of the Collapse Columns command.

As you can see, the Collapse Columns command removes the column from the data source. It does more than that, however. If you'd just chosen to remove the column, you'd still have unaggregated data by country (with no film title). The Collapse Columns feature re-aggregates the data and *then* removes itself from the query.

Google Analytics and Other Sources

The same behavior explained for the SSAS source can be found for other sources. One example of these is Google Analytics.

> Unfortunately, Google Analytics is only available in Power BI Desktop, not Excel.

Sources like Google Analytics and other SSAS databases most likely have all the data pre-aggregated for you, ready for consumption. In these cases, the main use of Power Query is not data cleaning but rather providing a method for the end users to discover what they need and integrate this data with other tables. Of course, you can still use the functionality of the Power Query user interface to further enrich the tables as well.

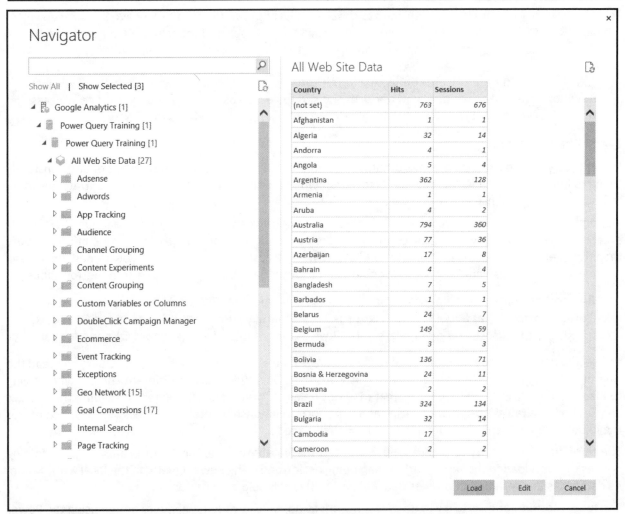

Figure 114 The Google Analytics connector in the Power BI Desktop uses an SSAS format.

Query Folding and Optimization

One of the great features that databases offer is the ability to take advantage of query folding to optimize query performance. While the technology is built in and will work by default for you when you build solutions using Power Query's user interface, you can also accidentally break it, in which case your queries will be processed by Excel alone. To understand how to avoid this mistake, you need to understand what query folding is and how it works at a rudimentary level.

What Is Query Folding?

Most people don't tend to think about what is happening behind the scenes as they're clicking the various commands to select, filter, sort, and group data. As you're aware by now, each of these steps is recorded in the Applied Steps box, letting you build a sequential macro. What you may not be aware of, however, is that Power Query is also translating as many of those commands as it can into SQL and sending those to the database.

What is even more amazing is that a server that has query folding capabilities will accept those individual queries and then attempt to fold them into a more efficient query. The impact of this is evident when you're issuing subsequent commands such as Select All Records in the Table followed by Filter to Exclude All Departments Except 150.

In lay terms, instead of loading all 100,000 records and then filtering down to the 1,500 for that department, the server instead takes the queries to build a more efficient query that reads:

```
Select * From tblTransactions WHERE Dept = '150'
```

The impact of this is massive: It saves the processing time involved in dealing with 98,500 records.

While not all commands can be folded, a great many can, pushing the processing workload to the server.

Query folding technology is restricted to databases. While it would be nice to have this function-ality for TXT, CSV, and Excel files, those files are not databases and therefore have no engine to fold the queries. You should also be aware that not all databases support query folding.

If the file or database you are connecting to is incapable of folding the queries, then Excel will just download the full set of data and perform the requested steps using its own engine to process them. Everything will still work, but it's just not as efficient.

Optimization

Power Query can be slow. It's an unfortunate fact, and one that Microsoft is keenly aware of and constantly trying to improve. Until Microsoft conquers this problem, it is important that you have some strategies to try to maximize performance where you can.

The first strategy is to *never* provide a custom SQL statement when setting up your initial query. (The only exception to this rule is if you are an SQL ninja and are confident that you can provide a more efficient query than the query folding steps can build for you.) By providing a custom SQL statement, you immediately break the query folding capabilities for any subsequent steps, potentially hurting your long-term performance.

Remember that Power Query was not built as a replacement for SQL Server Management Studio (SSMS). It was built as a tool to help Excel pros, who generally know very little—if any—SQL syntax, to extract, filter, sort, and manipulate data. Power Query's job is to build your SQL code for you.

The second strategy is to give preference to connecting to tables instead of views. Power Query can read the keys or indexes of a table but not of a view. This leads to Power Query making different choices when trying to load the data from a view—choices that may not be as efficient as those related to reading the indexes and keys from a table. Power Query also cannot perform relationship detection across views, which makes the initial design experience more difficult in the first place.

The third strategy is to try to push as much work to the database as possible. For example, query folding pushes the workload to the server, rather than being performed using Power Query on the local workstation. As databases are designed to process data efficiently, this will help with performance.

The fourth consideration is to try to do as much work as possible in your initial query design using the Power Query user interface commands rather than reaching to custom M code. While it will be tempting to inject parameters dynamically to control filters (especially after you read Chapter 23 on parameter tables), you should be aware that this will break the query folding capability.

Query folding cannot be executed against any line that contains a custom M or SQL statement. Even worse, M or an SQL statement stops any further query folding from taking place.

Chapter 9 Merging Tables and Queries

One of the classic issues that has presented itself to Excel pros for years is aggregating two separate data tables into one in order to serve a PivotTable. The route was to use a VLOOKUP() or INDEX(MATCH()) combination in order to read data from one table into the other.

The challenge with this is that many users were terrified of VLOOKUP() and didn't understand the INDEX() and MATCH() functions either. And while PowerPivot now allows you to aggregate two tables without using any VLOOKUP() functions, it carries its own complexities. Yet still the issue remains: Sometimes you just need an easy way to merge two tables' records together.

When Power Query hit the scene, it introduced yet another method to combine two tables together—one that didn't involve learning Excel formulas or building a relational database structure.

Merging Tables via Power Query

For this example, say that you have two separate tables that exist in an Excel worksheet. The first is the Sales table, which holds the Sale Date, Product SKU (number), Brand, and Sales Quantity of the sales transactions. But it doesn't hold any information about the price or cost of the products. That information (and more) is, however, held in the Inventory table. You'd like to merge the two tables together in order to get a comprehensive list of products with their finer details.

Creating "Pointer" Queries

In order to merge or append queries together, the queries must exist. Having a table in Excel isn't good enough; Power Query actually needs to recognize the data as a query. Yet it seems somewhat crazy to have to take an existing table, pull it into a Power Query, and then load it to an Excel table in order to reference it. And, indeed, you don't actually need to do that.

You do still need to pull the original table into Power Query, but the output is where you make a change.

Inside the Ch09 Examples\Merge.xlsx file, you'll find two tables set up: an Inventory table and a Sales table. In order to let Power Query read the contents of the Inventory table you need to:

- Click any cell inside the Inventory table
- Create a new query → From Table

Power Query opens its editor so you can make any transformations you need. In this case, however, you actually don't need to make any. All you want to do is create something that you can connect to later.

- On the Home tab, click the drop-down on the bottom of the Close & Load button
- Choose Close & Load To...
- In the Load To dialog, which now asks where to save your data, select Only Create Connection

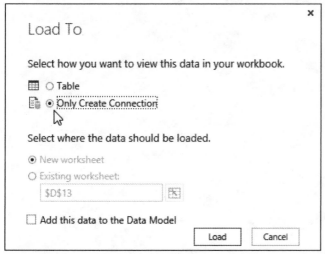

Figure 115 Choosing to create a connection-only query.

- Click Load

You see your query show up in the Workbook Queries pane, but Power Query doesn't create a new table for you.

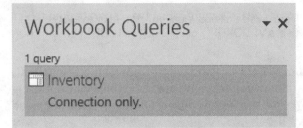

Figure 116 A new query created as a connection-only query.

> If you make a mistake and create a query with a table, you can fix it by right-clicking the query in the Workbook Queries pane and choosing Load To…. Power Query warns you that you're going to delete data when you commit the change, as you will be removing the newly created table. You can also add a table if you created a connection-only query by editing the Load To… behavior as above and changing the selected load behavior from Only Create Connection to Table.

With the Inventory table now available in Power Query, you need to repeat this process for the Sales table:

- Click any cell inside the Sales table → create a new query → From Table
- Home → Close & Load To… → Only Create Connection → OK

You're all set up and ready to merge the tables together.

Performing the Merge

You create a merged table in the same place where you create an append query from the Excel user interface. Here's what you do:

- Create a new query → Combine → Merge

The Merge dialog appears. Its two drop-downs allow you to pick the two tables that you'd like to merge together.

- Choose Sales as the top table
- Choose Inventory as the bottom table

Oddly, after you take these actions, the OK button is still not enabled:

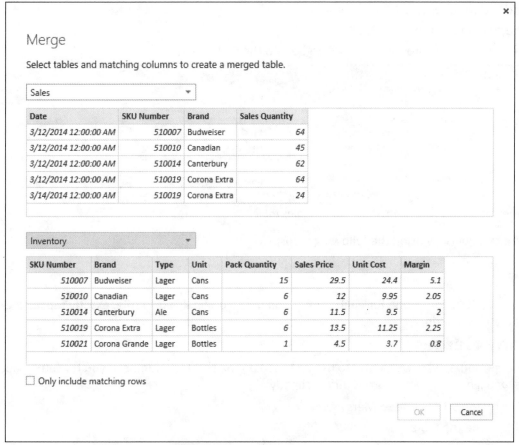

Figure 117 You've chosen tables, but why can't you proceed?

The issue at hand is that Power Query doesn't know which fields you want to use to perform the merge.

In order to perform a merge, you ideally want to have a column that contains unique values in one table but has repeating records in the other table. This is called a one-to-many structure, and using it is the best way to ensure that you end up with results that match what you'd expect.

Power Query supports one-to-one and many-to-many joins, as you'll see shortly.

In this case, the SKU Number column contains unique products in the Inventory table, and it repeats many times in the Sales table, so you can use those:

- Click the SKU Number header in each table
- Click OK

Power Query opens the editor, where you see a nice new column of tables on the right side of the Sales table:

SKU Number	Brand	Sales Quantity	NewColumn
4 12:00:00 AM	510007 Budweiser	64	Table
4 12:00:00 AM	510010 Canadian	45	Table
4 12:00:00 AM	510014 Canterbury	62	Table
4 12:00:00 AM	510019 Corona Extra	64	Table
4 12:00:00 AM	510019 Corona Extra	24	Table
4 12:00:00 AM	510021 Corona Grande	38	Table
4 12:00:00 AM	510021 Corona Grande	31	Table

PROPERTIES
Name
Merge1
All Properties

APPLIED STEPS
Source

Figure 118 A new column of tables, containing the matching Inventory table records.

You know what to do with a column of tables: Expand them! The only question here is which columns you need. Because the SKU Number and Brand columns already exist in the sales table, you don't need those, so make sure to exclude them during the expansion. Follow these steps:

- Click the expand icon

- Uncheck the SKU Number and Brand columns
- Uncheck the column prefix option → OK

As you can see, you now have the product details merged into the Sales table:

SKU Number	Brand	Sales Quantity	Type	Unit
510007	Budweiser	64	Lager	Cans
510010	Canadian	45	Lager	Cans
510014	Canterbury	62	Ale	Cans
510019	Corona Extra	64	Lager	Bottles
510019	Corona Extra	24	Lager	Bottles
510021	Corona Grande	38	Lager	Bottles
510021	Corona Grande	31	Lager	Bottles
510032	Granville Islan	24	Ale	Bottles

PROPERTIES
Name
Merge1
All Properties

APPLIED STEPS
Source
✕ Expanded NewColumn

Figure 119 Details from the Inventory table merged into the Sales table.

Now you can finalize this query by using the following steps:

- Rename the query OneToMany
- Go to Home → Close & Load

You'll find that you have 20 records, one for each transaction in the original Sales table, exactly replicating VLOOKUP()'s exact match scenario.

Many-to-Many Merges

When building a merge, you need to be careful to merge based on the correct columns. If you try setting up a merge as follows, you'll find that your output differs slightly:

- Create a new query → Combine → Merge
- Choose Sales as the top table
- Choose Inventory as the bottom table
- Click the Brand header in each table
- Click OK
- Click the expand icon
- Uncheck the SKU Number and Brand columns → OK
- Uncheck the column prefix option → OK
- Rename the query ManyToMany
- Go to Home → Close & Load

As you can see, the only two changes here are the column used to merge the tables and the final query name (which won't affect the output). Yet this time there are 22 records in the output table—2 more than the original count of transactions.

To understand why this is happening, you need to edit the ManyToMany query and step back to the Source step. If you go down the table to record 19 and click in the whitespace beside the word Table, you get a preview of the data in the table that will be merged into your Sales table.

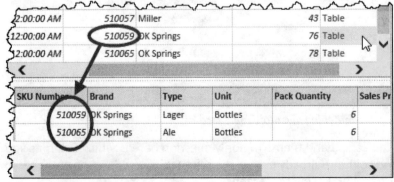

Figure 120 A many-to-many merge in action.

In the previous merge, you created the merge based on the SKU number, meaning that records would only be matched up if their item numbers matched. In this case, however, you matched based on the brand. Because the OK Springs brand shows twice in the Inventory table, when the Sales table has the brand OK Springs, it creates two matches. The fact that they have different SKUs is irrelevant to Power Query, as you asked for a match based on brand, not SKU.

You can see from this example that you need to be careful when creating matches. This feature can be very useful, but it can also be dangerous if you are not paying attention and are expecting a one-to-many match.

Dynamic Table Headers

Excel tables are fantastic, they truly are. But one issue with them is that they lock down the header row into hard-coded values. That prohibits you from having dynamic headers on your tables, driven by formulas.

The file Ch09 Examples\Dynamic Headers.xlsx contains a spreadsheet used for budgeting green fee rounds for a golf course. The author has set up a tabular setup and is able to change the year in B1 and update all headers in rows 3 and 32 of the document:

▲	A	B	C	D	E	
1	Most recent budgets supplied:	2014				
2						
3	Month	1/31/2014	2/28/2014	3/31/2014	4/30/2014	5/
4	Green Fee					
5	9 hole rounds (18 hole equivalent)	40	60	103	175	
6	18 hole rounds	100	250	400	670	
30						
31	Recap					
32	Month	1/31/2014	2/28/2014	3/31/2014	4/30/2014	5/
33	Total Green Fee Rounds	140	310	503	845	
34	Total Pass Rounds	50	50	90	180	
35	Member/Annual Pass Rounds	146	184	290	1,423	
36	Total Other Rounds	48	71	155	329	

Figure 121 A budget document with dynamic headers.

The Issue

The challenge here is that you need to load and unpivot the Recap table (rows 32:36). Since using Power Query is the easiest way to unpivot data, you obviously want to use it, but there are some challenges in getting the data into Power Query in the first place:

- Loading the data via a table would cause the column headers to be locked in, and you would lose the dynamic feel.

- Loading the data using a named range would allow the column headers to change in the worksheet but would potentially break any hard-coded steps in the query when the dates change.

The workaround in this case is to create a translation table and merge that back into the query.

Creating a Translation Table

The translation table for this example needs to be able to come up with a logical way to translate a static column header to the current dates. Using the notation CYMx (Current Year, Month x), you can build a table to hold these dates. Create the table as follows:

- Enter in cell A40:   Period
- Enter in cell B40:   Date
- Enter in cell A41:   CYM1
- Extend A41 down to A52 so that it reads CYM2, CYM3, and so on
- Select A40:B52 → Home → Format as Table

- Table Tools → Design → Table Name → name the table DateTranslation
- Copy B32:M32
- Right-click B41 → PasteSpecial
- Choose to paste Formulas & Number Formats and check the Transpose box

Your table should now be set up as follows:

	A	B
40	Period ▼	Date ▼
41	CYM1	1/31/2014
42	CYM2	2/28/2014
43	CYM3	3/31/2014
44	CYM4	4/30/2014
45	CYM5	5/31/2014
46	CYM6	6/30/2014
47	CYM7	7/31/2014
48	CYM8	8/31/2014
49	CYM9	9/30/2014
50	CYM10	10/31/2014
51	CYM11	11/30/2014
52	CYM12	12/31/2014

Figure 122 The DateTranslation table.

Naturally, in order to merge this into another table, you need Power Query to also know that it exists, so follow these steps:

- Select any cell in the table
- Create a new query → From Table
- Home → Close & Load To... → Only Create Connection

With a connection set up to this table, you're now ready to go.

Retrofitting the Source Table

Next, you need to pull in the Summary table. But in order to merge the data together, it will obviously need to have headers consistent with the CYM format. Yet at the same time, you'd like to keep the current dates showing. This is no big deal—you can fake it:

- Copy row 32
- Right-click row 33 → Insert Copied Cells
- Copy cells A42:A53
- Right-click B33 → Paste Special → Values + Transpose

The data range is now set up and ready for to use, and you just need to add a table to it:

	A	B	C	D
31	Recap			
32	Month	1/31/2014	2/28/2014	3/31/2014
33	Month	CYM1	CYM2	CYM3
34	Total Green Fee Rounds	140	310	503
35	Total Pass Rounds	50	50	90
36	Member/Annual Pass Rounds	146	184	290
37	Total Other Rounds	48	71	155

Figure 123 The summary table now has the alternate header.

The trick here is that you need to make sure the table only covers rows 33:37, as you don't want to lock down row 32's formulas. Follow these steps:

- Click inside the data range → Home → Format as Table

- Adjust the range to read =A**33**:$M$37
- OK → set the table name to StatsData
- Hide row 33

Depending on the style you choose, you can even hide all evidence that you've been tinkering with this and setting it up as a table:

	A	B	C	D
31	Recap			
32	Month	1/31/2014	2/28/2014	3/31/2014
34	Total Green Fee Rounds	140	310	503
35	Total Pass Rounds	50	50	95
36	Member/Annual Pass Rounds	146	184	290
37	Total Other Rounds	48	71	15

Figure 124 Table? What table?

Merging the Tables

And now for the magic moment—combining these tables:

- Click inside the StatsData table → create a new query → From Table
- Right-click the Month column → UnPivot Other Columns
- Right-click the Month column → Replace Values → "Total " (with a trailing space and no quotation marks) with nothing → OK

At this point the query is looking fairly decent. It's unpivoted, and it's ready to be merged. And guess what? You don't even have to leave Power Query to do it!

- Go to Home → Merge Queries
- Pick the DateTranslation table
- Choose the Attribute and Period columns → OK
- Expand the Date field (only) from the new column (unchecking the prefix) → OK
- Right-click the Date column → Change Type → Date
- Right-click the Attribute column → Remove
- Right-click the Value column → Rename → Rounds
- Change the query name to Budget
- Go to Home → Close & Load

The output is a very nice unpivoted set of data, with the correct dates associated with each transaction:

	A	B	C	D
1	Month	Rounds	Date	
2	Green Fee Rounds	140	1/31/2014	
3	Pass Rounds	50	1/31/2014	
4	Green Fee Rounds	310	2/28/2014	
5	Green Fee Rounds	503	3/31/2014	
6	Green Fee Rounds	845	4/30/2014	
7	Green Fee Rounds	2005	5/31/2014	
8	Green Fee Rounds	2355	6/30/2014	
9	Green Fee Rounds	2290	7/31/2014	
10	Green Fee Rounds	2320	8/31/2014	
11	Green Fee Rounds	2288	9/30/2014	
12	Green Fee Rounds	948	10/31/2014	

Figure 125 The unpivoted data set.

But how well does it update? Try this to see:

- Go to the Data worksheet
- Update cell B1 to 2015

It looks like the data entry worksheet is working:

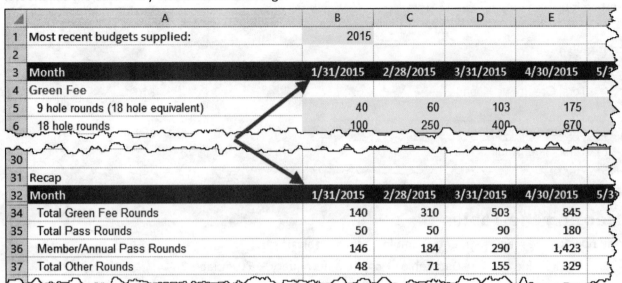

Figure 126 The data entry worksheet is still reacting dynamically.

Now check the Power Query:

- Select the worksheet that holds the Budget table
- Go to Data → Refresh All

It looks like the table is working nicely as well!

	A	B	C	D
1	Month	Rounds	Date	
2	Green Fee Rounds	140	1/31/2015	
3	Pass Rounds	50	1/31/2015	
4	Green Fee Rounds	310	2/28/2015	
5	Green Fee Rounds	503	3/31/2015	
6	Green Fee Rounds	845	4/30/2015	
7	Green Fee Rounds	2005	5/31/2015	
8	Green Fee Rounds	2355	6/30/2015	
9	Green Fee Rounds	2290	7/31/2015	
10	Green Fee Rounds	2320	8/31/2015	
11	Green Fee Rounds	2288	9/30/2015	
12	Green Fee Rounds			

Figure 127 The output table updates to reflect the current dates.

With the table headers now essentially dynamic and your ability to quickly unpivot the data into a table, you've now opened up great possibilities for the data. From merging this to other data sets to feeding it into PivotTables or Power Pivot, the possibilities are truly endless—and you still have a user-friendly front end.

Chapter 10 Query Loading Destinations

While the majority of the examples in this book to this point have focused on landing the Power Query output into Excel tables, that is certainly not the only option for where to place Power Query data.

In fact, you have three different loading destination options, some of which can be used in combination:

- Excel tables
- Connection-only queries
- The Power Pivot Data Model

 The ability to load directly to the Power Pivot Data Model is not supported in Excel 2010. Having said that, just because it isn't supported doesn't mean that it can't be done. You'll find out how to do it in this chapter.

Query Loading Methods

Each of the different loading options has different benefits, drawbacks, and caveats associated with it, which we will explore here.

Excel Tables

Excel tables are the default loading experience for Power Query queries. When you simply click Close & Load in the Power Query interface, Excel creates a new table on a new worksheet to hold the query's output. The newly created table inherits the name of the query, with a few modifications:

- Any spaces are converted to underscores.
- If the query's name is already used for an existing table or named range, it will then have an _# appended to the end.

 One caveat to be aware of here is that you should never give a query the same name as an existing Excel function. Excel tries to interpret named ranges before functions, so having a table named something like ROUND or LEFT will cause all cells using these functions to return #N/A errors.

If you are simply reading data from a table and making no manipulations to it, using the default option does give you a connection to the data in Power Query, but it also duplicates the data on another worksheet, increasing the file size and adding memory overhead to your file.

Connection-Only Queries

As you saw in Chapter 9, connection-only queries are set up to avoid landing data into a worksheet, but they still allow you to connect to the data via other Power Query queries.

This option is a fantastic one that gets used frequently in practice, as the queries set up in this fashion are loaded on demand only when called by a subsequent query. Since they don't load any data directly to the worksheet, they also don't increase the file size or memory overhead required to store the query output.

 Loading to a table and creating a connection-only query are mutually exclusive options. You can choose only one or the other.

For example, when you open Ch10 Examples\Load Destinations.xlsx, you'll find that the workbook contains two tables of sales items for a pet store. The analyst wants to merge these tables together for use in a business intelligence solution. How does she do it?

She could load each table into a query, load the queries into worksheets, and then create an append query that would also be loaded into a worksheet. She would essentially create three copies of the data, which seems a bit ridiculous.

A better alternative is to use connection-only queries to create pointers to the original data tables and then create an append query against those connections and land the output in a table. The final table would act as the source for the analyst's PivotTables, and there would not be an extra duplication step in the middle.

To set up this solution, you would follow these steps:

- Open Ch10 Examples\Load Destinations.xlsx

- Select a cell in the range of data on the May worksheet
- Create a new query → From Table
- Change the query name to Sales-May
- Go to Home → Close & Load To... → Only Create Connection
- Select a cell in the range of data on the Jun worksheet
- Create a new query → From Table
- Change the query name to Sales-Jun
- Go to Home → Close & Load To... → Only Create Connection

This process gives you two connection-only queries, without duplicating any data in the workbook:

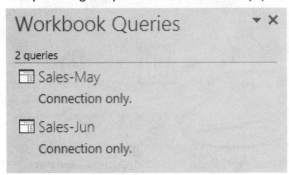

Figure 128 Two connection-only queries, ready for use.

You can now create an append query to merge the two connection-only queries together:

- Right-click the Sales-May query → Append
- Choose to append Sales-Jun → OK
- Rename the query Sales
- Right-click the Date column → Change Type → Date
- Go to Home → Close & Load

Power Query creates a new table that holds all the data and is ready to be pivoted:

	A	B	C	D	E	F
1	Date	Inventory Item	Sold By	Cost	Price	Commission
2	5/10/2014	Lovable Kitten	Fred	12	45	1.35
3	5/9/2014	Talkative Parrot	John	17	32	0.96
4	5/24/2014	Lovable Kitten	Jane	12	45	1.35
5	5/20/2014	Adorable Kitty Cat	John	25	35	1.05
6	5/8/2014	Lovable Kitten	Jane	12	45	1.35
7	5/23/2014	Sleepy Gerbil	Jane	25	39	1.17
8	5/11/2014	Cranky Crocodile	John	10	35	1.05
9	5/19/2014	Adorable Kitty Cat	Mary	25	35	1.05

Figure 129 An append query created from two connection-only queries.

When creating a new query against a connection-only query, it is not necessary to load the output to an Excel table. You could just as easily load it to another connection-only query if needed.

Loading to Power Pivot (Excel 2010)

There are actually two ways to load Power Query data to Power Pivot in Excel 2010. But only one is officially supported: loading via linked tables.

To link this data into the Power Pivot Data Model, you select anywhere inside the Sales table, go to the Power Pivot tab, and click Create Linked Table. The end result is a data flow that follows this process:

Excel table → connection-only query → append query → Excel table → Power Pivot

You might think it would be easier to just go directly from your monthly sales tables, link both tables to Power Pivot, and create a relationship—avoiding the necessity of creating the append query. The issue here is that Power Pivot is great at creating relationships horizontally (replicating VLOOKUP() functionality) but it's lousy at stacking two tables on top of each other (appending data).

The challenges with this approach are two-fold:

- Your data gets duplicated because it is loaded to the worksheet first and then to the Data Model.
- Your Power Pivot tables are capped at a maximum of 1,048,575 rows of data (1 less than the number of rows in the worksheet).

So while this works and is the supported method, using Power Query's supported loading methods definitely has some drawbacks for serious modelers.

Loading to the Data Model (Excel 2013+)

In Excel 2013 and higher, the process of linking to the Data Model is actually much easier: Excel gives you a little box that you can check to have Excel do the job for you. To see this in action, you can modify the existing Sales table connection:

- In the Workbook Queries pane, right-click the Sales query → Load To...
- Select Only Create Connection
- Check the Add This Data to the Data Model checkbox
- Click Load

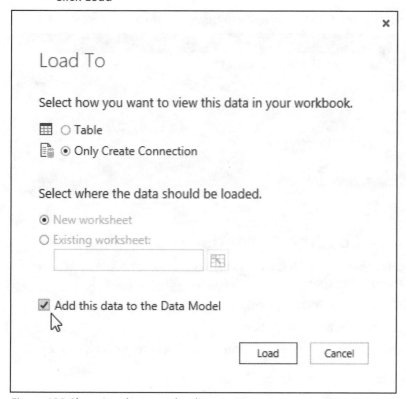

Figure 130 Changing the query loading options.

Making these changes triggers a warning about possible data loss. This happens because changing from Table to Only Create Connection tells Excel that you would like to remove the table that Power Query landed in the worksheet. Because that is to be expected, you can simply acknowledge the warning by clicking Continue.

Should you need to, you are able to load the data to both a table in a worksheet as well as the Data Model.

After Power Query takes a little bit of time to remove the table and set things up with the Data Model, you can head in to Power Pivot and go to the Power Pivot tab → Manage.

	Date	Inventory Item	Sold By	Cost	Price	Commission	A
1	5/31/2...	Slithering Snake	Fred	13	30	0.9	
2	5/31/2...	Rambunctious Pu...	John	9	30	0.9	
3	5/21/2...	Tubby Turtle	John	8	30	0.9	
4	5/4/20...	Tubby Turtle	Fred	8	30	0.9	
5	5/31/2...	Rambunctious Pu...	Fred	9	30	0.9	
6	5/21/2...	Tubby Turtle	Fred	8	30	0.9	
7	5/29/2...	Slithering Snake	John	13	30	0.9	

Figure 131 The data is comfortably loaded into the Power Pivot Data Model.

You'll also find that updates to the Power Query tables flow seamlessly into Power Pivot. Add a new column to the Sales table in Power Query to see how Power Pivot handles it:

- Return to Excel and edit the Sales query
- Select the Date column → Add Column → Date → Month → Month
- Go to Home → Close & Load
- Return to Power Pivot

The data is automatically updated for you, and you don't even need to trigger a refresh.

	Date	Inventory Item	Sold By	Cost	Price	Commission	Month	A
1	5/31/2...	Slithering Snake	Fred	13	30	0.9	5	
2	5/31/2...	Rambunctious Pu...	John	9	30	0.9	5	
3	5/21/2...	Tubby Turtle	John	8	30	0.9	5	
4	5/4/20...	Tubby Turtle	Fred	8	30	0.9	5	
5	5/31/2...	Rambunctious Pu...	Fred	9	30	0.9	5	
6	5/21/2...	Tubby Turtle	Fred	8	30	0.9	5	

Figure 132 A query update pushed directly into the Data Model.

Changing the Default Query Loading Settings

If you find that you're doing a lot of modifications to the default loading experience, you can make changes to your default experience. Where you make these changes depends on your version of Excel:

- Excel 2016:   Data → New Query → Query Options
- Excel 2010/2013:   Power Query → Settings → Options

Following either of these sets of instructions opens the Query Options dialog, where you can change your default loading behavior:

Query Options

GLOBAL

Data Load

Security

Account

Diagnostics

Default Query Load Settings

○ Use standard load settings ⓘ

◉ Specify custom default load settings:

☐ Load to worksheet

☑ Load to Data Model

Figure 133 Changing the default loading settings.

To overrule the default settings, select Specify Custom Default Load Settings and then configure these settings as you wish. The trick here is that by unchecking Load to Worksheet, you create a connection-only query. You can then optionally select the option Load to Data Model (in Excel 2013 or higher.)

Loading Directly to Power Pivot in Excel 2010

Let's be fair: Having to load data into the Excel 2010 Data Model via a table seems crazy. And, in fact, there is a way to go directly to the Data Model without going through a linked table first. A full caveat on this, however, is that this is *not supported by Microsoft*, which means you do this at your own risk.

Connecting to the Data Model

Connecting directly to the Data Model in Excel 2013 or higher is very easy, but in Excel 2010 you need to do a bit more work to pull it off. To see how it works, you'll use the Ch10 Examples\Load Destinations – Pre DataModel.xlsx workbook, which contains the Sales query you created earlier, loaded to a worksheet but not yet linked to Power Pivot.

As with working with Excel 2013 or higher, you want this to be a connection-only query, as the entire point is to avoid loading to a worksheet first. So you need to convert it:

- Open the Workbook Queries pane → right-click Sales → Load To… → Only Create Connection → Load
- Click Continue to accept the possible data loss warning

Now you need to link the Sales query directly to Power Pivot's Data Model. This is done inside the Power Pivot window:

- Go to Power Pivot → Power Pivot Window
- Go to Design → Existing Connections → scroll down to the end

This is perfect: The queries are all listed in Power Pivot already!

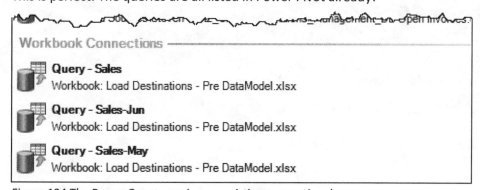

Workbook Connections

Query – Sales
Workbook: Load Destinations - Pre DataModel.xlsx

Query – Sales-Jun
Workbook: Load Destinations - Pre DataModel.xlsx

Query – Sales-May
Workbook: Load Destinations - Pre DataModel.xlsx

Figure 134 The Power Query queries are existing connections!

- Double-click Query – Sales → Next

You now see the following screen, which allows you to specify the SQL query to read from your query. Strangely, however, you can't edit the SQL statement.

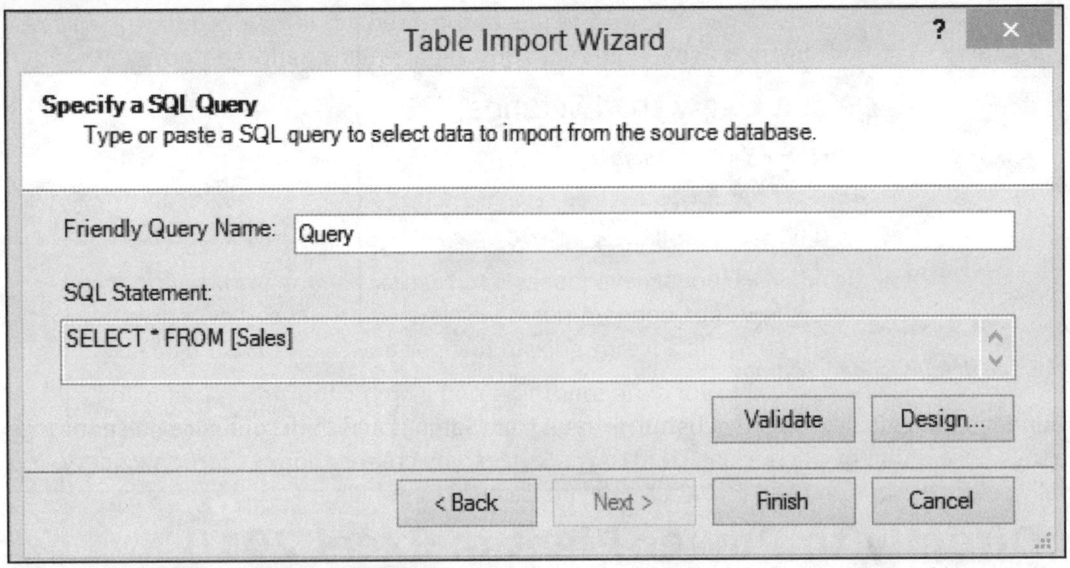

Figure 135 The query with un-editable SQL.

This is your *only* chance to set the Power Pivot table name . . . *ever*. Update the name of the query to something more logical here and make a mistake at your peril as it is un-editable after this point.

- Change the query name to Sales → Finish

The query is now loaded to the Data Model:

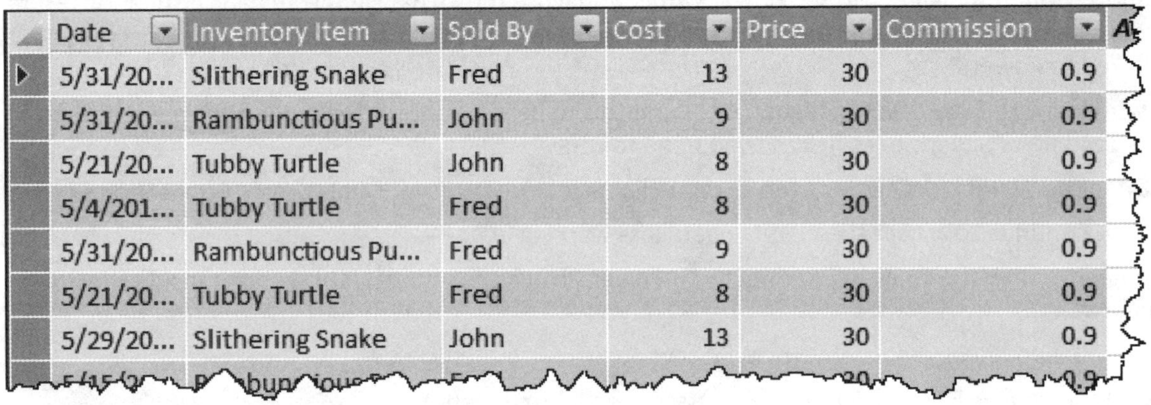

Date	Inventory Item	Sold By	Cost	Price	Commission	A
5/31/20...	Slithering Snake	Fred	13	30	0.9	
5/31/20...	Rambunctious Pu...	John	9	30	0.9	
5/21/20...	Tubby Turtle	John	8	30	0.9	
5/4/201...	Tubby Turtle	Fred	8	30	0.9	
5/31/20...	Rambunctious Pu...	Fred	9	30	0.9	
5/21/20...	Tubby Turtle	Fred	8	30	0.9	
5/29/20...	Slithering Snake	John	13	30	0.9	

Figure 136 A query loaded directly to the Excel Data Model.

Adding Columns to the Query

Now, what about adding that Month column? Go back to the Sales query and add it:

- Edit the Sales query
- Select the Date column → Add Columns → Date → Month → Month
- Go to Home → Close & Load

Now, take a look at how it updates:

- Return to Power Pivot
- Go to Home → Refresh

Things do not go well:

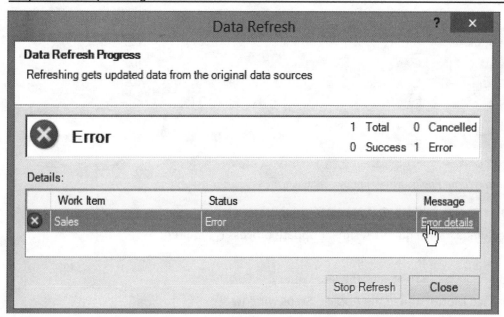

You get an error immediately. And clicking on Error Details yields a message that says this (and more):

```
The query 'Sales' or one of its inputs was modified in Power Query after
this connection was added. Please disable and re-enable loading to the
Data Model for this query.
```

This is obviously not good. So how do you fix it?

The issue is that Power Query queries are compiled into a complicated connection string. And every time a source query is modified, the connection string is changed. Because you linked to the connection string when setting up this query, you need to update that string, and this is how you do it:

- Dismiss the error
- Return to Excel
- Go to Data → Connections
- Select Query – Sales → Properties → Definition
- Click inside the Connection String box → press Ctrl+A to select the entire connection string
- Press Ctrl+C to copy the entire connection string
- Click OK → Close
- Return to Power Pivot → Design → Existing Connections → Query – Sales → Edit
- Select everything inside the connection string (Ctrl+A does not work here)
- Press Ctrl+V to paste the entire connection string you copied earlier
- Click Save → Close
- Go to Home → Refresh

But what's this? While the connection now refreshes, the new Month column isn't present?

As if the initial process weren't long enough, you need to re-confirm the table query as well by going to Design → Table Properties → Save.

Now you're done. A simple open and save, and you finally see your new column:

Date	Inventory Item	Sold By	Cost	Price	Commission	Month
5/31/20...	Slithering Snake	Fred	13	30	0.9	5
5/31/20...	Rambunctious Pu...	John	9	30	0.9	5
5/21/20...	Tubby Turtle	John	8	30	0.9	5
5/4/201...	Tubby Turtle	Fred	8	30	0.9	5
5/31/20...	Rambunctious Pu...	Fred	9	30	0.9	5
5/21/20...	Tubby Turtle	Fred	8	30	0.9	5
5/31/20...	Slithering Snake	John		30		5

Figure 137 The new month column finally arrives in Power Pivot.

Removing Columns from a Query

How do you remove columns from a query? A similar update process is required:

- Return to Excel
- Go to Workbook Queries → right click the Sales query → Edit
- Delete the Inserted Month step in the Applied Steps window
- Go to Home → Close & Load
- Go to Data → Connections
- Select Query – Sales → Properties → Definition
- Click inside the Connection String box → press Ctrl+A to select the entire connection string
- Press Ctrl+C to copy the entire connection string
- Click OK → Close
- Return to Power Pivot → Design → Existing Connections → Query – Sales → Edit
- Select everything inside the connection string (Ctrl+A does not work here)
- Press Ctrl+V to paste the entire connection string you copied earlier
- Save → Close
- Go to Design → Table Properties → Save
- Go to Home → Refresh

This process may seem incredibly painful, but if you follow these steps, you can easily update an Excel 2010 Power Pivot table when changes are made to your Power Query queries. The process is tedious, but at least it's always the same.

> The problem with loading directly to Power Pivot in Excel 2010 is that both Power Query and Power Pivot were separate add-ins for Excel 2010. Power Pivot was integrated into Excel 2013 and Power Query in 2016. So from Excel 2013 on, Power Query and Power Pivot were able to start talking to each other properly, and Excel can handle this process without manual intervention.

Data Model Dangers in Excel 2010 and 2013

Because Power Query is a separate add-in from Excel 2010 and 2013, there are some very dangerous idiosyncrasies that you need to be aware of when working with Power Query. Fortunately, these have been solved with Excel 2016 and for some people using Excel 2013, but if you are developing in earlier versions, you either need to go "all in" with Power Query or avoid using it.

How to Corrupt Your Model

Corrupting your model is deadly easy, and the worst part is that you may not realize for months that you've done it. Here is a very easy way to do it (and it's safe to try it here, so go for it!):

- Open the Ch10 Examples\Load Destinations – Complete that pertains to your version
- Open Power Pivot
- Rename the Sales worksheet Transactions

Your model is broken, but it certainly doesn't look like it, does it? In fact, it continues to refresh whether you go to Home → Refresh in Power Pivot or Data → Refresh All in Excel. So what's the big deal?

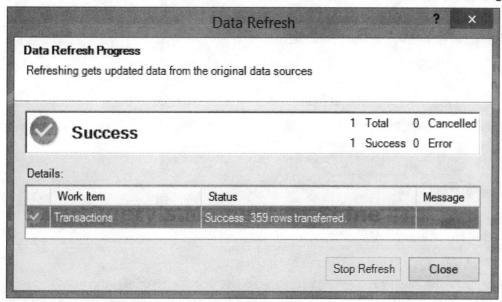

Figure 138 The model still refreshes, so what's the problem?

The model *is* damaged, but your workbook will continue to refresh, possibly for months, before you figure it out. What will trigger the issue to actually rear its ugly head? Any change to the underlying query.

To see what we mean, go back and add that month column again, using the steps outlined earlier in this chapter. Whether you use Excel 2010 or 2013, once you've followed the normal steps to update your table, the data will fail to load to the Power Pivot Data Model:

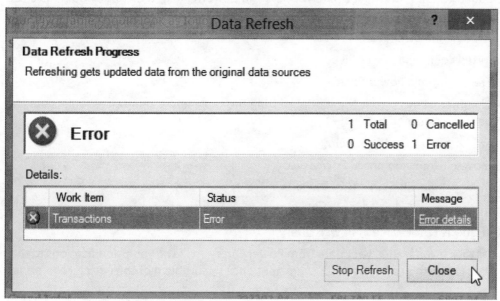

Figure 139 An error? But it refreshed yesterday!

What's even worse is that the error message provided only indicates that there is something wrong with the connection—but not what or how to fix it.

Can you even check a model to see if it's damaged? Yes, you can:

- In Excel go to Data → Connections
- Select your Power Query query → Properties → Definition

If the connection string is grayed out and you get a message in the bottom-left corner that reads "Some properties cannot be changed because this connection was modified using the PowerPivot Add-in," you're too late. The damage has been done, and it's irreversible.

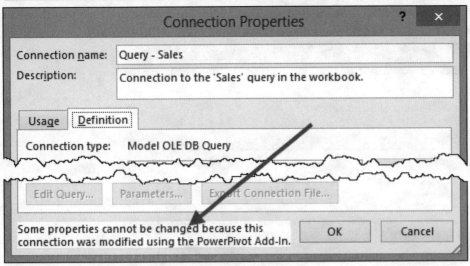

Figure 140 Power Query's game over screen.

The most awful news about this is that there is only one fix. You must:

1. Delete the table, including any measures and calculated fields that live on it, and then
2. Rebuild the table, measures, and calculated fields from scratch.

It's horrendous, it's ugly, and it's feared. It's also totally avoidable if you are disciplined.

Critical Do's and Don'ts to Avoid Corrupting Your Model

Using Power Query to source data for your Power Pivot Data Model is completely stable, provided that you follow certain rules.

If your data has been loaded to the Power Pivot Data Model from Power Query, then you should *never* do any of the following:

*   Change the table name in Power Pivot
*   Rename an imported column in Power Pivot
*   Delete an imported column in Power Pivot

Any of these actions will immediately corrupt the model, setting the table into a non-refreshable state the next time the Power Query query is modified.

Keep in mind that *it is safe to perform the following*:

*   Add/modify/remove custom columns in Power Pivot
*   Add/modify/remove relationships in Power Pivot
*   Add/modify/remove measures (calculated fields) in Power Pivot
*   Make any modifications to the table in Power Query

The basic rule of thumb is this: If you loaded your data from Power Query, make *all* your modifications to that table in Power Query. If you follow this rule, you won't ever experience the problem of corrupting your model.

Chapter 11 Defining Data Types

As Power Query matures, it is getting better and better at automatically setting appropriate data types on columns of data. Even so, there are still times when it pops up with an odd choice (or no choice at all). This can leave hidden traps in data sets that can rear their ugly heads when you least expect it and can cause all kinds of confusion.

What Data Types Are Recognized?

Power Query recognizes several data types—more, in fact, than Excel does. The complete list of Power Query's data types is:

- Number: Decimal Number, Whole Number, Currency
- Date/times: Date/Time, Date, Time, Date/Time/Timezone, Duration
- Text: Text
- Boolean: True/False
- Object: Binary
- Undefined: Any

The true killer is in the last data type. Any is a variant data type that Power Query will use to indicate that it isn't sure of the data type. The challenge here is that data defined as Any could take a variety of forms when being loaded or referenced in the future.

Why Data Types Are Important?

To demonstrate the importance of defining data types, in this chapter you will create a new query and remove the data types that Power Query defines for you. This will give you a good understanding of why declaring data types is important and not something you should leave to chance.

Tables and the Any Data Type

Start by loading a query with no defined data types into an Excel table:

- Open Ch11 Examples\Defining Data Types
- Select a cell in the May data table → create a new query → From Table
- Remove the Changed Type step

At this point, the data has no data types defined at all, which you can see by selecting a cell in the column and then looking on the Transform tab:

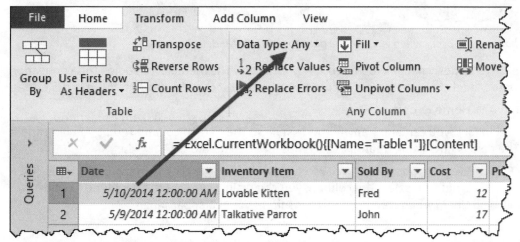

Figure 141 The Date column with a date type of Any.

- Interestingly, each column in this data set has the same data type, Any, yet they all look different. The dates look like they are in Date/Time format, and the numbers look like they are the Number data type. So what's the big deal? Follow these steps to find out:

- Rename the query May
- Go to Home → Close & Load

Here's the Excel table that shows up:

◢	A	B	C	D	E	F
1	Date ▼	Inventory Item ▼	Sold By ▼	Cost ▼	Price ▼	Commission ▼
2	41769	Lovable Kitten	Fred	12	45	1.35
3	41768	Talkative Parrot	John	17	32	0.96
4	41783	Lovable Kitten	Jane	12	45	1.35
5	41779	Adorable Kitty Cat	John	25	35	1.05
6	41767	Lovable Kitten	Jane	12	45	1.35
7	41782	Sleepy Gerbil	Jane	25	39	1.17
8	41770	Cranky Crocodile	John	10	35	1.05

Figure 142 What happened to that Date column?

As you can see, Excel didn't recognize the Date column as dates but instead placed the date serial numbers. While this is easily rectified (by formatting the column as dates), it is indicative of a more serious problem.

Power Pivot and the Any Data Type

At this point, make a change to the query and load it to the Data Model:

- In the Workbook Queries pane right-click the May query → Load To…
- Check the Add to Data Model checkbox (leaving the table option selected) → Load → Continue

Once you commit this change, the Excel table in the worksheet also changes!

◢	A	B	C	D	E	F
1	Date ▼	Inventory Item ▼	Sold By ▼	Cost ▼	Price ▼	Commission ▼
2	5/31/2014 12:00:00 AM	Slithering Snake	Fred	13	30	0.9
3	5/31/2014 12:00:00 AM	Rambunctious Puppy	John	9	30	0.9
4	5/21/2014 12:00:00 AM	Tubby Turtle	John	8	30	0.9
5	5/4/2014 12:00:00 AM	Tubby Turtle	Fred	8	30	0.9
6	5/31/2014 12:00:00 AM	Rambunctious Puppy	Fred	9	30	0.9
7	5/21/2014 12:00:00 AM	Tubby Turtle	Fred	8	30	0.9
8	5/29/2014 12:00:00 AM	Slithering Snake	John	13	30	0.9

Figure 143 Strange changes that occur when you add the data to the Data Model.

This is probably one of the oddest changes you'll see in Power Query. The mere act of adding this connection to the Power Pivot Data Model changes the field back to a date in the Excel table—or does it? To see if it does:

- Select column A → Home → Comma Style

There are no changes! In fact, you can apply any numeric style to the data in column A that you like, and it will not change it. The data is now being treated as text, not as a date at all.

What about inside Power Pivot? If you open Power Pivot, you see that the data is there, and it looks like a valid Date/Time value. But when you select the column, you can plainly see that the data type has been set to Text. That certainly won't help when creating a relationship to your calendar table!

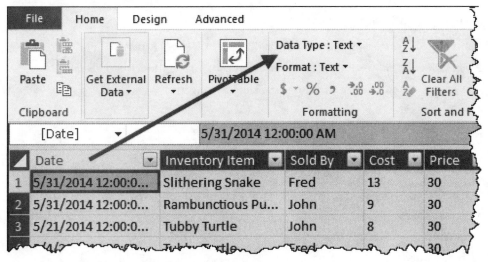

Figure 144 Dates that aren't really dates inside Power Pivot.

Dealing with Any Data Types

The fix for these issues is very simple. You edit the May query and set the data types, like this:

- In the Workbook Queries pane right-click May → Edit
- Set the Date column to a Date data type
- Set the Inventory Item and Sold By columns to a Text data type
- Set the Cost and Price columns to a Whole Number data type
- Set the Commission column to a Decimal Number data type
- Go to Home → Close & Load

If you now check the table and Power Pivot model, you'll find that everything is being treated as the data types you'd expect.

 Remember that Power Pivot formats valid dates in a Date/Time format, with 00:00:00 being 0 minutes after midnight of the provided date.

Combining Queries with Different Data Types

One of the tasks you're likely to perform often is appending two tables. But what happens when the columns in those tables have different data types?

Since you've already got the May query corrected, you can now create a new query for the June data without data types and see what happens when you append them:

- Select the June table → create a new query → From Table
- Remove the Changed Type step
- Rename the query June
- Go to Home → Close & Load To... → Only Create Connection

Appending Defined to Any Data Types

Now you can append the two queries:

- In the Workbook Queries pane right-click the June query → Append
- Select the May query → OK

At this point, if you check the data type in the Date column, you'll see that it is Any:

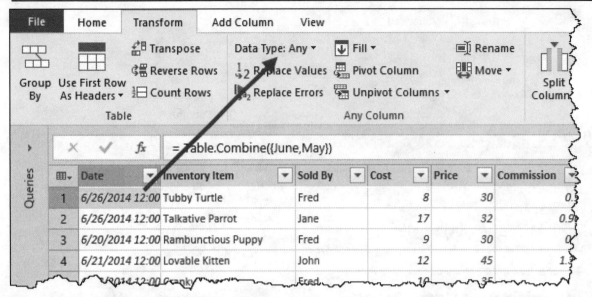

Figure 145 Combined tables with differing data types.

This probably isn't very surprising. After all, you started with a query where the Date column was defined as Any, so appending something else to an Any should probably yield a column of the same data type.

You can finalize this query and see what happens if you attack it from the other side:

- Rename the query Jun+May
- Go to Home → Close & Load To… → Only Create Connection

Appending Any to Defined Data Types

Now try this from the other direction, starting with a column that did have the data types defined:

- Go to the Workbook Queries pane → right-click the May query → Append
- Select the June query → OK

The data certainly looks better, but when you inspect the Date column, it still shows as an Any data type:

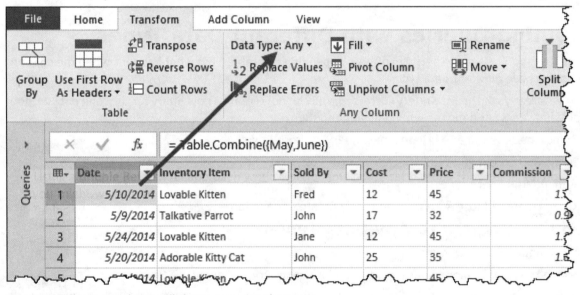

Figure 146 The Date column still shows as an Any data type.

By now it's fairly clear that it doesn't matter in which order you append the queries: If the data types are mismatched between the sets, they will be converted to Any data types.

You can now finalize this query and see what happens if you correct the issue in the underlying table:

- Rename the query May+Jun

- Go to Home → Close & Load To... → Only Create Connection

Appending Consistent Data Types

Since you already know the data types are defined in the May query, you can make the data types consistent in the June query and see how that affects the append queries:

- In the Workbook Queries pane right-click June → Edit
- Set the Date column to a Date data type
- Set the Inventory Item and Sold By columns to a Text data type
- Set the Cost and Price columns to a Whole Number data type
- Set the Commission column to a Decimal Number data type
- Go to Home → Close & Load

And now you can return to one of the two append queries to see the effects. No matter which you choose, you'll find that the values in the Date column show up properly defined as Date data types.

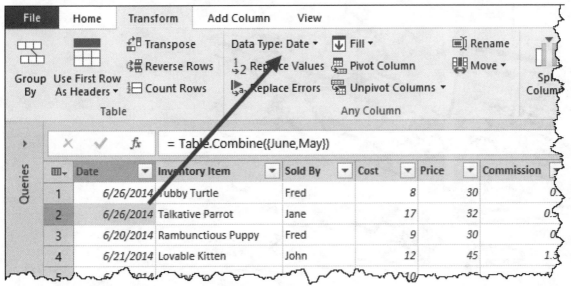

Figure 147 The Date data type is now applied to the append query's column.

Data Type Best Practices

While it can be tempting to just rely on Power Query to assign data types and continue on, we strongly recommend that you review the final step of every output query and define your data types there. Even though Microsoft is constantly improving the interface, there are still commands in the Power Query interface that will return an Any data type, even if it was defined before.

Until recently, an example of this was creating a month end from a date. Even though the column with the date was properly formatted as a date, the Month End function returned a value that looked like a Date but was, in fact, an Any. Although this specific issue is now fixed, there are bound to still be issues like this lurking in the program.

In addition, there are also certain commands that will not run on columns where the data type is defined as Any. One such command is the Replace Values command, which won't always find certain values. If the column is converted to Text, however, the command functions properly again.

As you've seen, the risk of having your data defined as an Any data type can cause issues in both Excel and Power Pivot, and these problems can manifest in different ways. Remember also that you fixed the two append queries in this chapter simply by changing the underlying data type. The flip side of this is that it would be just as easy to break things when modifying an underlying query and cause the final query to render Any data types. For the amount of effort compared to the peace of mind, it is highly recommended that you create a habit of defining data types for each and every column as the final step of a production query, even if the data types have been defined earlier. While it might seem tedious, remember that it is a one-time task for a query that could be rerun every single day of the year.

Chapter 12 Importing Web Data

One of the really interesting use cases for Power Query is when leveraging it to pull data relevant to your business from the web.

Power Query works very well when website data is stored in tables, and on occasion it even lets you directly access a text file that is holding information. If the data isn't formatted with table tags in the HTML code, however, things become very difficult, even if you have some HTML knowledge.

Connecting to Pages with Tables

For the example in this chapter, you will take the role of a marketing person who is trying to figure out the best countries in which to market a product. The primary statistic that you want to figure out up front is which 10 countries have the largest populations, as that seems to be a factor that could be reasonably construed to drive sales.

In order to get this information, you have been exploring the CIA World Factbook website, and you have come across a web page that lists the populations of the countries of the world. You would like to pull this data into Excel so that you can use it with other tables. Follow these steps:

- Create a new query → From Other Sources → From Web
- When prompted for the URL, enter the following: https://www.cia.gov/library/publications/the-world-factbook/rankorder/2119rank.html
- Click OK

You are now prompted with a set of authentication options:

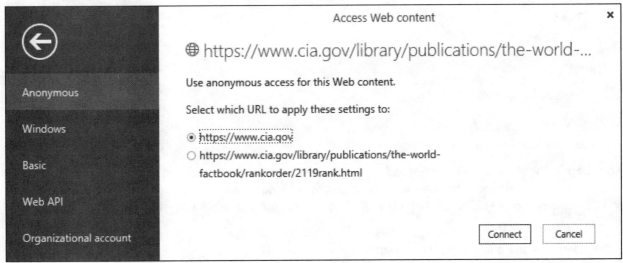

Figure 148 The web authentication dialog.

There are several options down the left side of the dialog, allowing you to choose from Windows or basic authentication, provide a Web API key, or even provide your Office 365 credentials. The important one to you at this point is the Anonymous option.

The question you are being asked here is if you'd like to use these credentials for the specific page or the root domain. While there are sometimes reasons to choose the specific page, chances are that you're probably going to want to stick with the default—the root domain—in most cases. So ensure that the first option is selected and click Connect.

At this point, Power Query inspects the document, looking for tables. Once it has worked out the content it recognizes, it sends you to the Navigator pane. In this case, there are two options to choose from—Table 0 or Document:

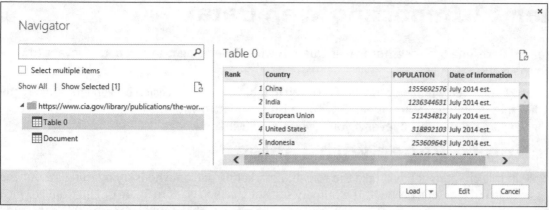

Figure 149 Previewing Table 0 in the Navigator.

In this case, Power Query recognizes that the HTML document contains a table denoted by table tags in the page code. It presents that table for you in an easy-to-use format.

If you select the Document option, you see that it doesn't look nearly as pretty:

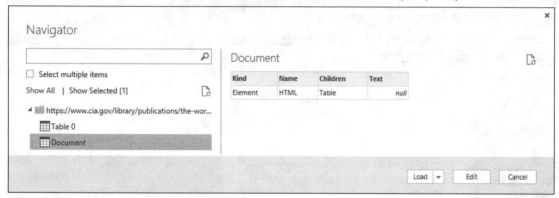

Figure 150 No good can come from this.

> The reality here is that it is going to be much more difficult to extract your data via the document interface than via a table.

Fortunately, the data looked pretty good in the preview of the Table 0 table. It was already organized in a beautiful table format, with headers in place. It was even already sorted into ascending order, just as it was in the web page. Your real goal is to filter to get the top 10 countries, so follow these steps:

- Select Table 0 → Edit
- Rename the query Top 10 Population
- Go to Home → Keep Rows → Keep Top Rows → 10 → OK

This is what you have now:

Rank	Country	POPULATION	Date of Information
1	China	1355692576	July 2014 est.
2	India	1236344631	July 2014 est.
3	European Union	511434812	July 2014 est.
4	United States	318892103	July 2014 est.
5	Indonesia	253609643	July 2014 est.
6	Brazil	202656788	July 2014 est.
7	Pakistan	196174380	July 2014 est.
8	Nigeria	177155754	July 2014 est.
9	Bangladesh	166280712	July 2014 est.
10	Russia	142470272	July 2014 est.

PROPERTIES

Name

Top 10 Population

All Properties

APPLIED STEPS

Source
Navigation
Changed Type
✕ Kept First Rows

Figure 151 You have your top 10 countries.

The query is now finished, so you can finalize it by selecting Home → Close & Load.

Connecting to Web-Hosted Files

As it happens, the World Factbook page actually makes use of a text file to feed the data displayed in the web page.

Now, if you happen to know the URL to the text file, can you connect directly to it? The answer is yes, and here's how it works:

- Create a new query → From Other Sources → From Web
- Enter the URL as follows: https://www.cia.gov/library/publications/the-world-factbook/rankorder/rawdata_2119.txt
- Click OK

You are launched directly into the Power Query editor.

 Notice this time that you bypass the website authentication step. The reason for this is that you specified that you wanted the authentication settings to apply to the website root (www.cia.gov) when you created the previous query. Had you not done that earlier, you would have been prompted to provide the authentication method.

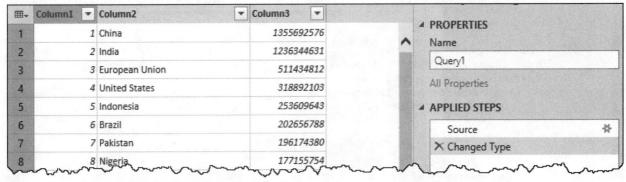

	Column1	Column2	Column3
1	1	China	1355692576
2	2	India	1236344631
3	3	European Union	511434812
4	4	United States	318892103
5	5	Indonesia	253609643
6	6	Brazil	202656788
7	7	Pakistan	196174380
8	8	Nigeria	177155754

PROPERTIES
Name
Query1
All Properties

APPLIED STEPS
Source
✕ Changed Type

Figure 152 Connecting directly to a text file over the web.

Based on the data you get back, you can assume that the column headers are not stored in the text file but rather were provided by the HTML of the web page. This is no big deal though, as you can fix this to make your data consistent with the previous experience:

- Go to Home → Keep Rows → Keep Top Rows → 10 → OK
- Right-click Column1 → Rename → Rank
- Right-click Column2 → Rename → Country
- Right-click Column3 → Rename → Population
- Rename the query From Text

It appears that the estimate date was also provided by the HTML page, not the text file, but since that's not a huge deal to you, you're not worried about it.

The truly important thing here is that you *can* connect *directly* to a file hosted on the web without going through the whole web page interface . . . if you know where it is.

Connecting to Pages Without Tables

If the web page you're connecting to doesn't contain table tags in the HTML source code, you're left with a horrendous experience of trying to drill into the HTML elements. This experience is about as much fun as navigating a subterranean labyrinth using a candle for light, where every signpost simply says "This way out."

The best way to get help in this situation is to open your web browser, turn on the developer tools, and try to find the element you want to extract. The following is the element inspector in Chrome (which you open by pressing F12) for the CIA web page:

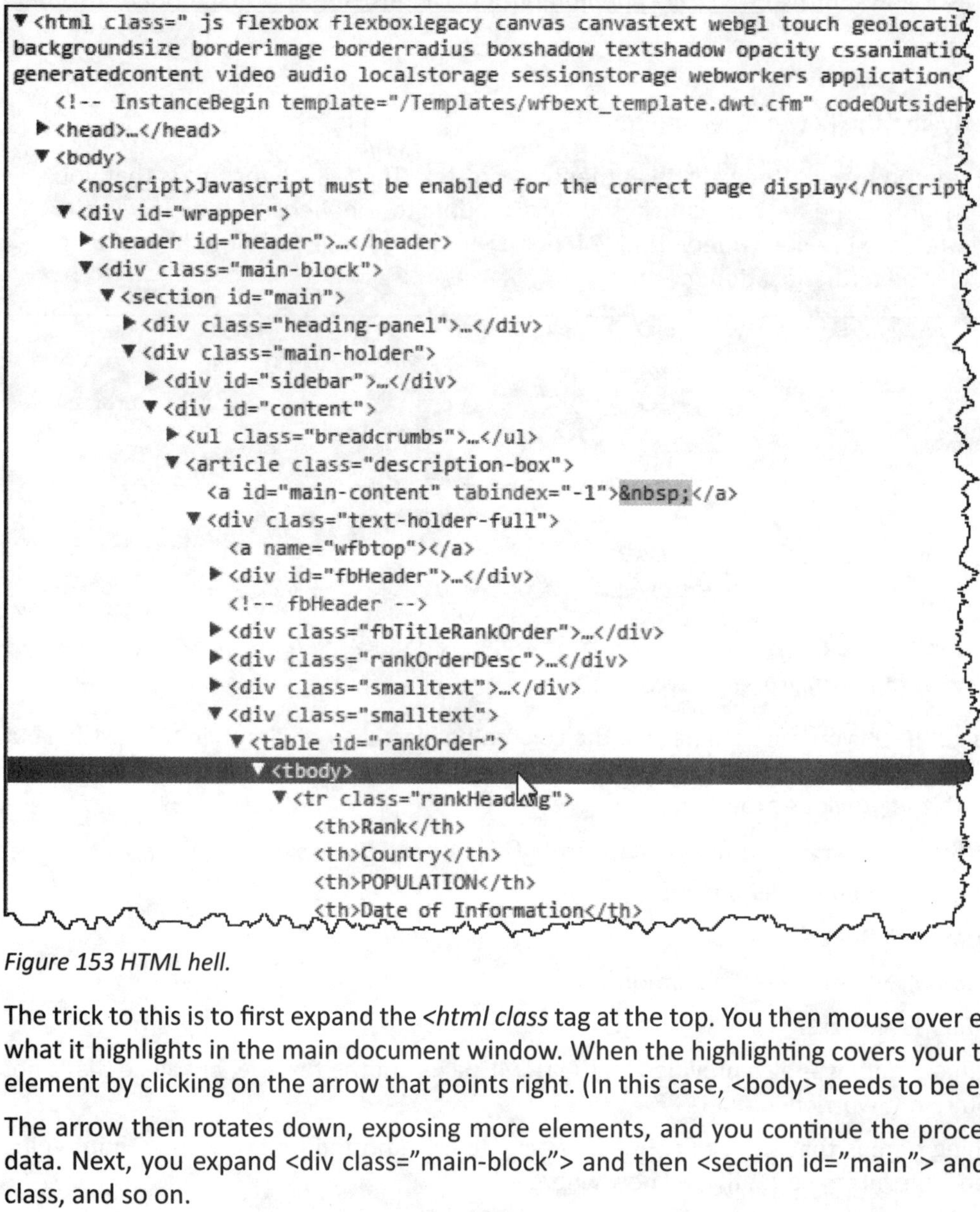

```
▼<html class=" js flexbox flexboxlegacy canvas canvastext webgl touch geolocatio
backgroundsize borderimage borderradius boxshadow textshadow opacity cssanimatio
generatedcontent video audio localstorage sessionstorage webworkers application
    <!-- InstanceBegin template="/Templates/wfbext_template.dwt.cfm" codeOutsideI
  ▶<head>…</head>
  ▼<body>
      <noscript>Javascript must be enabled for the correct page display</noscript
    ▼<div id="wrapper">
      ▶<header id="header">…</header>
      ▼<div class="main-block">
        ▼<section id="main">
          ▶<div class="heading-panel">…</div>
          ▼<div class="main-holder">
            ▶<div id="sidebar">…</div>
            ▼<div id="content">
              ▶<ul class="breadcrumbs">…</ul>
              ▼<article class="description-box">
                  <a id="main-content" tabindex="-1"> </a>
                ▼<div class="text-holder-full">
                    <a name="wfbtop"></a>
                  ▶<div id="fbHeader">…</div>
                    <!-- fbHeader -->
                  ▶<div class="fbTitleRankOrder">…</div>
                  ▶<div class="rankOrderDesc">…</div>
                  ▶<div class="smalltext">…</div>
                  ▼<div class="smalltext">
                    ▼<table id="rankOrder">
                      ▼<tbody>
                        ▼<tr class="rankHeading">
                            <th>Rank</th>
                            <th>Country</th>
                            <th>POPULATION</th>
                            <th>Date of Information</th>
```

Figure 153 HTML hell.

The trick to this is to first expand the *<html class* tag at the top. You then mouse over every arrow and watch what it highlights in the main document window. When the highlighting covers your table, you expand that element by clicking on the arrow that points right. (In this case, <body> needs to be expanded.)

The arrow then rotates down, exposing more elements, and you continue the process until you find your data. Next, you expand <div class="main-block"> and then <section id="main"> and then the second div class, and so on.

If you accidentally travel into a hole that doesn't have your data, you go back up one level and collapse that block of code by clicking the arrow. This rotates the arrow back from pointing down to pointing right, and it collapses the elements contained within that tag.

Once you have navigated through the process and found your data, you can begin the painful second portion: replicating the navigation in Power Query. Here's what you do:

- Create a new query → From Other Sources → From Web
- Enter the URL you used for the first example: https://www.cia.gov/library/publications/the-world-factbook/rankorder/2119rank.html
- Click OK → Document → Edit

You're now looking at this rather unfriendly view in the Power Query editor:

Figure 154 A most uninspiring view.

Now you need to very carefully replicate the steps you took in the web developer interface, drilling into Power Query's corresponding table element. There are some parallels between the two programs to help, but even so, it is easy to get lost.

The trick to navigating this process is to recognize that the Name field in Power Query contains the element shown in the web developer tools. In this case, you have HTML, and in Chrome you saw *<html class* at the top. These two items are the same.

Click on Table in the Children column to drill into it:

⊞▾	Kind	▾	Name	▾	Children	↕↔	Text	▾
1	Element		HEAD		Table		*null*	
2	Text			*null*		*null*		
3	Element		BODY		Table		*null*	

Figure 155 Children of the HTML element.

You now see the HEAD and BODY tags. Based on the HTML you expanded, you know you need to drill into the Body tag. You click the Table there and keep going.

The killer with this process is that in the HTML, the tags all have names, but in Power Query you don't see them, so it's very easy to get lost. In addition, the Applied Steps box doesn't trace the route; it just keeps combining steps together, giving you no way to back up one level. When that happens, your only recourse is to start over again from the beginning.

And as if that weren't bad enough, at the end of this navigation process, you end up extracting columns to drill into the detail, and it ends up stacked in a vertical table:

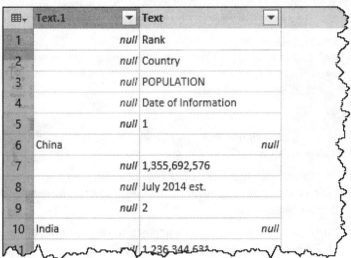

Figure 156 So much for a nice clean table!

The steps to make this table into a nice clean one are beyond the scope of this chapter, so we are going to abandon this approach at this point. (Rest assured, the steps *are* covered, just not until Chapter 15.)

The steps to complete this process have, however, been saved in the completed example, which can be found at Ch12 Examples\Importing Web Data – Complete.xlsx. This particular query has been saved as The-HardWay. Even with that query to review, you'll need to recognize that the Navigation step was generated as documented below.

Starting from the initial table:

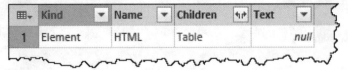

Figure 157 Starting the journey into HTML Hell.

Drill into Table in the Children column for:

- HTML (row 1)
- Body (row 3)
- DIV (row 4)
- The 1st DIV (row 4)
- SECTION (row 2)
- The 2nd DIV (row 4)
- The 2nd DIV (row 4)
- ARTICLE (row 4)
- DIV (row 4)
- The 5th DIV (row 12)
- TABLE (row 2)
- TBODY (row 2)

If you follow this drill-down carefully, you'll see that you drilled into exactly the same place as displayed in the Navigation step of the TheHardWay query, and you can follow the rest of the steps through to the end.

The job of drilling into the HTML document *can* be done, which is better than the alternative. However, it is not for the faint of heart and can be an incredibly frustrating process.

Caveats and Frustrations with the From Web Experience

The From Web experience is certainly a weakness in Power Query's otherwise incredible arsenal of tools. There are several things that we hope could be improved in this area, and there are things to watch out for as you develop solutions based on web data.

None of the factors discussed below should be seen as reasons not to develop solutions based on website data. Instead, they are intended to make sure you go into this area with both eyes open, seeing not only the benefits but also the risks of relying on web-sourced data you don't control.

The Collecting Data Experience

Building solutions against web data can be a very painful experience in Power Query. If there are table tags in the HTML code, everything works well. If not, however, all bets are off.

Compare this to Excel's classic Data → From Web experience, which kicks off a web browser that allows you to navigate the web to find the data you're looking for. Power Query does not give you this facility but instead leaves you to navigate web pages using a different browser.

In itself, this may not seem like a big deal, except for the issue that it is very difficult to tell if the data you are seeing in the web browser is in an easy-to-use table or not, without looking at the code.

The challenge here is that you'll grab the promising URL, drop it in the Power Query interface, and then spend a huge amount of time expanding columns, chasing each route down the rabbit hole of HTML tags, trying to find the data you're looking for. Even if you do understand the web debugging tools, it still doesn't make the job easy. Because Excel pros are not web developers, this is really an unnecessary burden that is being placed upon them.

Ideally, this experience should kick off a web browser, let you navigate to the page and select the data range you'd like to import, and then do the leg work of breaking the HTML down to do that for you. Until that happens, however, importing data that is not formatted in a tabular fashion will continue to be difficult.

Data Integrity

Another major concern with web data is the source and integrity of the data. Be cautious of connecting and importing data from sites such as Wikipedia or other sites that you don't have a business relationship with.

While demos love to use Wikipedia as a great example, the reality is that relying on this site can be dangerous. The content is curated, but it can also be changed by users. Although the site makes a great effort to curate data, the information there is far from perfect and may not be entirely factual.

The other issue is how readily the data is updated. Imagine investing time in building a complicated query against a web page, only to find out that the owner/curator doesn't update it on a timely basis. You need to be assured that when you refresh the data, the routine isn't merely refreshing out-of-date data but rather that it's refreshing current data. You're likely to invest a significant amount of time and make business decisions assuming that the last refresh you did pulled the most recent data.

Solution Stability

There is another very real concern when building your business logic against web sources that you do not own or control. Like your company, every other company that provides these feeds and pages wants to better serve its customers. Unfortunately for us, that doesn't mean that they are interested in putting out a consistent experience that never changes. In fact, quite the opposite is true. They are also trying to update things, changing the web pages to add new bells or whistles, or make the sites more attractive to the human eye. This has the very real side effect of blowing queries apart, usually without notice, and oftentimes when you don't have time to fix them.

Chapter 13 Loading Data from Exchange

In the past, trying to get data out of Microsoft Exchange was an absolute nightmare. It involved complex VBA scripts, significant development, and painful maintenance. The unfortunate part of this was that there is a significant amount of information buried in your email and calendar that can add great business value to you, but with it being so difficult to get at, it was a nonstarter. Power Query has changed that, allowing an easy way to connect to your Exchange database and start pulling out key drivers that can impact your business intelligence solutions.

Accessible Data

There are five main aspects that you can connect to in your Exchange database:

- Mail
- Calendar appointments
- People
- Tasks
- Meeting requests

Each of these can be pulled in to Power Query, cleaned and turned into a table, and then served up to a table or the Power Pivot Data Model.

Potential Use Cases

The most difficult question to wrap your head around related to Exchange as a data source is not how to connect to it but rather why you would want to. The main reason for this is that you've never had the ability, so you haven't thought about it much. Consider the following scenarios and how connection to your Exchange server could be used in your organization.

Aggregating Survey Data

With Power Query's ability to read email, you could create a simple survey with a table in the body and send it out to your audience. You could then use Power Query to read all the replies, extract the information from the individual tables, and combine the tables into a data source. Better yet, you don't have to worry if someone sends in a copy late, as you can just refresh the data source to pull it in.

Aggregating Budget Requests

It's a common practice for accountants to send Excel workbooks to key personnel and ask them to fill in budget information and return the spreadsheet via email. What if you could then use Power Query to scan for all emails with a certain subject and/or attachment and then open and combine each attachment and extract the data? This is entirely possible with Power Query.

Building an IT Alert Dashboard

In IT, we often get numerous email alerts from various servers and pieces of equipment. Some are informational and some critical, but depending on the volume of equipment you have and the frequency of alerts, they can quickly turn into information overload. Oftentimes these emails are automatically routed to a folder and ignored. But think about this: You can now use Power Query to aggregate the emails, chart the volume and severity, and build an entire systems alert dashboard from previously useless email.

Endless Possibilities

From extracting and matching contact details to appointments and emails, the real question today is not *if* you can use this feature but *how*. Maybe you need a dashboard of interaction you've had with a client, or you need to track who has replied to a critical email you sent out. There is a ton of valuable information sitting in your inbox that you now have access to in a way you never did before.

Building an Email Dashboard

For this example, you'll take the role of a website owner to see how previously useless email can be turned into something interesting. While you won't be able to replicate the steps in this chapter yourself (they are specific to the website owner's inbox), you'll see the process used to strip key information out of previously unread emails to drive a dashboard.

To begin with, you need to connect to Microsoft Exchange. This is done via the following process:

- Create a new query → From Other Sources → Microsoft Exchange
- Enter your username and password
- Click Allow when you're prompted to allow the Exchange Autodiscover Service

Figure 158 Trusting the Autodiscover Service.

This service is configured by your IT department and needs to be trusted in order to access the Exchange server. It is typically already installed and configured to allow cell phones to access their email remotely.

After a short delay while Power Query connects to the Exchange server, you are taken to a Navigator window.

- Select Mail → Edit

Don't ever click the Load button after choosing the Mail table in the Navigator. You'll be waiting for a *long* time as it loads your *entire* inbox!

Power Query launches and provides you with a preview of your inbox:

Figure 159 A list of emails in your inbox.

In order to reduce the number of emails to search through, you routed the relevant emails to a folder via a rule. This means that you need to filter the Folder Path column in order to locate only the emails that have been routed to that specific folder. Interestingly, when you attempt to set the filter, the relevant folder isn't listed:

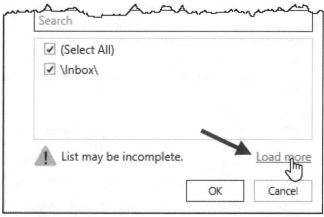

Figure 160 Locating the appropriate folder.

If you ever find that the values you're sure should be in the column just aren't there, look for the Load More option at the bottom right. By default, this list is shortened to the limited amount of data showing in the preview, but clicking the Load More button brings up all the folders in the inbox.

When the list appears in full, you select the correct folder, and the list of emails is filtered to show only those of interest—the earned commission emails from a specific affiliate source:

Figure 161 A list of emails with exciting subject lines.

While they don't show in the image, a huge variety of columns are included with email, including such useful fields as To, CC, Sender, Attachments, and more. For the purposes of this dashboard, however, only the Date-TimeSent and Body fields are required. For that reason, you select those two columns and use the Remove Other Columns command to remove the extraneous data:

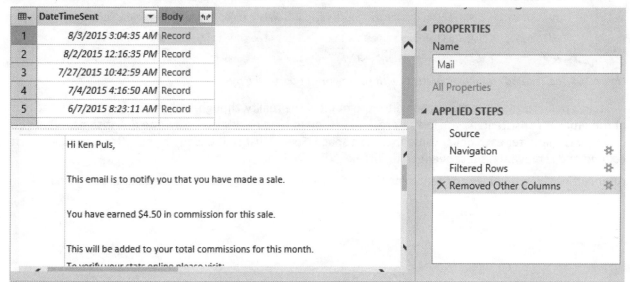

Figure 162 A column full of records.

The interesting part of the Body column is that it is full of records, which you can think of as the individual cells of a table. As it happens, these records contain some very interesting information in the body of the email. You can also see the expansion arrow at the top-right corner of the Body column, which means it is possible to expand these records into a column. Doing so gives you another option: the choice between TextBody and HTMLBody. Since working with text is far easier than working with HTML, you will usually elect to expand TextBody only and then clean and trim the resulting records.

The result is a consistent data set, which can then be further cleaned:

⊞▾	DateTimeSent	▾	TextBody
1	8/3/2015 3:04:35 AM		Hi Ken Puls,This email is to notify you that you have made a sale.You have earned $4.50 in c
2	8/2/2015 12:16:35 PM		Hi Ken Puls,This email is to notify you that you have made a sale.You have earned $3.00 in
3	7/27/2015 10:42:59 AM		Hi Ken Puls,This email is to notify you that you have made a sale.You have earned $11.70 in
4	7/4/2015 4:16:50 AM		Hi Ken Puls,This email is to notify you that you have made a sale.You have earned $4.50 in
5	6/7/2015 8:23:11 AM		Hi Ken Puls,This email is to notify you that you have made a sale.You have earned $3.00 in
6	6/?2015 ?:49:?8 AM		Ken Puls,This e?? ??is to notify you that ??? have made ? sale.You have ??rned $4.50 i

Figure 163 The body of all matching emails.

At this point, the email body can be pared down the email to get at the only part of real interest: the money.

One of the great things about Power Query is the preview window that appears when you select any cell in the Power Query grid. Not only can you see the data, you can select the data in that window and copy it. Rather than split by the $ sign and have to remove a column afterward or type a huge amount of text in the replace window, why not just replace the leading text with nothing? To do this, follow these steps:

- Copy the text from the preview window, starting with Hi and ending with $
- Right-click the TextBody column → Replace Values...
- Paste the copied text string into the Value to Find field
- Leave the Replace With field blank
- Click OK

The results are shown below, with the money at the left side of the column:

⊞▾	DateTimeSent	▾	TextBody
1	8/3/2015 3:04:35 AM		4.50 in commission for this sale.This will be added to your total commissions f
2	8/2/2015 12:16:35 PM		3.00 in commission for this sale.This will be added to your total commissions fo
3	7/27/2015 10:42:59 AM		11.70 in commission for this sale.This will be added to your total commissions,
4	7/4/2015 4:16:50 AM		4.50 in commission for this sale.This will be added to your total commissions f
5	6/7/2015 8:23:11 AM		3.00 in commission for this sale.This will be added to your total commissions f
6	?:?4M	4.50	?? ??ice ??.Thi? ??adde? ?ur total ?mission

Figure 164 The TextBody column now starts with the important part—the money.

Next, you need to get rid of the portion after the money. The reality, though, is that you aren't sure if the rest of the email is consistent, as you lost interest and stopped reading after you saw the dollar signs. What you do know is that after each dollar value there is a space. So you just split based on the leftmost space in that column and remove the subsequent column.

After setting the data types and renaming the columns, you are left with data that looks much better:

Date	Commission
1	8/3/2015	4.5
2	8/2/2015	3
3	7/27/2015	11.7
4	7/4/2015	4.5
5	6/7/2015	3

Figure 165 Date sourced from email, cleaned and ready to be used.

The final step for this data source is to load it to Excel and build a PivotChart from it:

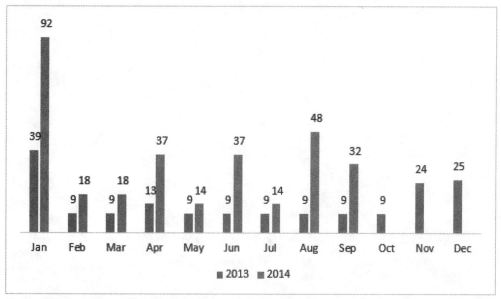

Figure 166 A profit-tracking chart built from previously useless email.

Consider the impact here where you've been collecting these emails for the better part of two years and never reading them. Suddenly they now have business value. These emails can be used as part of an email dashboard to review the profitability of one of the income streams that supports your website.

Best Practices for Exchange Sources

There are two main issues to consider when building a solution against a Microsoft Exchange service: portability and performance.

Portability

The very first thing you need to take into account is how long this solution is intended to survive and whether we will need to pass it on to another user. Why? Because you are targeting your own email account. Building a solution against your email account locks it down so that only you can use it. It can't be shared, and it's difficult to port to others later, as the source files for the solution (emails, attachments, and so on) are in your inbox.

The reality is that if you leave the organization, voluntarily or otherwise, the solution will most likely become useless to others. And if you stay and get promoted, you'll be stuck updating the solution that is bound to your email account.

If you intend to use the solution for a longer period, or it serves other users, it may be best to try to figure out how to extract the data from your inbox first and build the solution against that source. For email attachments, that is fairly easy: Just save them to a folder. For the email itself, it may not be practical, and maybe Power Query *is* the method to use to extract the emails and archive them in another format. Regardless, you should definitely give some thought to a succession plan for your solution once it starts to get reused.

Performance

The other major consideration you should take into account is performance, including speed.

Let's face it: Most of us don't keep extremely organized email inboxes. Instead, they are huge buckets of email spanning back sometimes months but more often years. As a result, retrieving data from Exchange can be very slow.

The solution to this is to use rules to reroute key emails into subfolders. When the subfolders contain only relevant data, retrieving, transforming, and loading the finished product will happen much more quickly.

Chapter 14 Grouping and Summarizing

In many ways, grouping and summarizing sums up the life of an Excel pro. You've got all kinds of tools for the purpose, including Excel's ability to subtotal, aggregate, and perform various other operations using PivotTables. Sometimes, however, when working with large data sets you need to group the records at the source before analysis.

Power Query adds another set of tools that you can use to quickly group and summarize data. Interestingly, it even gives you the ability to quickly remove extra columns, thereby thinning the data set to a truly manageable level.

Applying Grouping

To demonstrate how grouping works in Power Query, consider the case of a T-shirt manufacturer that has provided this table of data:

	A	B	C	D	E
1	Date	ProductID	ProductName	ChannelName	Amount
2	3/6/2015	1001	Cap Sleeve	Reseller	164.7
3	3/6/2015	1002	Long Sleeve	Online	180.43
4	3/10/2015	1003	Short Sleeve	Online	229.92
5	3/10/2015	1004	Sleeveless	Online	118.4
6	3/11/2015	1005	3/4 Sleeve	Store	184.02
7	3/12/2015	1003	Short Sleeve	Online	230.67
8	3/13/2015	1003	Short Sleeve	Online	133.98

Figure 167 A list of sales transactions.

Your goal is to take this list and figure out two things:

- Total sales for each day by channel
- The largest product's proportion as a percentage of daily sales

Connecting to the Data

Start by loading your data in Power Query:

- Open Ch14 Examples\Grouping.xlsx
- Select a cell in the table on the Sales worksheet → new query → From Table
- Right-click the Date column → Change Type → Date

You now have your table in a nice state, ready to group and summarize the data:

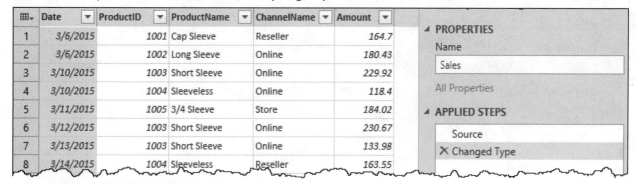

Figure 168 The table is ready to summarize.

Grouping the Data

To group the data by date and by channel.

- Select the Date column

- Go to Transform → Group By

In this interface, you have the ability to define the items you want to group by, as well as how you'd like them grouped. Power Query starts with only the Date column in the Group By section. If you left that setting as is, you wouldn't have the data broken down by Date and ChannelName, so you need to change that:

- Click the + beside the Group By header

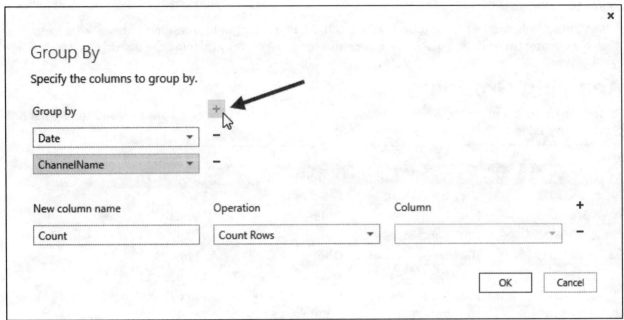

Figure 169 Adding grouping levels

Next, you need to determine how you want the data grouped. Because you are looking for a total of all channels, as well as a total of the products by channel, you need to take the following steps:

- Change the new column name from Count to Products Sold
- Click the + next to Column on the right side to add a new calculation
- Give the new column a name of Sales $ and set it to Sum the Amount column

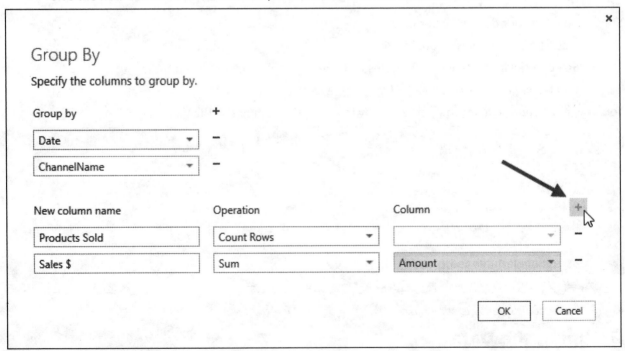

Figure 170 The grouping level is configured correctly.

- Click OK

The data is grouped for you, as shown below:

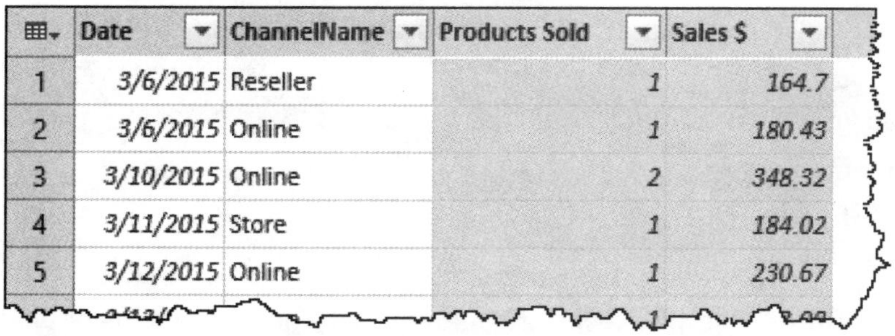

#	Date	ChannelName	Products Sold	Sales $
1	3/6/2015	Reseller	1	164.7
2	3/6/2015	Online	1	180.43
3	3/10/2015	Online	2	348.32
4	3/11/2015	Store	1	184.02
5	3/12/2015	Online	1	230.67

Figure 171 The data is nicely grouped by Date and ChannelName.

Notice that the grouping feature works quite nicely to get your data grouped, and you can have multiple levels stacked very easily for both grouping levels and calculations. You can aggregate the data in different ways here as well, including counting rows, counting distinct rows, or performing Sum, Average, Median, Min, or Max operations.

As an added bonus, the Group By feature removes all columns that were not specified in the original Group By section at the top of the dialog. This saves you the step of removing the unneeded columns before or after the operation is complete.

Now you can load this data to a table:

- Change the query name to Grouped
- Go to Home → Close & Load

Creating Summary Statistics

You've managed to accomplish the first of your goals in grouping the data by Date and by ChannelName. Now you need to work out the top-selling product in each segment and what it represented as a percentage of total sales for that group.

Duplicating Queries

In order to accomplish your goal, you actually need to modify and add some steps to the original query. Rather than potentially break it, it's not a bad idea to create a copy to work from. That gives you a fallback plan if things don't work out the way you wanted:

- Display the Workbook Queries pane
- Right-click the Grouped query → Duplicate
- Change the query name to Performance

You now have an exact copy of the previous query that we can load to the workbook:

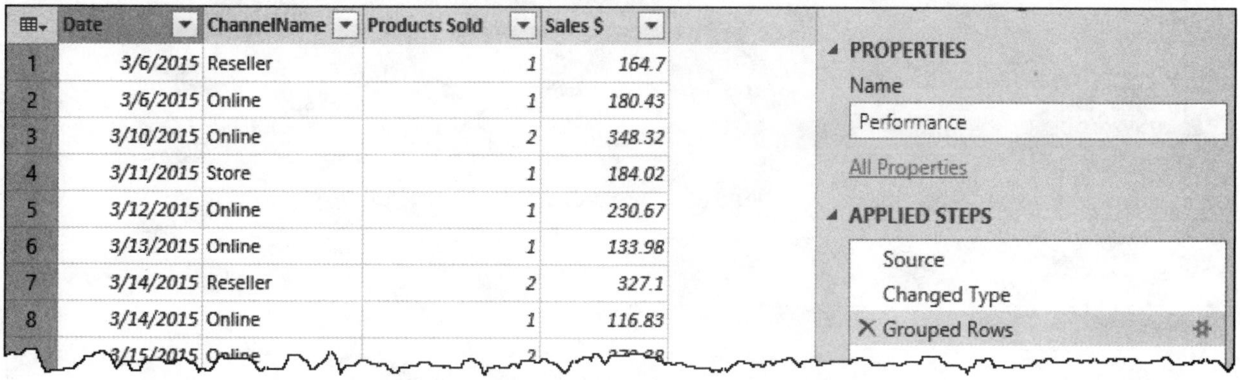

#	Date	ChannelName	Products Sold	Sales $		PROPERTIES
1	3/6/2015	Reseller	1	164.7		Name
2	3/6/2015	Online	1	180.43		Performance
3	3/10/2015	Online	2	348.32		
4	3/11/2015	Store	1	184.02		All Properties
5	3/12/2015	Online	1	230.67		
6	3/13/2015	Online	1	133.98		APPLIED STEPS
7	3/14/2015	Reseller	2	327.1		Source
8	3/14/2015	Online	1	116.83		Changed Type
	3/15/2015	Online	2	232.28		✕ Grouped Rows

Figure 172 An exact copy of the Grouped query.

Determining the Top Seller

Now you can set about determining the top-selling product. To do this, you are going to modify the Grouped Rows step and add another step:

- Click the gear beside the Grouped Rows step
- Add a new column at the bottom of the query
- Set the column name to Details and set the Operation to All Rows
- Click OK

This adds a column of tables to your query. These tables, however, are quite special. They contain the details of which rows from the previous step were summarized in order to come up with each row's totals!

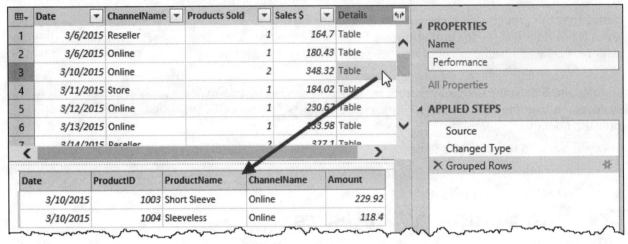

Figure 173 A peek at which rows were used to generate the grouped values.

The question is, how can you use these tables?

Your goal here is to work out the top-selling sales item for each day. You can identify that by looking at the highest value in the Amount column shown in the preview for each table. But how do you extract it? The answer is to reach to a custom column and use a formula. To do so, follow these steps:

- Go to Add Column → Add Custom Column
- Call the column MaxRecord and use the following formula

      =Table.Max([Details],"Amount")

- Click OK

You now have a column of records listed:

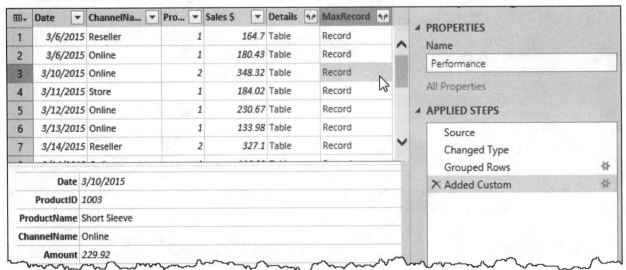

Figure 174 A column of . . . records?

Let's circle back for a moment and look at what happened first and then look at what you got from it.

The formula you used examines a table and extracts the max value from the given column. For the parameters, you provide the [Details] column of the query, as that holds the tables to be examined. The column within that table, Amount, was then provided, wrapped in quotes as the function requires.

Unlike previous formulas you've seen, however, this function doesn't return just the value. It returns a record. This is fantastic because the record doesn't just hold the maximum value. It holds *all* of the details that go with that data point.

You'll learn more about records in Chapter 19.

In addition, you can expand the MaxRecord column by using the double-headed arrows on the top right to get the individual components into columns:

- Click the Expand arrow on the MaxRecord column
- Expand the ProductName and Amount columns and uncheck the Prefix option at the bottom → OK
- Right-click the Details column → Remove
- Right-click the ProductName column → Rename → TopSeller
- Right-click the Amount column → Rename → TopSeller $

The result is that you now have a table that summarizes sales by Date and Channel and clearly shows the top-selling item, as well as its contribution:

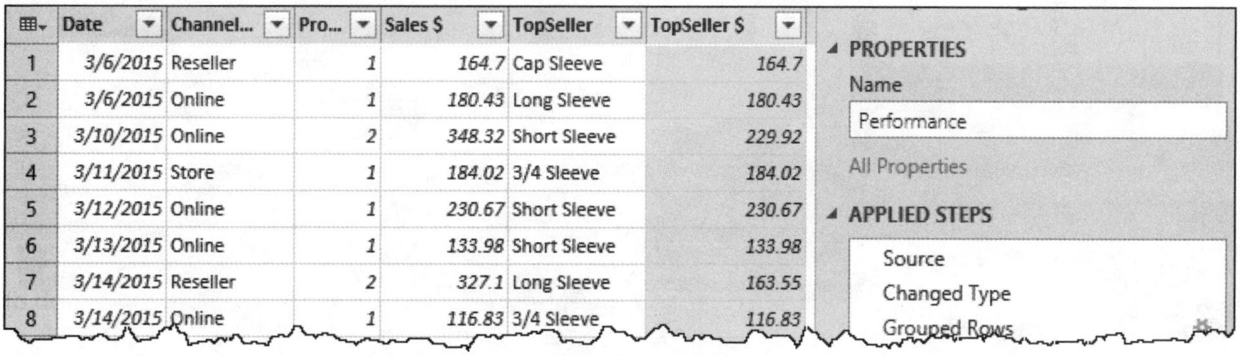

#	Date	Channel...	Pro...	Sales $	TopSeller	TopSeller $
1	3/6/2015	Reseller	1	164.7	Cap Sleeve	164.7
2	3/6/2015	Online	1	180.43	Long Sleeve	180.43
3	3/10/2015	Online	2	348.32	Short Sleeve	229.92
4	3/11/2015	Store	1	184.02	3/4 Sleeve	184.02
5	3/12/2015	Online	1	230.67	Short Sleeve	230.67
6	3/13/2015	Online	1	133.98	Short Sleeve	133.98
7	3/14/2015	Reseller	2	327.1	Long Sleeve	163.55
8	3/14/2015	Online	1	116.83	3/4 Sleeve	116.83

PROPERTIES
Name
Performance
All Properties

APPLIED STEPS
Source
Changed Type
Grouped Rows

Figure 175 The data grouped by Date and Channel with TopSeller details.

There is only one thing left to do: work out the percentage that the top seller represents of the total daily sales. That is easily accomplished with a simple calculation:

- Go to Add Column → Add Custom Column
- Set the column name to TS % of Sales and enter the following formula:

```
[#"TopSeller $"]/[#"Sales $"]
```

Don't let the hash marks and quotes mess you up here. The easiest way to build the formula is by clicking the field names on the right, and Power Query will put them in for you. You'll learn more about why they show up when you read Chapter 21.

The result is a little ugly, with some numbers showing no decimals, some showing one, and others showing a ton. You can round them off quite easily:

- Select the TS % of Sales column → Transform → Rounding → Round... → 2

Make sure you return to the Transform tab to perform this operation. If you don't, Power Query will create a new column for you, and you'll have to remove the previous column manually.

The results are nicely rounded for you, but they do show as decimal values like 1, 0.66, and so on. They certainly don't show as nice percentages, but that's okay. You can load the query to an Excel table and apply a percentage style to the column there. As you can see, this gets you to your original goal:

	A	B	C	D	E	F	G
1	Date	ChannelName	Products Sold	Sales $	TopSeller	TopSeller $	TS % of Sales
2	3/6/2015	Reseller	1	164.7	Cap Sleeve	164.7	100%
3	3/6/2015	Online	1	180.43	Long Sleeve	180.43	100%
4	3/10/2015	Online	2	348.32	Short Sleeve	229.92	66%
5	3/11/2015	Store	1	184.02	3/4 Sleeve	184.02	100%
6	3/12/2015	Online	1	230.67	Short Sleeve	230.67	100%
7	3/13/2015	Online	1	133.98	Short Sleeve	133.98	100%
8	3/14/2015	Reseller	2	327.1	Long Sleeve	163.55	50%
9	3/14/2015	Online	1	116.83	3/4 Sleeve	116.83	100%

Figure 176 The completed analysis.

Number styles applied to a table column stay in place after a Power Query query is updated.

Chapter 15 Transposing and Unpivoting Complex Data

When working with real-world data, Excel pros often encounter data that needs to be treated in a variety of ways. While unpivoting is extremely common, on occasion you may need to reverse this process and pivot data before making more complex transformations. Another technique that can be extremely useful is transposing data—for example, flipping data that's laid out in a vertical manner and so that it's displayed horizontally (or vice versa). Both of these functions are, fortunately, built in to the Power Query user interface and can aid in transforming data into useful tables.

Unpivoting Subcategorized Tables

The first complex issue we will deal with in this chapter is unpivoting a subcategorized table. While we looked at unpivoting in Chapter 6, this scenario, based on the figure below, adds an additional dimension to the issue.

	April				Account	Month	Measure	Value
	Actual	Budget	Variance		Alcohol	April	Actual	15,747.28
Alcohol	15,747.28	25,012.00	(9,264.72)		Food	April	Actual	34,523.71
Food	34,523.71	44,740.00	(10,216.29)		Other	April	Actual	237.79
Other	237.79	3,867.00	(3,629.21)		Alcohol	April	Budget	25,012.00
	50,508.78	73,619.00	(23,110.22)		Food	April	Budget	44,740.00
					Other	April	Budget	3,867.00

Figure 177 A challenging unpivot scenario

What makes this problem any more challenging than a standard unpivot? It's the additional level of having the month with the measure type.

When you unpivot, the data is de-aggregated, using the column names as data points. But what should the column names be here? If you promote the second row to headers, you will lose some key information about the month. It's just not going to work.

But there is most certainly a way to unpivot this data; you'll just need to use a bit of imagination and some more advanced tricks.

Loading the Data

For this example, you will unpivot the financial statement found in Ch15 Examples\UnPivot Sub Categories.xlsx:

⏷	A	B	C	D	E	F	G	H
8				April			May	
9			Actual	Budget	Variance ($)	Actual	Budget	Variance ($)
10	Revenues							
11		Alcoholic Beverages	15,747.28	25,012.00	(9,264.72)	22,133.53	41,881.00	(19,747.47)
12		Food & Non-Alc Beverages	34,523.71	44,740.00	(10,216.29)	51,007.02	71,125.00	(20,117.98)
13		Incidental Revenue	237.79	3,867.00	(3,629.21)	186.59	4,334.00	(4,147.41)
14	Total Revenues		50,508.78	73,619.00	(23,110.22)	73,327.14	117,340.00	(44,012.86)
15								
16	Expenses							
17		Cost of Sales	21,977.81	24,296.00	2,318.19	23,442.63	40,284.00	16,841.37
18		Labour & Benefits	35,166.60	45,327.25	10,160.65	34,266.40	52,415.50	18,149.10
19		Other Operational	10,830.99	13,210.00	2,379.01	9,078.01	14,447.00	5,368.99
20	Total Expenses		67,975.40	82,833.25	14,857.85	66,787.04	107,146.50	40,359.46
21	Net Income (Loss)		(17,466.62)	(9,214.25)	(8,252.37)	6,540.10	10,193.50	(3,653.40)

Figure 178 A challenging data set to unpivot.

You begin by loading the data into Power Query. You can do that by setting up a named range, as you don't really want to lock down the column headers with a table. Follow these steps:

- Select A8:H21 → Formulas → Defined Names → Define Name
- Enter Statement in the Name field → OK
- Create a new query → From Table

Power Query opens, showing you a somewhat ugly yet informative view of the data:

⊞▾	Column1 ▾	Column2 ▾	Column3 ▾	Column4 ▾	Column5
1	null	null	April	null	
2	null	null	Actual	Budget	Variance (S
3	Revenues	null	null	null	
4	null	Alcoholic Beverages	15747.28	25012	(
5	null	Food & Non-Alc Beverages	34523.71	44740	(1
6	null	Incidental Revenue	237.79	3867	(
7	Total Revenues	null	50508.78	73619	(2
8	null	null	null	null	
9	Expenses	null	null	null	

PROPERTIES
Name
Statement
All Properties

▲ APPLIED STEPS
Source
✕ Changed Type

Figure 179 The data set is rife with null values.

There are some key points to notice in this data set:

- Every blank cell in the original data table has come in as a *null*
- Column4's row 1 value is also *null*

Now you have to figure out what you are going to do with this. You can start by looking at Column1.

Filling Vertically

You can't get rid of Column1 because it contains information that tells if the account is a revenue classification or an expense classification. The problem is that the account classification doesn't exist in the same row as the account description and values. This means you need to find a way to get the classification to fill down into the *null* areas.

As it happens, this is exactly how Power Query's Fill Down command works:

- Select Column1 → Transform → Fill → Down

Now you've got your classifications on each row where required:

⊞▾	Column1 ▾	Column2 ▾	Column3 ▾	Column4 ▾	Colum
1	null	null	April	null	
2	null	null	Actual	Budget	Variance
3	Revenues	null	null	null	
4	Revenues	Alcoholic Beverages	15747.28	25012	
5	Revenues	Food & Non-Alc Beverages	34523.71	44740	
6	Revenues	Incidental Revenue	237.79	3867	
7	Total Revenues	null	50508.78	73619	
8	Total Revenues	null	null	null	
9	Expenses	null	null	null	
10	Expenses	Cost of Sales	21977.81	24296	

Figure 180 The account classification has been filled down.

Power Query's Fill Down command fills the value above into any cell that is *null,* but it does not overwrite any other data. The Fill Up command works the same way but fills up instead of down.

> A blank cell is not the same as a *null*. If you need to fill into blank areas, you must replace the data on the column, asking to replace an empty value (leave the field blank) with null. Power Query will convert the text-based null to *null*.

You now need a strategy to deal with the column headers. They seem to have the same issue, with April being in Column3 and missing from Column4 and Column5. Unfortunately, there is no Fill Right command in Power Query. So how do you deal with this?

Transposing Data

In order to fill data to the right in Power Query, you must transpose the table, flipping it on its ear:

- Go to Transform → Transpose

The view changes drastically, with the former column headers now becoming rows and vice versa:

▦▾	Column1 ▾	Column2 ▾	Column3 ▾	Column4 ▾	Column5
1	null	null	Revenues	Revenues	Revenues
2	null	null	null	Alcoholic Bevera	Food & No
3	April	Actual	null	15747.28	3
4	null	Budget	null	25012	
5	null	Variance ($)	null	(9264.72)	(1
6	May	Actual	null	22133.53	5
7	null	Budget	null	41881	
8	null	Variance ($)	null	(19747.47)	(2

PROPERTIES
Name
Statement
All Properties

APPLIED STEPS
Source
Changed Type
Filled Down
✕ Transposed Table

Figure 181 The result of transposing the table.

This opens up a couple of useful features. One of the issues you had earlier is that you couldn't fill right, but now you can fill down on Column1. In addition, the main challenge with unpivoting subcategorized data is that you have to unpivot based on the column names, which means you can't use two rows of column names to perform the task. But what if you were to temporarily merge Column1 and Column2, resulting in a single header? Try it to see what happens:

- Select Column1 → Transform → Fill → Down
- Select Column1 → hold down Ctrl → select Column2 → Transform → Merge Columns
- Set a Custom delimiter of a | (pipe) character → OK

 The reason you use a | character is that this character is seldom found in the average data set. This means you can use this character later, confident that you're not going to accidentally pick up a character that already existed in the data.

You now have a single column of labels that you can use for headers:

▦▾	Merged ▾	Column3 ▾	Column4 ▾	Column5 ▾	Column6 ▾	Colun
1	|	Revenues	Revenues	Revenues	Revenues	Total
2	|	null	Alcoholic Bevera	Food & Non-Alc Bev	Incidental Reve	
3	April|Actual	null	15747.28	34523.71	237.79	
4	April|Budget	null	25012	44740	3867	
5	April|Variance ($)	null	(9264.72)	(10216.29)	(3629.21)	(;
6	May|Actual	null	22133.53	51007.02	186.59	
7	May|Budget	null	41881	71125	4334	
8	May|Variance ($)	null	(19747.47)	(20117.98)	(4147.41)	(;

PROPERTIES
Name
Statement
All Properties

APPLIED STEPS
Source
Changed Type
Filled Down

Figure 182 Merging the categories and subcategories into a single column.

Now you can flip the data back and promote the new headers:

- Go to Transform → Transpose
- Go to Transform → Use First Row as Headers
- Right-click the | column → Rename → Class
- Right-click the |_1 column → Rename → Account

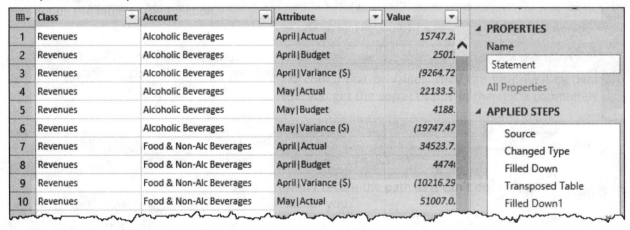

⊞▾	Class	▾	Account	▾	April|Actual	▾	April|Budget	▾	April|
1	Revenues			null		null		null	
2	Revenues		Alcoholic Beverages		15747.28		25012		
3	Revenues		Food & Non-Alc Beverages		34523.71		44740		
4	Revenues		Incidental Revenue		237.79		3867		
5	Total Revenues			null	50508.78		73619		
6	Total Revenues			null	null		null		
7	Expenses			null	null		null		
8	Expenses		Cost of Sales		21977.81		24296		
9	Expenses		Labour & Benefits		35166.6		45327.25		
10	Expenses		Other Operational		10830.99		13210		

PROPERTIES
Name
Statement
All Properties

APPLIED STEPS
Source
Changed Type
Filled Down
Transposed Table
Filled Down1

Figure 183 You're getting closer!

Unpivoting the Data

The rest of the process is fairly straightforward and standard for an unpivot scenario:

- Filter the Account column to remove *null* values
- Select the Class and Account columns
- Right-click the selected headers → Unpivot Other Columns

Now you have an unpivoted list:

⊞▾	Class	▾	Account	▾	Attribute	▾	Value	▾
1	Revenues		Alcoholic Beverages		April|Actual		15747.2?	
2	Revenues		Alcoholic Beverages		April|Budget		2501.	
3	Revenues		Alcoholic Beverages		April|Variance ($)		(9264.72	
4	Revenues		Alcoholic Beverages		May|Actual		22133.5	
5	Revenues		Alcoholic Beverages		May|Budget		4188.	
6	Revenues		Alcoholic Beverages		May|Variance ($)		(19747.47	
7	Revenues		Food & Non-Alc Beverages		April|Actual		34523.7.	
8	Revenues		Food & Non-Alc Beverages		April|Budget		4474(	
9	Revenues		Food & Non-Alc Beverages		April|Variance ($)		(10216.29	
10	Revenues		Food & Non-Alc Beverages		May|Actual		51007.0.	

PROPERTIES
Name
Statement
All Properties

APPLIED STEPS
Source
Changed Type
Filled Down
Transposed Table
Filled Down1

Figure 184 The list is finally unpivoted.

Finally, you need to split the Attribute column back into its respective pieces and clean up the column headers:

- Right-click the Attribute column → Split Column → By Delimiter → Custom → | → OK
- Right-click the Attribute.1 column → Rename → Month
- Right-click the Attribute.2 column → Rename → Measure
- Select the Class, Account, Month and Measure columns → right-click → Change Type → Text
- Right-click the Value column → Change Type → Decimal Number
- Right-click the Value column → Rename → Amount

The query is now finished, unpivoted, and ready to load:

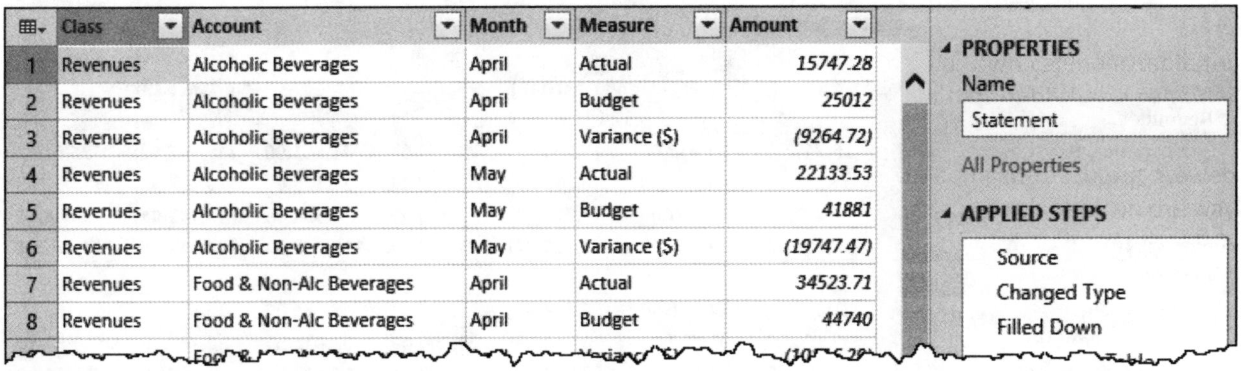

	Class	Account	Month	Measure	Amount
1	Revenues	Alcoholic Beverages	April	Actual	15747.28
2	Revenues	Alcoholic Beverages	April	Budget	25012
3	Revenues	Alcoholic Beverages	April	Variance ($)	(9264.72)
4	Revenues	Alcoholic Beverages	May	Actual	22133.53
5	Revenues	Alcoholic Beverages	May	Budget	41881
6	Revenues	Alcoholic Beverages	May	Variance ($)	(19747.47)
7	Revenues	Food & Non-Alc Beverages	April	Actual	34523.71
8	Revenues	Food & Non-Alc Beverages	April	Budget	44740

PROPERTIES

Name

Statement

All Properties

APPLIED STEPS

Source

Changed Type

Filled Down

Figure 185 The subcategorized list, fully unpivoted.

Method Recap

As you've seen in this chapter, the process for unpivoting subcategories involves the following eight-step process:

1. Load the data.
2. Transpose the data.
3. Fill the major heading into null areas.
4. Merge the major headings and subheadings into a single column.
5. Transpose the data back.
6. Promote the consolidated headings into header rows.
7. Unpivot the data.
8. Split the consolidated headings back into their individual components.

This technique is not limited to only two levels of headings. The secret is to combine all the headings and subheadings into one text string that can be promoted to headers. As long as you've done that, you can unpivot a dozen levels of subheadings if needed.

Replicating the Original Data

With the data completely unpivoted, the original data table can quickly be rebuilt using a PivotTable with the following configuration:

- Class and Account on Rows
- Month and Measure on Columns
- Amount on Values

However, in order to rebuild the PivotTable so it's laid out consistently with the original data, you also need to make the following modifications:

- Go to PivotTable Tools → Design → Subtotals → Show all Subtotals at Bottom of Group
- Select the Revenues cell in the first column and drag it above the Expenses row
- Right-click the April column header → uncheck Subtotal Month
- Right-click any value cell → Value Field Settings → Number Format
- Choose Accounting → 2 decimals → No Symbol
- Click OK (twice) to return to the worksheet

At this point, you should have replicated the original report so that it looks as shown below:

Sum of Amount	Column Labels						Grand Total
	April			May			
Row Labels	Actual	Budget	Variance ($)	Actual	Budget	Variance ($)	
Revenues							
Alcoholic Beverages	15,747.28	25,012.00	(9,264.72)	22,133.53	41,881.00	(19,747.47)	75,761.62
Food & Non-Alc Beverages	34,523.71	44,740.00	(10,216.29)	51,007.02	71,125.00	(20,117.98)	171,061.46
Incidental Revenue	237.79	3,867.00	(3,629.21)	186.59	4,334.00	(4,147.41)	848.76
Revenues Total	50,508.78	73,619.00	(23,110.22)	73,327.14	117,340.00	(44,012.86)	247,671.84
Expenses							
Cost of Sales	21,977.81	24,296.00	2,318.19	23,442.63	40,284.00	16,841.37	129,160.00
Labour & Benefits	35,166.60	45,327.25	10,160.65	34,266.40	52,415.50	18,149.10	195,485.50
Other Operational	10,830.99	13,210.00	2,379.01	9,078.01	14,447.00	5,368.99	55,314.00
Expenses Total	67,975.40	82,833.25	14,857.85	66,787.04	107,146.50	40,359.46	379,959.50
Grand Total	118,484.18	156,452.25	(8,252.37)	140,114.18	224,486.50	(3,653.40)	627,631.34

Figure 186 The original data, reconstructed via a PivotTable.

Transposing Stacked Tables

Another complicated transformation scenario is one where the details for a transaction are stacked vertically on top of each other, with blank rows separating the transactions:

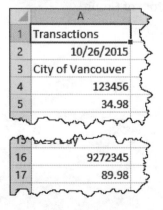

Figure 187 Data where repeating the transpose operation is necessary.

In this scenario, you essentially need to transpose each block of data, then stack the blocks into one tall table. The issue, however, is that Power Query doesn't really have an out-of-the-box command to do this. If you transpose the table, you'll get one row of data and a large number of columns rather than getting each record transposed individually the way you need.

Again, getting the outcome you want is entirely possible, but it requires a little creative thinking and some tricks.

Loading the Data

In this example, you will transpose the list of credit card transactions found in Ch15 Examples\Transpose Stacked Tables.xlsx:

Figure 188 A stacked list of transactions in a single column.

Before you can do anything else, you need to get the data into Power Query:

- Select A1 → create a new query → From table
- Extend the table boundaries to cover A1:A17

The data is now ready for you, and it's time to figure out how to approach it.

Creating a Modulo Column

Rather than try to transpose the records at this point, you're going to take a different approach. You're going to number the records, and you're going to do it twice. To make this happen:

- Go to Add Column → Add Index Column → From 0

At this point, you have a numeric list of the transactions, starting from 0:

	Transactions	Index
1	10/26/2015 12:00:00 AM	0
2	City of Vancouver	1
3	123456	2
4	34.98	3
5	null	4
6	null	5
7	10/27/2015 12:00:00 AM	6
8	Earl's Restauarant	7
9	323511	8

Figure 189 Each line of the file now has an index number.

You currently have a number indicating the numeric data line in the file. What we actually want is a number as it corresponds to each line of the transaction. In other words, the transaction date should always be 0, the vendor 1, and so on. To get that, you need to add a modulo column.

Before you do this, you need a key piece of information from the table: You need to know the value in the first row of the second record. In this case, the value you are looking for is 6, as shown in the Index column. (Power Query starts counting from 0, not 1.) That number is going to be the factor for the modulo calculation.

The modulo essentially takes a value, subtracts the closest multiple of the factor from the value provided, and returns the remainder. So if the value is 8, the modulo subtracts 6 and returns the remainder, which is 2. Try it out:

- Select the Index column
- Go to Add Column → From Number → Standard → Modulo → 6

You now have a list of the transaction line numbers!

	Transactions	Index	Inserted Modulo
1	10/26/2015 12:00:00 AM	0	0
2	City of Vancouver	1	1
3	123456	2	2
4	34.98	3	3
5	null	4	4
6	null	5	5
7	10/27/2015 12:00:00 AM	6	0
8	Earl's Restauarant	7	1
9	323511	8	2

Figure 190 You now have a transaction line number for each item.

This looks interesting, but why set this up in the first place? The answer lies in the solution to this data set.

Pivoting the Data

When you have a list of repeating transaction numbers as you do in this example, you can pivot them. It will look a little ugly at first, but you'll see how incredible this truly is.

- Select the Inserted Modulo column → Transform → Pivot Column

Now comes the tricky part: The pivot needs to be set up correctly.

By default, when you ask to pivot a column, the values in that column will be used as the column headers. Power Query then asks which values you want in the values (or body) area of the pivoted data set. The trick here is that pivoting data is usually done to summarize the values, and you aren't interested in doing that. You want the original values, so follow these steps:

- Set the Values column to Transactions
- Expand the Advanced Options
- Set the Aggregate Value Function to Don't Aggregate
- Click OK

The table changes shape and fills with null values everywhere:

Index	0	1	2	3	4	5
1	0	10/26/2015 12:00:00 AM	null	null	null	null	null
2	1	null	City of Vancouver	null	null	null	null
3	2	null	null	123456	null	null	null
4	3	null	null	null	34.98	null	null
5	4	null	null	null	null	null	null
6	5	null	null	null	null	null	null
7	6	10/27/2015 12:00:00 AM	null	null	null	null	null
8	7	null	Earl's Restauarant	null	null	null	null
9	8	null	null	323511	null	null	null
			null	null	89.98		

Figure 191 The pivoted table, full of null values.

This is actually amazing.

Filling in the Blanks

The next step is to fill in the holes in the pivoted data set:

- Select column 1 → hold down Shift → select column 5
- Go to Transform → Fill → Up

The transactions now cascade up to fill in the blanks:

Index	0	1	2	3	4	5
1	0	10/26/2015 12:00:00 AM	City of Vancouver	123456	34.98	null	null
2	1	null	City of Vancouver	123456	34.98	null	null
3	2	null	Earl's Restauarant	123456	34.98	null	null
4	3	null	Earl's Restauarant	323511	34.98	null	null
5	4	null	Earl's Restauarant	323511	89.98	null	null
6	5	null	Earl's Restauarant	323511	89.98	null	null
7	6	10/27/2015 12:00:00 AM	Earl's Restauarant	323511	89.98	null	null
8	7	null	Earl's Restauarant	323511	89.98	null	null

Figure 192 The data, filled up.

Believe it or not, you're very close to finished here:

- Filter column 0 → uncheck (null)
- Select columns 0 through 3 → right-click → Remove Other Columns

You now have a data set that has been fully transposed from a single column of stacked records:

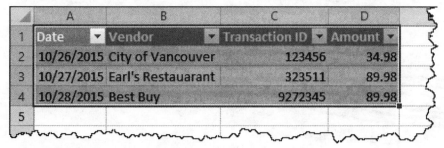

	0	1	2	3
1	10/26/2015 12:00:00 AM	City of Vancouver	123456	34.98
2	10/27/2015 12:00:00 AM	Earl's Restauarant	323511	89.98
3	10/28/2015 12:00:00 AM	Best Buy	9272345	89.98

Figure 193 The transformation from stacked tables to useful data is almost complete.

The final thing to do to this query is to provide better column names and set the data types. As soon as that's done, you're finished!

- Rename column 0 Dates and format it as Date
- Rename column 1 Vendor and format it as Text
- Rename column 2 TransactionID and format it as Whole Number
- Rename column 3 Amount and format it as Decimal Number
- Rename the query Transactions
- Go to Home → Close & Load

The data is finally transformed:

	A	B	C	D
1	Date	Vendor	Transaction ID	Amount
2	10/26/2015	City of Vancouver	123456	34.98
3	10/27/2015	Earl's Restauarant	323511	89.98
4	10/28/2015	Best Buy	9272345	89.98
5				

Figure 194 The transformed data set.

Method Recap

This is the process for transposing and pivoting a single column of data:

1. Load the data.
2. Add an Index column from 0.
3. Add a modulo column, using the value that indicates the first value in the second data set.
4. Pivot the modulo column using the text as values with aggregation.
5. Fill the data up for every column after the initial one.
6. Filter out null rows in the first data column.
7. Do the final cleanup.

With practice, this process actually becomes quite quick, which is a good thing. You'll be amazed how many times you need to do this in the real world.

Chapter 16 Automating Refreshing

As you build more and more solutions that leverage Power Query, and as you realize how much time it saves you, you're bound to become hungry for more automation in your life. Yes, you can simply right-click a table that comes from Power Query, but even that will begin to feel so . . . manual. Wouldn't it be better if you could just schedule an update, or maybe control the order in which things update?

Options for Automating Refreshing

You can actually use a few different methods of automating the refreshing of Power Query solutions:

- Refresh when the workbook is opened
- Refresh every *x* minutes
- Refresh a connection on demand via VBA
- Refresh all connections on demand via VBA
- Schedule refreshes via a third-party add-in

Each works differently and has its own benefits and drawbacks, as you'll see in this chapter.

Scheduling Refreshes Without Code

The first two methods for automating refreshing that we'll explore are both set through the user interface and don't require any VBA code whatsoever. They can be configured on a connection-by-connection basis, and you can even automate the refresh to Power Pivot if desired. Each of these connections is controlled by navigating to the Workbook Connections dialog in Excel (not Power Query):

- Go to Data → Connections → select your query → Properties

This launches the following dialog, where you can check the box to update the query when the file is opened:

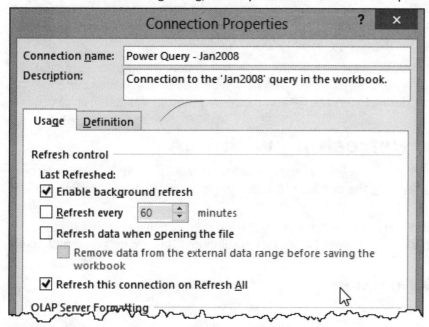

Figure 195 Setting connection options.

Background Refreshing

In the Connection Properties dialog, notice that the Enable Background Refresh checkbox is selected by default. This setting allows you to specify whether you'd like to keep working in Excel while the data refreshes. If you uncheck this box, you could potentially decrease the amount of time it takes to refresh your solution, but you'll also lock out the user interface, which means you won't be able to do other things until it is complete.

If you want to prevent users from working with the data until it is fully refreshed, you want to disable this setting. If you need to do other things while you wait, however, this setting is best left alone.

Refreshing Every x Minutes

The next available setting in the Connection Properties dialog lets you tell Excel to refresh the Power Query query every *x* minutes. When you check the box, you can set how often you'd like the data to be refreshed. This setting is fantastic if you're pulling data from a web source that is constantly changing or if you are targeting a database that is being updated regularly, as it assures you that your data is always kept up-to-date while you're in the file.

Keep in mind that the workbook needs to be open in order for this refresh to occur. And if you're going to be scheduling frequent refreshes while you are actively working in the workbook, you'll want to make sure the Enable Background Refresh setting is checked.

> Valid values for this setting run from 1 to 32,767, which means you can refresh once every minute up to once every 22.75 days.

Refreshing When the Workbook is Opened

This selection in the Connection Properties dialog actually allows you to specify two components:

- Refreshing the data when opening the file
- Removing the data before saving

The first one is rather self-explanatory, and checking the box for this will change the behavior of the workbook to do exactly what it says: refresh the data each time you open the file. This helps ensure that your data is always up-to-date when you start working with the file.

If you have a significant number of data sources, or if the data takes a significant amount of time to refresh, then it may be a good idea to leave the Enable Background Refresh setting enabled so that you can use the workbook while the refresh is occurring.

The second choice in this section controls whether to save the data in the workbook or only the query definition. This setting is actually a security setting, as it ensures that your users have access to the data source when they open the workbook. If they don't, they'll be greeted by a blank table, as the connection cannot be refreshed. If they do have access, the query will run and bring in the data.

> There is currently a bug in all versions of Excel that affects the last option. If you open Excel and then open the workbook, the query will refresh, and the data will be loaded. If you then close the workbook and reopen it (without closing Excel), the data will not refresh automatically. Closing Excel fixes the problem.

Automating Query Refreshing with VBA

The options described so far in this chapter allow you to refresh Power Query queries with no macro security warnings at all. In addition, workbooks using the options described above are easier to port to Power BI, as they don't cause any blocking issues.

If you're working purely in a desktop Excel instance, however, there are times when you may want to give a user an easy-to-use and obvious way to update your Power Query solutions. This can be accomplished via recording VBA macros.

Refreshing a Single Connection

You can build a macro to refresh a single Power Query connection. To see how this works, open Ch16 Examples\Automating Refresh.xlsx and navigate to the Transactions worksheet.

On this worksheet you'll find a Transactions table, as well as a PivotTable. Say that you'd like to create a macro to update the Transactions table and then the PivotTable.

To do this, you can record a simple macro by using the following steps:

- Navigate to the Developer tab

> If you don't see the Developer tab, right-click any tab on the ribbon and choose Customize Ribbon. Check the box on the right-hand side, next to Developer, and then click OK.

- In the upper-left, click Record Macro

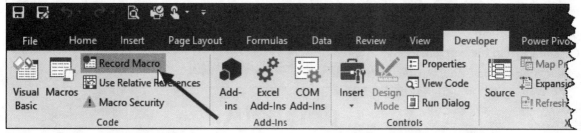

Figure 196 Start recording a macro.

Once you've clicked this button, Excel starts recording every worksheet click, every keystroke, and every mistake you make. Follow the steps below with precision to make sure you get a clean macro!

- Name the Macro Refresh and store it in This Workbook → OK
- Go to Data → Connections → Power Query – Transactions → Refresh
- Click Close
- Right-click the PivotTable → Refresh
- Go to Developer → Stop Recording

The macro is now recorded and ready to use. To test it:

- Go to Developer → Macros

You now see the Macro dialog, which allows you to see what macros are in your file and run any of them. Select the Refresh macro—it may be the only one you have—and click Run:

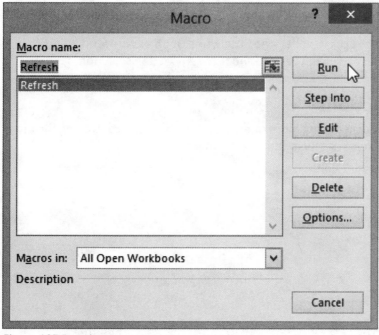

Figure 197 Running your macro.

When you run the macro, you can see that the Transactions table refreshes, followed by the PivotTable. (Of course, this would be more obvious if the data changed, but the data source is static.)

As great as this is, sending your users back to the Developer tab to run the macro on a regular basis is a little scary. Rather than do that, why not give them a button to refresh the macro? Follow these steps:

- Go to Developer → Insert → choose the top-left icon
- Find an empty space on the worksheet
- Hold down the left mouse button → drag down and right → let go of the mouse

The Assign Macro dialog pops up with your macro in it.

- Select the Refresh macro → OK

- Right-click the button → Edit Text
- Rename it Refresh
- Click any cell in the worksheet

You now have a nice, shiny, new button, all ready to use:

	A	B	C	D	E	F	G
1	Date ▼	Account ▼	Dept ▼	Amount ▼			
2	1/2/2008	61510	150	-26.03		Sum of Amount	Column Labels ▼
3	1/2/2008	61520	150	-55.07		Row Labels ▼	110
4	1/2/2008	61530	150	-10.6		⊟ 2008	
5	1/2/2008	61540	150	-0.29		Jan	(7,568.20)
6	1/2/2008	61550	150	-48.02		Feb	(32,777.28)
7	1/2/2008	61560	150	-1.35		Mar	(45,802.53)
8	1/2/2008	61570	150	-77.04		Grand Total	(86,148.01)
9	1/2/2008	62010	150	-305.95			
10	1/2/2008	62020	150	-95.15			
11	1/2/2008	62099	150	8.79		Refresh	
12	1/2/2008	62510	120	-56.74			
	1/2		120	-41			

Figure 198 Launch button, ready to activate!

Go ahead and click the Refresh button and revel in the fact that any user can now refresh your query.

> If you ever need to edit the button, right-click it. When the little white bubbles surround it, it is in Design mode and can be modified. Select a cell in the worksheet to remove the selection handles and put it back into Active mode.

Refreshing Multiple Connections

The next concern that you might want to tackle is adding more queries to the macro and controlling the order in which they refresh. You can easily do these things by modifying the macro.

- Go to Developer → Macros → Refresh → Edit.

At this point you see code like this:

```
Sub Refresh()
'
' Refresh Macro
'
'
    ActiveWorkbook.Connections("Power Query - Transactions").Refresh
    Range("G6").Select
    ActiveSheet.PivotTables("PivotTable1").PivotCache.Refresh
End Sub
```

Here's what this macro code does:

- The first four lines after the Sub Refresh() line are simply comments, so you really don't need to keep them.
- The line that starts with ActiveWorkbook refreshes the connection.
- The next line selects a range on the active worksheet.
- The final line refreshes the PivotTable on the active worksheet.

You can make some modifications to this macro to not only control the order in which all the connections refresh but also make the code a bit more bulletproof. (Right now it would fail if someone tried to run it from a different worksheet since it wouldn't have the PivotTable on it.) Here's what the code should look like after you revise it:

```
Sub Refresh()
    ActiveWorkbook.Connections("Power Query - Jan2008").Refresh
    ActiveWorkbook.Connections("Power Query - Feb2008").Refresh
    ActiveWorkbook.Connections("Power Query - Mar2008").Refresh
    ActiveWorkbook.Connections("Power Query - Transactions").Refresh
    Worksheets("Transactions").PivotTables("PivotTable1"). _
        PivotCache.Refresh
End Sub
```

 The space and underscore characters are the characters you use to indicate a line break in VBA code. The code will run equally well if the PivotCache.Refresh line remains on the same line as Worksheets("Transactions").PivotTables("PivotTable1"). Just make sure that there is no space between the period at the end of the first line and PivotCache.Refresh.

You can see that you need to remove the unneeded code comments first. After that you simply inject new lines in order to refresh the specific connections in the order in which you want them refreshed.

In addition, by specifying Worksheets("Transactions") in place of ActiveSheet, you eliminate the need to select the PivotTable, and you also ensure that you are always refreshing the PivotTable on the Transactions worksheet.

Be aware that connections may or may not include the name *Power Query*. These names must match the names that are shown in the Workbook Connections dialog, as shown below:

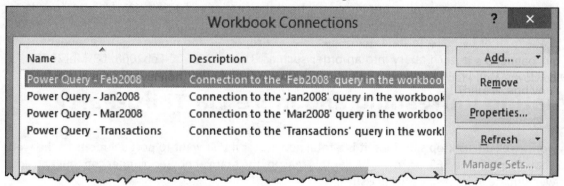

Figure 199 Determining the names of your query connections.

 In midsummer 2015 Microsoft decided to rebrand (or debrand) Power Query due to concern that the term *Power* scared users away from the feature set. To this end, queries that you create today are not prefixed with "Power Query –" as they are in the dialog above.

When you click the Refresh button now, each query refresh is kicked off in turn, and the PivotTable is refreshed.

 One thing to be aware of is that you *cannot* save your workbook in XLSX format once you have a macro inside it. Instead, you need to save the workbook in XLSM or XLSB format to preserve the macros. This way, users get a macro security warning message when they open the workbook before they can use your button to refresh the data.

Refreshing All Power Query Queries

In order to refresh all Power Query queries in a workbook, you need to use a slightly different block of code. The following macro will look through all connections in the workbook and identify whether they are created by Power Query (and it ignores all others):

```
Public Sub UpdatePowerQueriesOnly()
    Dim lTest As Long, cn As WorkbookConnection
    On Error Resume Next
    For Each cn In ThisWorkbook.Connections
        lTest = InStr(1, cn.OLEDBConnection.Connection, _
            "Provider=Microsoft.Mashup.OleDb.1")
        If Err.Number <> 0 Then
            Err.Clear
            Exit For
        End If
        If lTest > 0 Then cn.Refresh
    Next cn
End Sub
```

This macro can be stored in the same workbook as the one created in the previous section, or it can replace the previous code (although you'd need to relink your button to the new macro instead).

> Be aware that the code above will not necessarily refresh the queries in the order in which they need to be refreshed, as Excel refreshes queries in alphabetical order. Fortunately, you can change the name of the queries by going to Data → Connections → Properties and modifying the connection name. You can rename each query into an order such as 01-Jan2008, 02-Feb2008, 03-Mar2008, 99-Transactions. By doing this, you can ensure that a Power Query refresh runs in the correct order.

Automating Refreshing and more via Third-Party Add-ins

While VBA works well on desktop solutions, it is a total nonstarter if you want to port solutions to the web, whether to SharePoint, Office 365, or Power BI. For this reason, the team at power-planner.com built an add-in called Power Update to help solve these issues.

Here's how the company describes the product in its own words:

Power Update is a brand-new software utility designed from the ground-up as a "companion" to Power Pivot, Power Query, and the entire Power BI stack.

It allows you to schedule ANY Power Pivot / Power BI workbook for refresh, regardless of data sources used, and automatically deploys/publishes the resulting workbook to a destination of your choice: SharePoint (both on-premises and cloud), OneDrive, Power BI online, file folders and network shares, and even Tabular SSAS servers.

Even when paired with O365, Power BI, or other cloud server, Power Update does NOT require the configuration of gateways, VPN's, or firewall ports. Furthermore, Power Update supports auto-refresh of Power Query workbooks as well as loading Power Query and PowerPivot data into SQL Server, finally allowing the industry to utilize PQ in "on-premises" production environments.

Finally, Power Update is NOT restricted to "once a day" refresh, nor is it subject to "rowset throttling" by Power BI version 2's 10k rows/hr (free version) or 1MM rows/hr (Pro) limitations.

If this product sounds interesting to you, or if you'd like to read more about the features in Power Update, see the following blog posts by Rob Collie of PowerPivotPro.com:

http://mrx.cl/intropowerupdate, http://mrx.cl/freepowerupdate, http://mrx.cl/ssisalternative, http://mrx.cl/buildingdatazen

The free version of the Power Update tool can be downloaded directly from:

http://www.power-planner.com/Products/ProdID/10

Chapter 17 Power Query Formulas

Power Query's user interface is amazing, and many of the things you need to do are already built in. Having said that, there are sure to be times when you need to do things that aren't built in to the user interface. Even without easy-to-click buttons, there are ways to get such jobs done. You just have to reach in to Power Query's programming language: M.

Getting Started with M

While aspects of M can get quite technical, the easiest way to get some exposure to the language is to start with custom columns and add formulas to them.

Because Power Query was built for Excel pros, you might expect that its formula language would be just like Excel's—much like Power Pivot's DAX formulas are identical in name to those from Excel. Unfortunately, this is not the case, as you'll see, and you'll have to temper your initial instincts to use those formulas as you learn a new formula syntax.

Creating Custom Columns

It is relatively straightforward to create a custom column. While inside your query:

- Go to Add Column → Add Custom Column

You see this dialog, which allows you to create a new formula:

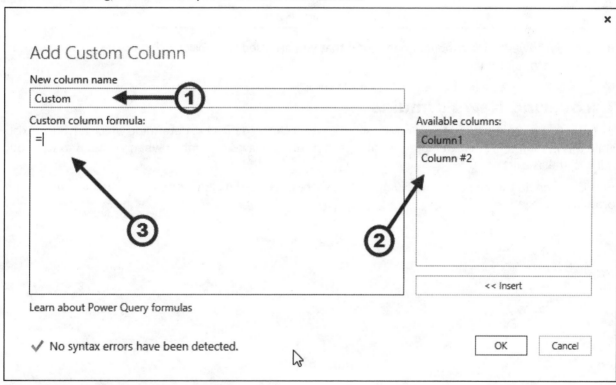

Figure 200 The Add Custom Column dialog.

Three portions to this dialog that are important:

- **New Column Name**—Whatever you type here will be used as the name of the column you are creating when you click OK.
- **Available Columns**—This box lists the names of all the columns in your query. Double-clicking any item in this box places it into the formula area with the correct syntax to refer to the field.
- **Custom Column Formula**—This is where you actually create the formula that will be used.

You can easily do simple aggregations in the formula area, using syntax that you're used to in Excel. For example, to join the two fields listed above as text, you would build a formula in the following manner:

- Double-click Column1 in the Available Columns list
- Type the & character
- Double-click Column #2 in the Available Columns list

From this, Power Query would build the following formula:

```
=[Column1]&[#"Column #2"]
```

The great thing about using the double-click interface is that, at this point, it doesn't matter to you that the syntax of Column1 and Column #2 must be handled differently. The interface will get it right, and you can get on with completing the job.

> This specific syntax is explained in Chapters 19 and 20.

As you might expect, you can perform regular mathematical equations as well, including the following:

Operation	Power Query Formula Equivalent
Addition	`=[Column1]+[#"Column #2"]`
Subtraction	`=[Column1]-[#"Column #2"]`
Multiplication	`=[Column1]*[#"Column #2"]`
Division	`=[Column1]/[#"Column #2"]`

Interestingly, however, the exponent operator ^ that you are used to in Excel will not work. Exponentiation requires a custom formula:

```
=Number.Power([Column1],[#"Column #2"])
```

Discovering New Formulas

Currently, Power Query doesn't have any IntelliSense, so it can be difficult to determine which formulas exist. While this is something that we hope will change in future, it leaves us hunting when we need to work out which formulas exist.

For this reason, in the Add Custom Column dialog, there is a hyperlink just underneath the Custom Column Formula box.

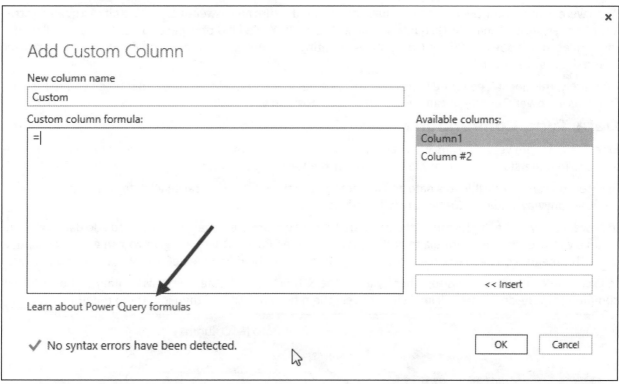

Figure 201 How to find more Power Query formulas.

Click this link to go to a web page that promises to help you learn about Power Query formulas. If you scroll down that page, you'll find a link to Power Query Formula Categories, which then links you through to the MSDN documentation site. This site lists all formula categories and allows you to browse and find the ones you need.

 We highly recommend bookmarking the landing page for the MSDN site. This will prevent you from having to open the Add Custom Column dialog in order to access this documentation.

Formula Gotchas

Power Query and Excel have some significant differences in terms of how they handle inputs. The following table summarizes some of the issues that will certainly frustrate you in the beginning:

Excel	Power Query
Formulas are *not* case sensitive	Formulas *are* case sensitive
Counts using base 1	Counts using base 0
Data type conversions are implicit	Observes strict data typing

Case Sensitivity

The case sensitivity aspect is a headache but something you get used to. The trick to remember here is that in 99% of cases, the first letter of each word in a Power Query formula is capitalized, and the rest are lower-case. Whereas Excel doesn't care which case you use and converts formulas to uppercase by default, Power Query just returns an error.

Base 0 versus Base 1

The difference between base 0 and base 1 is where the number line starts. Consider the following word: *Excel*. If you were to ask yourself the position of the x character, you'd probably say 2. Character E is 1, and x is 2. Does that sound correct?

Counting in this fashion follows a base 1 rule, where the first character has an index position of 1, the second character 2, and so on. It's the way you count, and it's the way Excel counts.

If you were to ask Power Query the same question, it would return an answer of 1. That's a bit of a head-scratcher at first, especially since Excel counts in a base 1 fashion. You'd kind of expect Power Query to follow the same rules, but it doesn't. Power Query starts counting at 0, not 1. So in the word *Excel*, the E is character 0, and the x is character 1.

Ultimately, this doesn't generate issues that can't be dealt with, but it does mean that when you're building formulas in Power Query, you can end up off by one position very easily.

Data Type Conversions

Excel formulas are very forgiving with data types, using implicit conversion, unlike Power Query explicit Conversion. To understand what that means, consider the following scenarios.

In Excel you can add a value to a date and increment it to the next day. Because all dates are really just serial numbers anyway, adding 1 to the date will work perfectly.

In Power Query, if the date is formatted as a date type, you must use a specific formula to add days to it. And if you try to use the same formula to add days to a number, Power Query will give you an error as it's not a date. This means you need to explicitly convert your fields to the data type before using them in formulas.

In Excel you can join two cells together by using the & function. Whether the cells contain text or values is completely irrelevant. Excel will implicitly convert them both to text and then join them together:

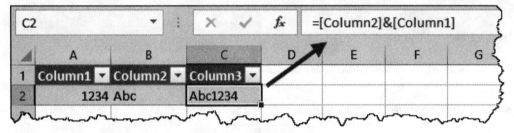

Figure 202 Implicit conversion in action: Number and text converted to text.

Observe what happens when you pull this data into Power Query and create a new column using the following formula:

```
=[Column1]&[Column2]
```

As you can see, you get a completely different result:

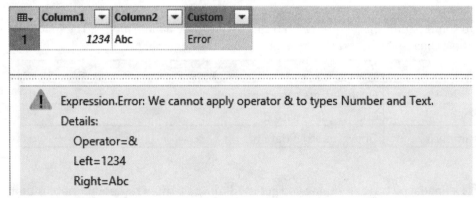

Figure 203 Power Query can't join numbers and text together.

In order to fix this issue, you have to tell Power Query explicitly to convert the number to text before it tries to join the two text strings together. You do that by wrapping Column1's input in a conversion function:

```
=Text.From([Column1])&[Column2]
```

When you explicitly convert the data in Column1 to a text value, the concatenation will work as you originally intended:

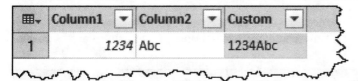

Figure 204 Explicit conversion of data types ensures that the formula works.

There are actually two ways to deal with data types in Power Query:

- Set the data type for the column you are referring to *before* using it in a custom function.
- Use a data type conversion function to force the input to convert to the required data type.

Useful Data Type Conversion Functions

There are several data type conversion functions in Power Query. Some of the most important of them are described in the following sections.

Converting to Text

For the most part, if you need to convert the values in a column to text, you just use the Text.From() function. There are also some additional functions, however, you can use to keep your data typing even more explicit. The following table shows how to convert different data types into a Text data type:

To Convert	Formula	Example
Anything	Text.From()	Text.From([Column1])
A date	Date.ToText()	Date.ToText([Column1])
A time	Time.ToText()	Time.ToText([Column1])
A number	Number.ToText()	Number.ToText([Column1])

Keep in mind that Text.From() will do the job of all the others, whereas Time.ToText() will not convert a number to a text value.

Dates

There are two types of dates that you need to be concerned with: those that are based on numbers, and those that come as textual dates. Different conversion functions are provided for each data type in order to turn them into a Date data type:

To Convert	Formula	Example
Numeric dates	Date.From()	Date.From([Column1]) Date.From(42986)
Text dates	Date.FromText()	Date.FromText([Column1]) Date.FromText("Jan 31, 2015")

Again, Date.From() actually performs the function of Date.FromText, although the reverse case is not true.

Times

Like dates, time values can arrive as either numeric time values or textual ones. Again, there are two functions for these:

To Convert	Formula	Example
Numeric times	Time.From()	Time.From([Column1]) Time.From(0.586)
Text times	Time.FromText()	Time.FromText([Column1]) Time.FromText("2:03 PM")

And, just as with dates, Time.From()performs the function of Time.FromText(), but again, the reverse case is not true.

Durations

A duration is the difference between two date/time values, and it allows you to work out the days, hours, minutes, and seconds to complete a task. Two functions exist, where the .From() variant can perform the job of the other:

To Convert	Formula	Example
Numeric durations	Duration.From()	Duration.From([Column1]) Duration.From(2.525)
Text durations	Duration.FromText()	Duration.FromText([Column1]) Duration.FromText("15:35")

Values

There are actually a large variety of numeric conversion functions. Again, while Number.From() will perform the job of all of them, there are others included as well, in case you want to force your numbers to a specific numeric type:

Convert Value To	Formula	Example
Decimal number	Number.From()	Decimal.From([Column1]) Number.From(2.525)
Decimal number (from text)	Number.FromText()	Number.FromText([Column1]) Number.FromText("15.35")
Decimal number	Decimal.From()	Number.From([Column1]) Decimal.From(15)
Whole number	Int64.From()	Int64.From([Column1]) Int64.From(2)
Currency	Currency.From()	Currency.From([Column1]) Currency.From(2.52)

Comparing Excel and Power Query Text Functions

When we Excel pros are trying to land and clean data, we often need to clean and split text.

If you've worked with Excel's text functions for a long time, you'll find that you are naturally inclined to try to use them to extract components from your data. And you'll find that they just don't work. For that reason, in this section you'll explore how to replicate Excel's five most commonly used text functions.

Each of the examples in this section can be found in Ch17 Examples\5 Useful Text Functions.xlsx. Each of the examples in this section begins with a set of data like the one below:

Word	LEFT(x,4)
Football	Foot
Doorknob	Door
Bookkeeper	Book
Automobile	Auto
Mountain	Moun
Truck	Truc
Car	Car

Figure 205 A sample of the data you'll work with.

There is a set of words down the left column, and there are some extractions in the right column. Each of these extractions was performed with Excel formulas, using the function listed in the header of the second column.

The following sections compare how to get Power Query to accomplish the same thing using different functions.

 In August 2015, the Power Query team added the ability to extract the first character, the last character, and a range of characters to the Transform tab. Despite this, the following sections walk through the process of replicating and comparing these formulas to those of Excel as this not only provides an understanding of how to work with the M code formulas but also allows you to build more robust solutions than you can with the user interface commands alone.

Replicating Excel's LEFT() Function

Follow these steps to pull the data into Power Query:

- Select a cell in the table of data on the LEFT worksheet → create a new query → From Table
- Rename the query pqLeft
- Go to Add Column → Add Custom Column
- Call the new column pqLeft(x,4) and enter the following formula:

```
=LEFT([Word],4)
```

This should work, shouldn't it? Power Query certainly isn't indicating that it won't:

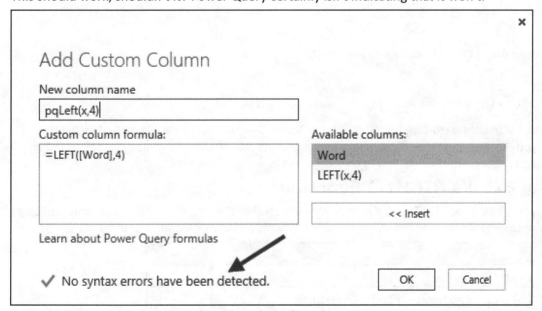

Figure 206 Power Query seems comfortable with the formula.

Click OK, and despite the green checkmark, things are not as good as you'd hoped:

 Expression error: The name 'LEFT' wasn't recognized. Make sure it's spelled correctly.

Figure 207 You're pretty sure you spelled left correctly.

So despite the tool being built for Excel pros, the design team elected to use a completely different formula term to refer to the x left characters of a cell. Here is a direct comparison of the syntax between the two programs:

	Syntax	Example	Result
Excel	=LEFT(text,num_chars)	=LEFT("Excel",2)	Ex
Power Query	=Text.Start(text,num_chars)	=Text.Start("Excel",2)	Ex

This means you need to edit the formula:

- Click the gear icon next to the Added Custom step
- Modify the formula to read as follows:

```
=Text.Start([Word],4)
```

- Click OK

Don't forget that the formula is case sensitive. Text.start, TEXT.START, and other variants will return errors!

This works, and better yet, it delivers results consistent with the Excel formula set:

⊞	Word	LEFT(x,4)	pqLeft(x,4)
1	Football	Foot	Foot
2	Doorknob	Door	Door
3	Bookkeeper	Book	Book
4	Automobile	Auto	Auto
5	Mountain	Moun	Moun
6	Truck	Truc	Truc
7	Car	Car	Car

Figure 208 Replicating Excel's LEFT() function with Text.Start().

You can now finalize the query:

- Go to Home → Close & Load To… → Only Create Connection

Never use the name of an existing function as your Power Query table name. If you had called this table LEFT, you would experience #N/A errors in the original table's Excel formulas, as table names are evaluated before functions.

Replicating Excel's RIGHT() Function

Based on what you know about LEFT(), you've probably guessed that using =RIGHT() won't work in Power Query, and you're correct. Again, the Power Query team chose a different function name, as shown below:

	Syntax	Example	Result
Excel	=RIGHT(text,num_chars)	=RIGHT("Excel",2)	el
Power Query	=Text.End(text,num_chars)	=Text.End("Excel",2)	el

Follow these steps to see how the results stack up:

- Select a cell in the table of data on the RIGHT worksheet → create a new query → From Table
- Rename the query pqRight
- Go to Add Column → Add Custom Column

- Call the new column pqRight(x,4) and enter the following formula:

```
=Text.End([Word],4)
```

- Click OK

The results are shown below:

⊞▾	Word	▾	RIGHT(x,4)	▾	pqRight(x,4)	▾
1	Football		ball		ball	
2	Doorknob		knob		knob	
3	Bookkeeper		eper		eper	
4	Automobile		bile		bile	
5	Mountain		tain		tain	
6	Truck		ruck		ruck	
7	Car		Car		Car	

Figure 209 Replicating Excel's RIGHT() function with Text.End().

Once again, the results are consistent with Excel's, which is a good thing. You can now finalize this query as well:

- Go to Home → Close & Load To… → Only Create Connection

Replicating Excel's LEN() Function

This isn't looking difficult so far, is it? Now try the LEN() function, whose syntax is listed below:

	Syntax	Example	Result
Excel	=LEN(text)	=LEN("Excel")	5
Power Query	=Text.Length(text)	=Text.Length("Excel")	5

Based on this, the results should be exactly the same as Excel's. Follow these steps to see what happens:

- Select a cell in the table of data on the LEN worksheet → create a new query → From Table
- Rename the query pqLen
- Go to Add Column → Add Custom Column
- Call the new column pqLen(x) and enter the following formula:

```
=Text.Length([Word])
```

- Click OK

The results are shown below:

⊞▾	Word	▾	LEN(x)	▾	pqLen(x)	▾
1	Football		8		8	
2	Doorknob		8		8	
3	Bookkeeper		10		10	
4	Automobile		10		10	
5	Mountain		8		8	
6	Truck		5		5	
7	Car		3		3	

Figure 210 Replicating Excel's LEN() function with Text.Length().

The results line up perfectly again. You're ready to load them to a connection as well:

- Go to Home → Close & Load To… → Only Create Connection

Replicating Excel's FIND() Function

By now you're wondering what the big deal is. It's obvious that the Power Query team just changed the way we reference formulas. In fact, the team has even injected some logic to group all the text formulas together, as they all start with Text.FunctionName.

But the changes are actually a bit bigger. Let's take a look by replicating Excel's FIND() function.

The following base table is using the FIND() function to find a lowercase o in the words. Naturally, that works in some cases, and it returns errors in the case of words that don't contain the specified character.

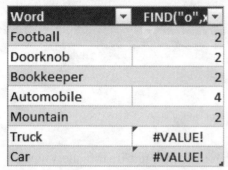

Figure 211 The FIND() function you want to replicate.

Follow these steps to see how Power Query handles this:

- Select a cell in the table of data → create a new query → From Table
- Change the query name to pqFind

Before you add the custom column, you should know that the new name for FIND in Power Query is Text.PositionOf(). Based on the syntax of the FIND() function, that means that you should be able to go with this:

```
=Text.PositionOf("o",[Word])
```

Try it:

- Go to Add Column → Add Custom Column
- Name the new column pfFind("o",x) and enter the formula above
- Click OK

The results are far from what you'd predict:

⊞▾	Word	▾	FIND("o",x)	▾	pfFind("o",x)	▾
1	Football		2		-1	
2	Doorknob		2		-1	
3	Bookkeeper		2		-1	
4	Automobile		4		-1	
5	Mountain		2		-1	
6	Truck	Error			-1	
7	Car	Error			-1	

Figure 212 What the heck is going on here?

In Power Query, the -1 result for the function informs you that Text.PositionOf() found no match. But how is that possible? The letter *o* plainly appears in a bunch of those words.

To find the answer, examine the full syntax for this function, as compared to Excel's:

	Syntax	Example	Result
Excel	=FIND(find_text,within_text)	=FIND("xc","Excel")	2
Power Query	=Text.PositionOf(text, find_text)	=Text.PositionOf("Excel","xc")	1

Do you see the big difference? Not only is the FIND() function masquerading under a new name, but the order of the parameters has flipped! That will certainly cause an issue. Now you need to follow these steps:

- Click the gear icon next to the Added Custom step
- Modify the formula to flip the order of the parameters:

    ```
    =Text.PositionOf([Word],"o")
    ```

- Click OK

The results are better but still not quite consistent with Excel:

▦▾	Word	▾	FIND("o",x)	▾	pfFind("o",x)	▾
1	Football		2		1	
2	Doorknob		2		1	
3	Bookkeeper		2		1	
4	Automobile		4		3	
5	Mountain		2		1	
6	Truck		Error		-1	
7	Car		Error		-1	

Figure 213 Every result is off by one.

It looks like the values returned here follow the base 0 rule. (Counting F as 0, the first *o* in Football would be character 1, not character 2.)

This is not a huge issue; it just means that you need to modify the formula and add 1 to the result in order to make it consistent with Excel. Follow these steps to do so:

- Click the gear icon next to the Added Custom step
- Modify the formula as follows:

    ```
    =Text.PositionOf([Word],"o")+1
    ```

- Click OK

And now things are looking . . . almost the same:

▦▾	Word	▾	FIND("o",x)	▾	pfFind("o",x)	▾
1	Football		2		2	
2	Doorknob		2		2	
3	Bookkeeper		2		2	
4	Automobile		4		4	
5	Mountain		2		2	
6	Truck		Error		0	
7	Car		Error		0	

Figure 214 The numeric results line up nicely, but the errors don't.

This case is actually an interesting one, as Power Query actually gives a nicer result than Excel when a value isn't found. Wouldn't it be great if you didn't have to wrap your FIND() function in an error handler in case the character wasn't located? You can now finalize this query:

- Go to Home → Close & Load To... → Only Create Connection

One thing you cannot do is replicate the #VALUE! error. Trying to replace 0 with #VALUE! will fail unless you convert the column to text first. Even if you did so, you would then land a column of textual numbers into Excel, which would obviously impact your ability to use the values in formulas.

Replicating Excel's MID() Function

The last function you will attempt to replicate is Excel's MID() function. This is a tricky one, as it actually throws an additional wrinkle into the mix as well.

In order to replicate the MID() function, you need to use Power Query's Text.Range() function, which has the following syntax:

	Syntax	Example	Result
Excel	=MID(text,start,num_chars)	=MID("Excel",2,2)	ex
Power Query	=Text.Range(text, start,num_chars)	=Text.Range("Excel",2,2)	ce

As you can see, the function has a different name, but the parameters are listed in the same order as the Excel equivalent. That is good news, at least. And yet, as you can see, the end result seems to be a character off. This is due to the fact that Power Query counts letters using base 0 instead of base 1, as Excel does. But armed with this information, you should be able to make this work. To start the process:

- Select a cell in the table of data on the MID worksheet → create a new query → From Table
- Rename the query pqMid
- Go to Add Column → Add Custom Column
- Name the new column pqMid(x,5,4) and enter the following formula:

```
=Text.Range([Word],5,4)
```

- Click OK

The results are, once again, underwhelming:

⊞▾	Word ▾	MID(5,4) ▾	pqMid(x,5,4) ▾
1	Football	ball	Error
2	Doorknob	knob	Error
3	Bookkeeper	keep	eepe
4	Automobile	mobi	obil
5	Mountain	tain	Error
6	Truck	k	Error
7	Car		Error

Figure 215 A couple of these worked, but why not all?

This is a bit of a shock. You were expecting the word to be off by a character but not to have errors everywhere. What happened?

Before dealing with the errors, you need to correct the position of the starting character. You can see that Bookkeeper should be returning "keep," and it's coming in late by one letter, returning "eepe." That's doesn't require a huge fix; you just need to adjust the formula to subtract 1 from the starting parameter:

- Click the gear icon next to the Added Custom step
- Modify the formula as follows:

```
=Text.Range([Word],5-1,4)
```

- Click OK

Interestingly, the results look much better:

⊞▾	Word ▾	MID(5,4) ▾	pqMid(x,5,4) ▾
1	Football	ball	ball
2	Doorknob	knob	knob
3	Bookkeeper	keep	keep
4	Automobile	mobi	mobi
5	Mountain	tain	tain
6	Truck	k	Error
7	Car		Error

Figure 216 Why are these formulas now returning consistent results?

One of the great features of Excel's MID() function is that you never have to worry about how many characters are remaining in the text string. If the final parameter you provide is higher than the number of characters remaining, it will simply return all remaining characters without triggering an error. Not so in Power Query.

In order to fix this, you obviously have to make a modification to how many characters are being returned, as you don't want to provide a number higher than the number of characters remaining. In other words, you want to return the minimum of four characters, or the number of characters still remaining in the text string.

You're going to learn a lot more about required functions in Chapter 20. Right now, however, just know that you need to use a List function to do this, specifically List.Min().

Rather than just try to build this into your function, follow these steps to see if you can build this in a separate column:

- Go to Add Column → Add Custom Column
- Enter the following formula
  ```
  =List.Min({Text.Length([Word])-(5-1),4})
  ```
- Click OK

You can see that you have a table that clearly indicates that Truck has only one extra character:

▦▾	Word	▾	MID(5,4)	▾	pqMid(x,5,4)	▾	Custom	▾
1	Football		ball		ball			4
2	Doorknob		knob		knob			4
3	Bookkeeper		keep		keep			4
4	Automobile		mobi		mobi			4
5	Mountain		tain		tain			4
6	Truck		k		Error			1
7	Car				Error			-1

Figure 217 You have determined the number of characters remaining.

You'll get a lot more exposure to lists in Chapter 19, but here's a quick breakdown of the formula:

- Text.Length([Word])-(5-1) simply takes the length of the word in the Word column and subtracts the starting position. You used (5-1) as you wanted the fifth character, but you need to correct it for base 0. (You could simplify this to 4 if desired.)
- The final 4 represents the maximum number of characters you want to return
- In order to use these in the List.Min() function, they need to be surrounded by curly braces and separated by commas.

With this working, you can simply edit your original column to use this formula in place of the final 4:

- Click the gear icon next to the Added Custom 1 step
- Copy the formula you just wrote
- Click OK
- Click the gear icon next to the Added Custom step
- Modify the formula and nest the copied formula in place of the final 4:
  ```
  =Text.Range([Word],5-1, List.Min({Text.Length([Word])-(5-1),4}))
  ```
- Click OK

When you preview the Added Custom step, your MID function equivalent should now be working:

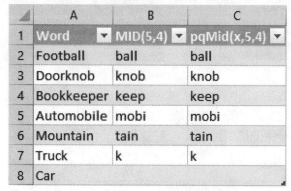

▦▾	Word	▼	MID(5,4)	▼	pqMid(x,5,4)	▼
1	Football		ball		ball	
2	Doorknob		knob		knob	
3	Bookkeeper		keep		keep	
4	Automobile		mobi		mobi	
5	Mountain		tain		tain	
6	Truck		k		k	
7	Car				Error	

Figure 218 The query is working for all but the last line.

Once you are comfortable that the query is working, you can take the following steps:

- Remove the Added Custom 1 step
- Go to Home → Close & Load

Despite the error, you can call this done and load the query to an Excel table. Why? Because errors just show up as empty cells anyway:

◢	A	B	C
1	Word ▼	MID(5,4) ▼	pqMid(x,5,4) ▼
2	Football	ball	ball
3	Doorknob	knob	knob
4	Bookkeeper	keep	keep
5	Automobile	mobi	mobi
6	Mountain	tain	tain
7	Truck	k	k
8	Car		

Figure 219 Errors disappear when loaded to a table, giving the output a consistent feel.

Observations

It is a real shame that not all the functions in Power Query have full equivalency with those in Excel, especially since Power Query is a tool for Excel users. Hopefully this will change in future versions; we'd like to see a new library of functions added that allow you to port your existing Excel formula knowledge directly into Power Query without needing to learn new formula names and syntaxes. Until that time, however, it is important that you test the results from the Power Query functions that seem to be Excel's equivalents and make sure they match what you expect, as you will occasionally have to tinker with the output to get it to line up correctly.

Chapter 18 Conditional Logic in Power Query

As you build more solutions using Power Query, you're bound to come across a scenario where you need to perform some kind of logic in a column. And while Power Query has a method to do this, it's not consistent with the way an Excel Pro would approach this issue.

IF Scenarios in Power Query

This example looks at the issues that appear when you import the following timesheet from a text file:

```
Date:    Work Date
From:    3/1/2015
To:      3/14/2015

Work Date       Out      Reg Hrs OT Hrs  Misc Hrs        Expenses
Contingent Worker:       John Thompson
3/3/2015       6:00 PM 8.50    0.00    0.00    0.00
3/4/2015       6:00 PM 8.00    0.00    0.00    0.00
3/5/2015       6:00 PM 8.50    0.00    0.00    0.00
3/6/2015       6:00 PM 8.50    0.00    0.00    0.00
3/7/2015       3:30 PM 6.50    0.00    0.00    0.00
3/10/2015      6:00 PM 8.50    0.00    0.00    0.00
3/11/2015      6:00 PM 8.50    0.00    0.00    0.00
```

Figure 220 A text file with some challenges.

The data doesn't seem so bad at first glance. And it seems like even less of an issue when you realize that you don't really need the top four rows, as the dates are included on each row of the data table. But then you notice an issue: The employee name is not included in rows but rather is buried in the middle of the data. How do you get it out of there?

The challenge in this scenario is to figure out how to get the employee name associated with each row of data—and that is not going to be possible without some conditional logic.

Connecting to the Data

You need to connect to the data to see how it looks in Power Query, as this may give you some ideas about how to proceed:

- Starting in a new workbook, create a new query → From File → From Text
- Browse to Ch18 Examples\2015-03-14.txt
- Go to Home → Reduce Rows → Remove Rows → Remove Top Rows → 4 → OK
- Transform → Use First Row as Headers

And the problem is now fully exposed:

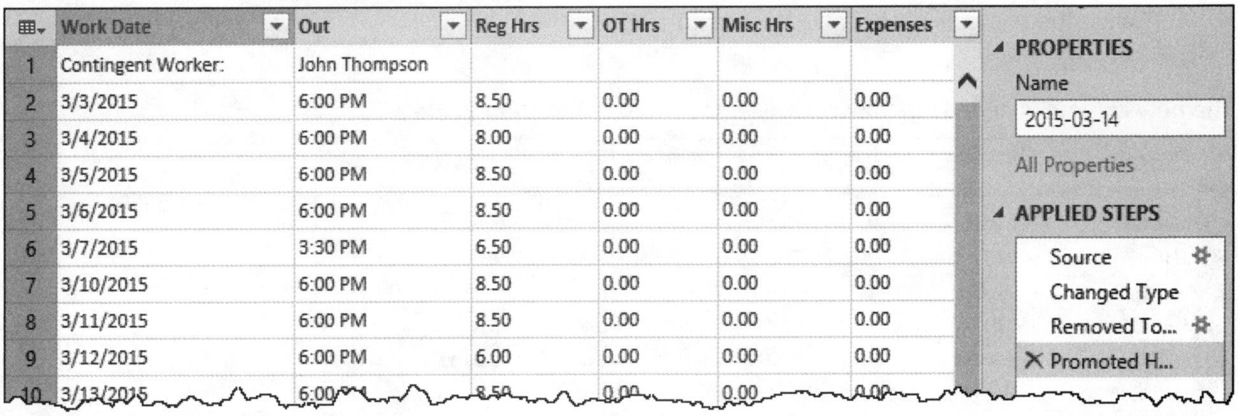

Work Date	Out	Reg Hrs	OT Hrs	Misc Hrs	Expenses
Contingent Worker:	John Thompson				
3/3/2015	6:00 PM	8.50	0.00	0.00	0.00
3/4/2015	6:00 PM	8.00	0.00	0.00	0.00
3/5/2015	6:00 PM	8.50	0.00	0.00	0.00
3/6/2015	6:00 PM	8.50	0.00	0.00	0.00
3/7/2015	3:30 PM	6.50	0.00	0.00	0.00
3/10/2015	6:00 PM	8.50	0.00	0.00	0.00
3/11/2015	6:00 PM	8.50	0.00	0.00	0.00
3/12/2015	6:00 PM	6.00	0.00	0.00	0.00
3/13/2015	6:00 PM	8.50	0.00	0.00	0.00

PROPERTIES — Name: 2015-03-14 — All Properties

APPLIED STEPS: Source, Changed Type, Removed To..., Promoted H...

Figure 221 John Thompson, hanging out in the Out column.

At first glance, you might be tempted to transpose this data and fill John Thompson's name down. But there are other rows as well, and you have no idea how many. Building a solution to use this approach could be very difficult to maintain, so you need to find a better way.

A more sensible approach in this case would be to add a new column and put a formula in it—a formula that checks whether the Out column is a time and pulls the data in that column if the test fails. But how do you do that?

Replicating Excel's IFERROR() Function

Try an experiment here:

- Right-click the Out column → Change Type → Time

As you'd expect, the times all convert nicely, but the employee name returns an error:

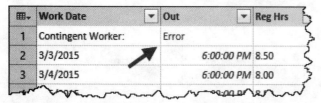

Figure 222 John Thompson doesn't have the time.

This is entirely to be expected, but can you use your knowledge of this behavior to solve the problem? What if you tested to see if converting this column to a time data type returns an error? If it did, then you could return *null*, and if it did not, you could return the time.

You can use Power Query's Time.From() function to attempt to convert the data to a valid time. And based on your Excel knowledge, you'd kind of expect this to work:

```
=IFERROR(Time.From([Out]),null)
```

Unfortunately, this will get you nothing but an error, as Power Query doesn't recognize the IFERROR function. All is not lost, however, as Power Query *does* have a function to do this, although the syntax is very different:

```
=try <operation> otherwise <alternate result>
```

Just like Excel's IFERROR(), Power Query's *try* statement attempts to perform the operation provided. If it succeeds, that result will be returned. If, however, the result is an error, then it will return the value (or other logic) specified in the *otherwise* clause.

This means that IFERROR() can be written in Power Query as follows:

```
=try Time.From([Out]) otherwise null
```

It should return null for any row that contains an employee name in the Out column and the time for any row that has a valid time in it. Give it a try:

- Remove the Changed Type step
- Add Column → Add Custom Column
- Leave the name as is but enter the formula above
- Click OK

The new column is added, and it works nicely to meet the current goal:

Work Date	Out	Reg Hrs	OT ...	Misc ...	Exp...	Custom
Contingent Worker:	John Thompson					null
3/3/2015	6:00 PM	8.50	0.00	0.00	0.00	6:00:00 PM
3/4/2015	6:00 PM	8.00	0.00	0.00	0.00	6:00:00 PM
3/5/2015	6:00 PM	8.50	0.00	0.00	0.00	6:00:00 PM
3/6/2015	6:00 PM	8.50	0.00	0.00	0.00	6:00:00 PM
3/7/2015	3:30 PM	6.50	0.00	0.00	0.00	3:30:00 PM
3/10/2015	6:00 PM	8.50	0.00	0.00	0.00	6:00:00 PM

Figure 223 Returning null instead of an error.

You may get a different time format, like 18:00:00 instead of 6:00:00 PM, depending on the regional settings in your computer.

This is fantastic, as it means you can now do some other tests to work out what you really want to know.

Replicating Excel's IF() Function

You've now got something you can test using simple logic: If the Custom column contains *null*, then give us the value in the Out column. If it doesn't, return null.

This should be pretty easy—just create a custom column and use the following function, right?

```
=IF([Custom]=null,[Out],null)
```

Not so fast! That isn't going to work either.

Power Query doesn't use the same syntax as Excel does for its IF() function, either. Instead, the Power Query syntax is as follows:

```
=if <logical_test> then <result> else <alternate_result>
```

Yes, you're reading that correctly. You actually have to spell the whole thing out for Power Query. Try it:

- Add Column → Add Custom Column
- Set the new column name to Employee
- Enter the following formula:

```
= if [Custom]=null then [Out] else null
```

- Click OK

The column is added to the data, and you can see some real potential here:

	Out	Reg Hrs	OT ...	Misc ...	Exp...	Custom	Employee	
ker:	John Thompson						null	John Thompson
	6:00 PM	8.50	0.00	0.00	0.00	6:00:00 PM	null	
	6:00 PM	8.00	0.00	0.00	0.00	6:00:00 PM	null	
	6:00 PM	8.50	0.00	0.00	0.00	6:00:00 PM	null	
	6:00 PM	8.50	0.00	0.00	0.00	6:00:00 PM	null	
	3:30 PM	6.50	0.00	0.00	0.00	3:30:00 PM	null	
	6:00 PM	8.50	0.00	0.00	0.00	6:00:00 PM	null	

Figure 224 John Thompson finally has his own column.

Naturally, with this in place, you can fill the employee name into the null areas:

- Right-click the Employee column → Fill → Down

Even better, because Power Query processes the steps in the Applied Steps box as completely self-sufficient steps in sequential order, you don't need to keep the precedent information around. You can remove that column and clean up the rest of the data, like this:

- Right-click the Custom column → Remove
- Right-click the Work Date column → Change Type → Date
- Select the Work Date column → Home → Reduce Rows → Remove Errors
- Right-click the Out column → Change Type → Time
- Select the Reg Hrs through Expense columns → Transform → Data Type → Decimal Number
- Right-click the Employee column → Change Type → Text
- Rename the query to Timesheet

The query is now final and ready to be loaded:

⊞ ▾	Work Date ▾	Out ▾	Reg Hrs ▾	OT ... ▾	Misc ... ▾	Exp... ▾	Employee ▾
1	3/3/2015	6:00:00 PM	8.5	0	0	0	John Thompson
2	3/4/2015	6:00:00 PM	8	0	0	0	John Thompson
3	3/5/2015	6:00:00 PM	8.5	0	0	0	John Thompson
4	3/6/2015	6:00:00 PM	8.5	0	0	0	John Thompson
5	3/7/2015	3:30:00 PM	6.5	0	0	0	John Thompson
6	3/10/2015	6:00:00 PM	8.5	0	0	0	John Thompson
7	3/11/2015	6:00:00 PM	8.5	0	0	0	John Thompson
8	3/12/2015	6:00:00 PM	6	0	0	0	John Thompson
9	3/13/2015	6:00:00 PM	8.5	0	0	0	John Thompson
10	3/14/2015	6:00:00 PM	8.5	0	0	0	John Thompson
11	3/3/2015	6:00:00 PM	9.5	0	0	0	Bob Johnson
12	3/4/2015	6:00:00 PM	8	0	0	0	Bob Johnson
13	3/5/2015	6:00:00 PM	8.5	0			

Figure 225 The timesheet with employees filled down the last column.

The key to working with Power Query's logic functions is to remember to spell them out in full and make sure to keep the function names in all lowercase.

Chapter 19 Power Query Objects

Before we take a closer look at programming with Power Query's M language, we first need to take a detailed look at the different objects and functions that are available. Having a sound understanding of how to create these objects, sometimes from each other, will be useful when working with more advanced programming concepts.

Be aware that the focus on this chapter is not how to use these new-found powers in anything extremely practical. This chapter focuses on how to actually talk to these objects, providing a reference for you to return to when you need to talk to these objects (or portions thereof) when working in more complex scenarios.

If you're following along on your own computer, you'll notice that all of the key objects in this chapter (tables, lists, records, values, binaries, and errors) show up in a green font when included in a column. In addition, each can be previewed by clicking the whitespace beside that key word.

Tables

Table objects can show up in numerous places in Power Query, and we always appreciate it when they do, as they are very easy to work with. Follow these steps to see for yourself:

- Open Ch19 Examples\Power Query Objects.xlsx
- Create a new query → From Other Sources → Blank Query
- Type the following formula in the formula bar:

```
=Excel.CurrentWorkbook()
```

You can see that there is one table in the workbook:

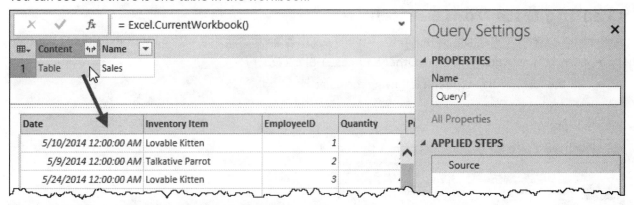

Figure 226 The sole table in the workbook being previewed.

The benefits of tables are numerous in Power Query:

- You can preview the data in a table.
- The data contained in a table has rows and columns (even though you can't guarantee that a header row will already be in place).
- You can drill into specific tables listed in the column or expand them all.
- Once you've expanded a table, you have a full set of transformation ribbon tabs available to you, and you can use them to further transform and manipulate the data.

Tables do not, of course, only mean Excel workbook tables—far from it, in fact. You can find tables in many data sources, including those extracted using formulas like Excel.CurrentWorkbook(), Csv.Document(), database tables, and more, as you've seen in earlier chapters.

You should finalize this query before you move on:

- Rename the query Table
- Go to Home → Close & Load To... → Only Create Connection

Lists

Power Query lists are incredibly robust and useful, and in many cases they are required in order to use some of Power Query's most powerful formulas.

The main way that lists differ from tables is that, when viewed, a list only ever has a single column of data. If you picture a list as being equivalent to your grocery list, you would simply list the names of the items you want to purchase. As soon as you start adding price comparisons between different stores, you have moved from a list to a table.

Syntax

When working with Power Query, a list can be identified by the presence of curly braces, with the list items separated by commas. In addition, textual items must be surrounded by quotes, just as they would need to be in an Excel formula. Here are two examples of lists:

- A list of numbers:

    ```
    ={1,2,3,4,5,6,7,8,9,10}
    ```

- A list of text values:

    ```
    ={"A","B","C","D","E","F","G","H","I","J"}
    ```

Lists are not restricted to containing only numeric values, however. They can mix any data types at all, including other lists:

```
={1,465,"M","Data Monkey",{999,234}}
```

The key items to remember here are that the individual list items are separated by commas, and each individual list is surrounded by curly braces.

Creating Lists from Scratch

You will now create some lists from scratch to see how they work, starting with a list of individual numbers:

- Create a new query → From Other Sources → Blank Query
- In the formula bar, type the following formula:

    ```
    ={1,2,3}
    ```

- Press Enter

You now have a nice list of numbers from 1 through 3:

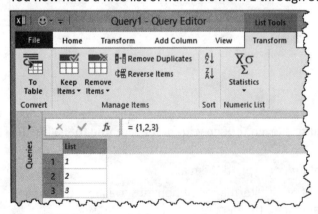

Figure 227 Creating a list from scratch.

In addition to the fact that you've created a list of values, you'll also notice that you're now working with the List Tools → Transform contextual tab active. Virtually all of the commands on the other tabs will be inactive at this point, making this feel like a very limited experience. Despite this, you'll see that you still have access to keeping/removing rows, sorting, de-duplicating, and even performing some basic statistical operations on your data.

Now, as great as it is to be able to create a list from scratch like this, creating a list of numbers from 1 to 365 would be a bit of a pain. For this reason, you also have the ability to use a coding shortcut to create a consecutive list from one number through another. Change the formula in the formula bar to read as follows:

```
={1..365}
```

You get a nice consecutive list from 1 to 365:

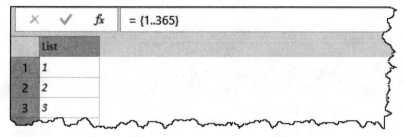

Figure 228 Using the .. characters to create a consecutive list.

 You can create consecutive alphabetical lists in this manner as well, provided that you wrap the characters in quotes and use only a single character. For example, ={"A".."J"} will work, but ={"AA".."ZZ"} will not.

You can also use commas inside lists, provided that they are inside the quotes. Replace the formula in the formula bar with the following:

```
= {"Puls,Ken","Escobar,Miguel"}
```

Upon committing it, you get two list items, showing the names of this book's authors:

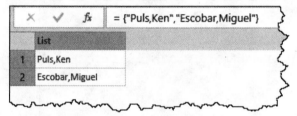

Figure 229 You can still use commas in list output.

Converting Lists into Tables

Say that you really want to split your data into two columns, but that is not possible with a list as lists are restricted to a single column of data. In this case, you really need the richer transformational toolset that tables offer.

Not to worry: It is super easy to transform a list into a table. Just click the big To Table button in the top left of the List Tools contextual tab. This interesting dialog appears:

To Table

Create a table from a list of values.

Select or enter delimiter

Comma

How to handle extra columns

Show as errors

OK   Cancel

Figure 230 What's this about delimiters?

You can set the delimiter setting to Comma and click OK, and your data will load nicely into a two-column table:

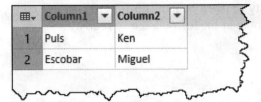

Figure 231 Data loaded from a comma-separated list.

> This dialog shows up whether there are delimiters in your data or not. If you don't have delimiters, just click OK, and the dialog will go away.

Finalize this query:

- Change the query name to List_Authors
- Go to Home → Close & Load To… → Only Create Connection

Creating Lists from Table Columns

Sometimes you'll want to extract the data from a single column of a query into a list. To see how this works, connect to the Sales table:

- Go to the Sales worksheet and select any cell in the Sales table
- Create a new query → From Table

You now have the full table showing:

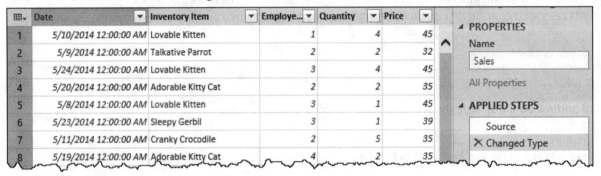

Figure 232 The raw table of data.

Now, what would you do if you wanted to get a unique list of the inventory items? If you were comfortable leaving it in the form of a table, you could simply remove all the other columns and then go to the Transform tab and remove duplicates. The challenge here is that it would still be in table form, and you wouldn't be able to feed it into a function if you needed to. Instead, you'd like to get those unique items, but as a list, which gives you that flexibility. Follow these steps:

- Remove the Changed Type step from the Applied Steps box
- Right-click the Inventory Item column → Drill Down

You now see a list of all the inventory items:

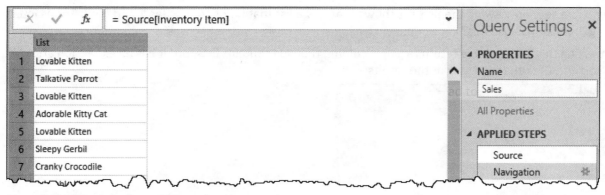

Figure 233 The column extracted to a list.

Before you move on, look at the formula bar. In there, you see this line of code:

```
=Source[Inventory Item]
```

This line of code refers to the Inventory Item column, as it was calculated during the Source step of this query. This gives you the M code shortcut to extract all column values into a list without using the user interface commands—something you'll find *very* useful later.

With the column contents extracted to a list, you are able to perform further list operations on it, such as de-duplicating the data, like this:

- Go to List Tools → Transform → Remove Duplicates

You now have a list of unique items that you could feed into a different function.

It's time to finalize this query:

- Rename the query List_FromColumn
- Go to Home → Close & Load To... → Only Create Connection

Creating Lists of Lists

We mentioned earlier that it is possible to create lists of lists. This might seem like an odd concept, so let's explore this scenario.

Say that you have four employee IDs (from 1 through 4) involved in your sales table. These values represent Fred, John, Jane, and Mary, in that order. Wouldn't it be nice to be able to convert those values to their names, without having to create a separate table? Follow these steps to see if you can use a list to do this:

- Create a new query → From Other Sources → Blank Query
- Create a new list in the formula bar as follows:

```
= {{1,"Fred"},{2,"John"},{3,"Jane"},{4,"Mary"}}
```

Notice that here you have four separate lists, each surrounded by curly braces and separated by commas. These four lists are in turn surrounded by a single set of master curly braces, defining a master list made up of four sublists. When you commit this formula to the formula bar, Power Query gives you a list containing four lists:

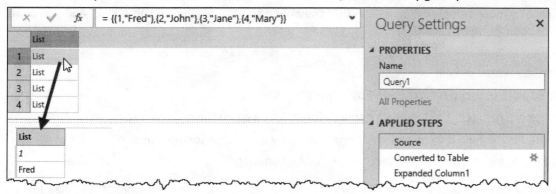

Figure 234 A list of lists.

As you can see, previewing the first list shows that it is a list that holds the values 1 and Fred. This is interesting, but can you use this?

Converting this list to a table returns a single column that still contains lists, but it has an expansion arrow in the top left. Click that and look at the results:

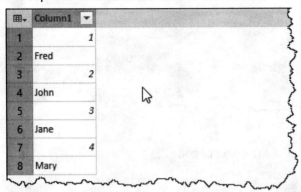

Figure 235 The lists have expanded vertically, not horizontally!

Plainly, aggregating the lists combines them by stacking the rows, not treating each as an individual row. While you could transform this by using the index/modulo/pivot approach from Chapter 15, it is a bunch of extra work that you should be able to avoid.

> In order to make this work, you would have needed to define your list as is done in the author example above—not as a list of lists but rather as a list of items with the commas inside the quotes.

Finish this example with the following steps:

- Rename the query List_of_Lists
- Go to Home → Close & Load To… → Only Create Connection

There are two key things to recognize here when working with lists:

- Lists *can* contain other lists
- Expanding lists of lists does not change their orientation

Let's look at an alternative.

Records

While a list can be described as a single vertical column of data, a record is a list's horizontal, multi-column counterpart. A record can be visualized as one row of a database, containing all the pertinent information related to a particular customer or transaction.

In Power Query, records can appear in table columns or in lists as you retrieve data. They can also be created on-the-fly if needed.

Syntax

Records are slightly more complex than lists in that they need to have a value of some kind, and you must also define the column names, like this:

```
=[Name="Ken Puls", Country="Canada", Languages Spoken=2]
```

Observe these key syntax points:

- Every complete record is surrounded by square brackets.
- Every record field (column) needs a name defined, followed by the = character.
- The data for the field is then provided, surrounded by quotes for textual data.
- Each field name and data pair is then separated by commas.

> Field (column) names do not need any punctuation surrounding them, whether they include spaces or not.

What happens when you need to create multiple records at once? The answer is that you reach to a list:

```
={[Name="Ken Puls", Country="Canada", Languages Spoken=2],
    [Name="Miguel Escobar", Country="Panama", Languages Spoken=2]}
```

Creating a Record from Scratch

It's time to circle back to your prior attempt at building the records for an employee ID table:

- Create a new query → From Other Sources → Blank Query

Here you need to create a single record:

- In the formula bar, enter the following formula:

```
=[EmployeeID=1,EmployeeName="Fred"]
```

- Press Enter

Power Query returns your record:

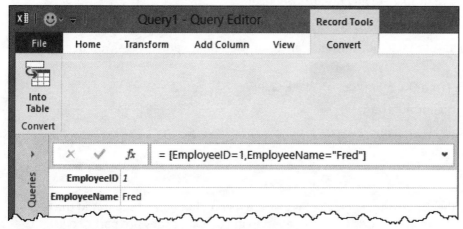

Figure 236 Your first record.

As you can see, the record's field names are listed down the left, with the corresponding data down the right. Interestingly, the data is arranged vertically, not horizontally, as you'd expect. This isn't an issue, just something to get used to.

Also notice that you have a new Record Tools → Convert contextual tab and, if you explore the rest of the ribbon tabs, you'll find out that they are all grayed out.

Converting a Record into a Table

Since there's obviously not a lot that you can do with records, you can just go ahead and turn this one into a table to see what happens:

- Go to Record Tools → Convert → Into Table

The result is probably not exactly what you expected:

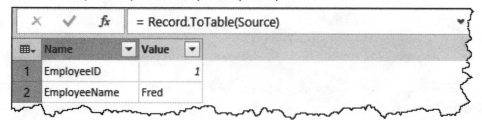

Figure 237 A single record converted to a table.

You may have expected that this would show up with the field names across the top and the values in the first row. Although it doesn't work this way, it's easy to fix since it's now a table:

- Go to Transform → Transpose
- Transform → First Row as Headers

The result looks more like what you would have originally expected:

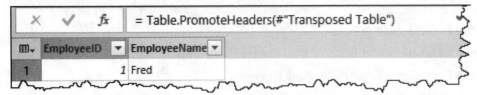

Figure 238 The record now looks like a proper table.

In this case, this is fine, but what is going to happen if you have a bunch of records that you need to convert to a table? Finalize the query so you can move on to the next section and find out:

- Rename the query Record_Single
- Go to Home → Close & Load To… → Only Create Connection

Creating Multiple Records from Scratch

Now say that you want to build your table out so that it encompasses all the employees. You need to build a list of records to do that:

- Create a new query → From Other Sources → Blank Query
- Enter the following in the formula bar:

  ```
  = {[EmployeeID=1,EmployeeName="Fred"], [EmployeeID=2,EmployeeName="-
  John"],
  [EmployeeID=3,EmployeeName="Jane"],
  [EmployeeID=4,EmployeeName="Mary"]}
  ```

Notice that you are still using the same format you use for a single record, but you've separated the records with commas and surrounded them in the curly braces needed to indicate that they are part of a list.

When you commit the formula above, it returns a list of records:

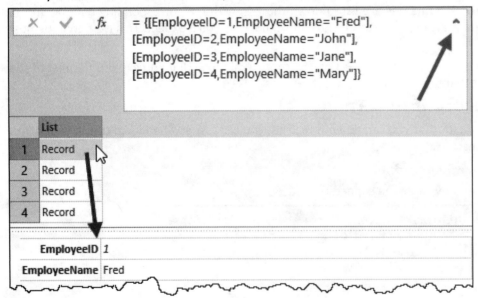

Figure 239 A list of records, with the preview showing that you got it right.

The arrow in the top right of the formula bar allows you to expand it to show multiple lines at once.

Converting Multiple Records into a Table

Now you can convert this list of records to a table and see what kind of a disaster you have on your hands:

- Go to List Tools → Transform → To Table → OK

The result is a column of records that can be expanded. Interestingly, clicking that expand icon indicates that there are columns to be expanded:

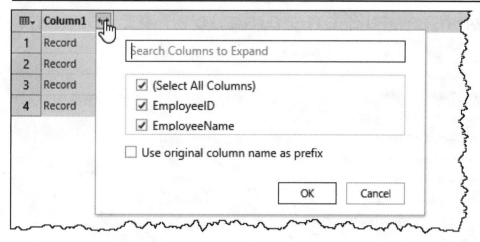

Figure 240 This is looking better!

Clicking OK returns a nice set of columns and rows, exactly as you were looking for with the single record!

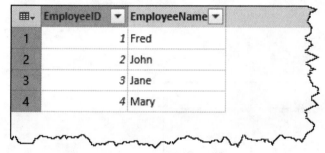

Figure 241 You just built a table from scratch!

It goes against conventional wisdom, but creating multiple records actually feels like it unwinds into a table more logically than a single record. The true difference is that you convert a *list* of records into a table in the second instance, not a single record into a table. With the records in a table column, Power Query then reads the record information correctly in order to expand it into the requisite column and rows.

You're now at a stage where this table can be saved—and even merged into other queries if you like. Save it like this:

- Rename the query Table_From_Records
- Go to Home → Close & Load To... → Only Create Connection

Creating a Record from a Table Row

When you were working with lists, you saw how you can convert a column into a list if you ever need to do this for any reason. You can also convert a row into a record. To do this, you can start with a new query:

- Go to the Sales worksheet and select any cell in the Sales table
- Create a new query → From Table

As with earlier examples, you now have the full table showing. To extract the first record, you need to create a blank query step. To do this:

- Click on the Source step in Applied Steps → OK
- Click the fx button next to the formula bar

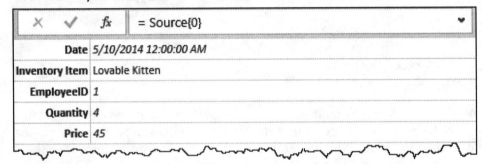

Figure 242 Creating a blank query step.

You now get a new step with the following formula in the formula bar:

        =Source

- Modify this formula to add {0} to it:

        =Source{0}

The result is your first record:

Date	5/10/2014 12:00:00 AM
Inventory Item	Lovable Kitten
EmployeeID	1
Quantity	4
Price	45

Figure 243 {0} = Record 1?

What just happened here?

When treated in this way, the Source step returns a list of records. Because Power Query is base 0, record 0 returns the first value in the list. (If you'd made this =Source{1}, you would have retrieved the record for the Talkative Parrot.)

Even more interestingly, you can drill in even further by appending the field name in square brackets. Try modifying the query to the following:

        =Source{0}[Price]

As you can see, you just drilled right in and extracted the price for the first record in the table:

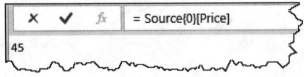

Figure 244 Drilling into record 0's price.

To understand the relevance of this, consider a situation where you need to drill into a specific record in order to control filters. In Chapter 20 you'll see where this technique allows you to do exactly that.

You can now finalize the query:

- Rename the query Record_From_Table
- Go to Home → Close & Load To... → Only Create Connection

Creating Records from Each Table Row

To convert each row in a table into records, you need to use a little trick. Start like this:

- Go to the Sales worksheet and select any cell in the Sales table
- Create a new query → From Table

Next, you want to convert each row in the table to a record. The challenge is that you need the index number of each row to do that. So you can reach to the Index column:

- Go to Add Column → Add Index Column → From 0

Now you are going to rename this *step* (not the column) in the Applied Steps box:

- Right-click the Added Index step → Rename → AddedIndex (without a space)

The query now looks as follows:

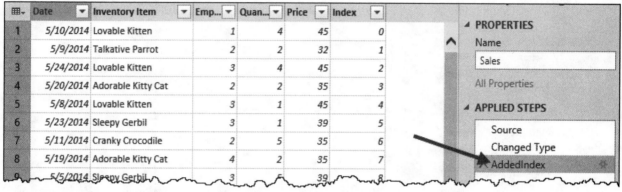

Figure 245 The Index column has been added, and the step has been renamed without the space.

Now you can reach to a custom column to convert your rows to records. The trick in this is creating an Index column, as you now have the value you need to extract your records. Why do you need this trick? You're not going to operate on the current row but rather on the AddedIndex step's output. This way, rather than getting a specific value (such as the first row), you can dynamically feed it into the query to get each row. Follow these steps:

- Go to Add Column → Add Custom Column
- Name the column Records
- Use the following formula:

```
=AddedIndex{[Index]}
```

The result is that a new column is created, and it contains the rows as records:

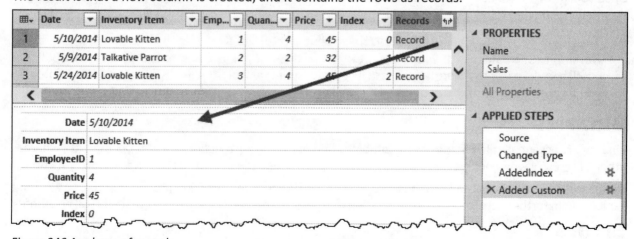

Figure 246 A column of records.

 Strictly speaking, you didn't need to rename the Added Index column to remove the space. Doing that just makes things a lot easier in the user interface.

At this point, you could remove all other columns, and you'd simply have a column of records:

- Right-click the Records column → Remove Other Columns
- Rename the query Records_From_Table
- Go to Home → Close & Load To... → Connection Only

Values

If you are working with databases, you will occasionally see columns containing values:

SalesLastYear	CostYTD	CostLastYear	Person.CountryRegion	Person.Sta
3298694.494	0	0	Value	Table
3607148.937	0	0	Value	Table
3205014.077	0	0	Value	Table
5366575.71	0	0	Value	Table
3925071.432	0	0	Value	Table
5693988.86	0	0	Value	Table
2396539.76	0	0	Value	Table

CountryRegionCode	US
ModifiedDate	6/1/2002 12:00:00 AM
Person.StateProvince	Table
Sales.CountryRegionCurrency	Table
Sales.SalesTerritory	Table

Figure 247 The elusive value object.

This particular object shows up only in certain cases. In order for it to appear, you must be working with a database that has a primary key and foreign key relationship set up between the tables. What's really strange is that a value is just the way a database returns a record.

> This particular table can be located in the AdvertureWorks2012 database that you connected to in Chapter 8. Use the same method to connect as described in Chapter 8, connect to the Sales. SalesTerritory table, and remove the columns other than those shown.

Once you know what values you have, working with them is the same as working with the other data types that they are related to.

> The direction of the relationship determines what is returned to a related column when you're working with a database. If you are in a fact table, and the link is going to the dimension table, you'll receive a value (record). If you are in a dimension table and the link is going to a fact table, you'll receive a table.

Binaries

Binaries are essentially files. Some can be combined and read by using functions like Csv.Document(), whereas others, like Excel workbooks, cannot be combined and must be read using the Excel.Workbook() function.

The process of extracting data from these workbooks is covered extensively in Chapters 3 and 4, so we don't explore them further here, other than to mention that they are a Power Query object that you will encounter.

Errors

There are two types of error messages that you can encounter in Power Query: step-level errors and row-level errors.

Row-Level Errors

Row-level errors typically occur when you're trying to convert data to the wrong data type or trying to operate on data before it has been converted to the correct type. You've seen several examples of these types of errors throughout this book. Here's one:

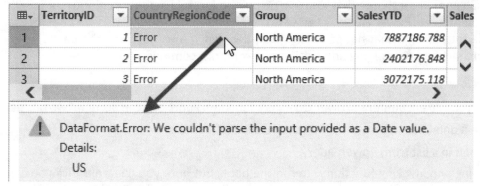

Figure 248 A row-level error triggered by trying to convert countries to a Date data type.

These errors generally aren't show-stoppers, and they can even be very useful when you're cleaning data, as they can be treated in two ways:

- Used as filters to keep/remove rows
- Replaced with other data using the Transform → Replace Errors command

Despite the fact that there is no debugging engine in Power Query, these errors are usually identifiable and often (although not always) are related to incorrect data types.

Step-Level Errors

Step-level errors are a bit more serious to deal with than row-level errors. These messages block Power Query from showing anything in the output window except the error, like these examples:

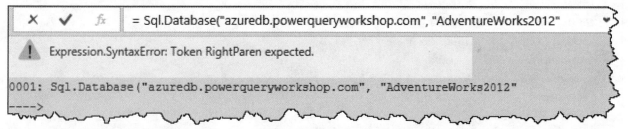

Figure 249 An expression syntax error, triggered by a missing) at the end of the line.

Figure 250 A general expression error, triggered by referring to SQL rather than Sql.

Unfortunately, Power Query's debugging tools are particularly weak, as you can see with the following issue:

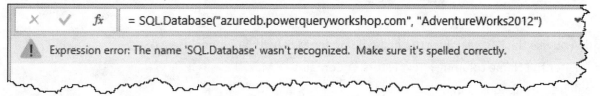

Figure 251 A syntax error caused by a missing } character but with the error message asking for a comma.

The error message debugging offering is presented on a single row (though it had to be cut and wrapped for this image). At the very end of the string is a helpful ^ character which indicates where Power Query thinks you need to place your comma. The issue, however, is that a curly brace was not provided to close the YTD Sales list, as indicated by the upward-pointing red arrow.

These issues today are challenges. It's a shame that we have no built-in formula indenter, coloring, or Intelli-Sense today to help with such issues. Power Query is frequently being updated, though, and we hope to see changes in this area in the future. Until that happens, however, debugging must be done the painful way: reviewing the line and watching for key opening and closing syntax marks, commas, and the like.

Functions

The last type of object that you will encounter in Power Query is a function. Functions can occur in two places:

1. They can be inside a database, where they indicate a stored procedure.

2. They can be returned in a list from Power Query.

You'll learn more about using and invoking functions later in the book, but here you'll learn a trick you can use to see how functions manifest and also to discover the Power Query function list. Try this:

*   Create a new query → From Other Sources → Blank Query

*   In the formula bar enter the following formula:

    ```
    =#shared
    ```

*   Go to Record Tools → Convert → Into Table

Power Query generates a table of all Power Query tables in the current workbook, but more importantly, it follows the list of tables with a list of all functions included in the product. You can access the documentation for any function from this list:

▦ ▾	Name	▾	Value	▾
10	List.NonNullCount		Function	
11	List.MatchesAll		Function	
12	List.MatchesAny		Function	
13	List.Range		Function	
14	List.RemoveItems		Function	
15	List.ReplaceValue		Function	
16	List.FindText		Function	
17	List.RemoveLastN		Function	
18	List.RemoveFirstN		Function	

Figure 252 A table of functions.

How do you use this? To see, filter the first column for Max (with an uppercase *M*):

*   Filter the Name column → Text Filters → Contains → Max

The search turns up four offers:

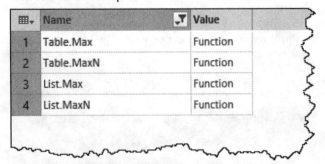

▦ ▾	Name	▾	Value
1	Table.Max		Function
2	Table.MaxN		Function
3	List.Max		Function
4	List.MaxN		Function

Figure 253 All functions containing Max.

If you click on Function beside Table.Max, you see two things happen—documentation pops up behind and an invocation dialog pops up in front:

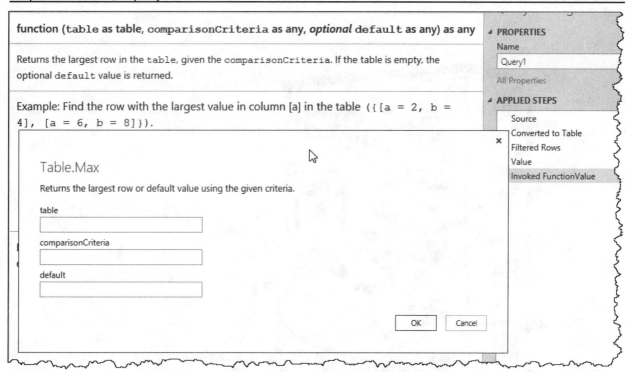

Figure 254 An invocation dialog appears in front of the documentation.

This box allows you to test the function out, but clicking Cancel makes it go away. Behind it you'll find the full documentation for the function, so you can determine whether it does what you need.

Note that you're not restricted to using the #shared command from a blank query. Any time you want to check Power Query's formula documentation, you can do the following:

1. Click the fx on the formula bar to add a new step
2. Replace the code in the new step with =#Shared
3. Convert the records to a table
4. Drill into the function you want to explore

You can then step back into the earlier steps in the Applied Steps box to implement the function, and you can delete all the #Shared steps when you are finished.

Chapter 20 Understanding the M Language

Now that you've explored the different objects you can use in Power Query, it is time to take a deeper look at the M language that is used to perform Power Query's magic. While mastering M isn't truly necessary, it will certainly add some incredible power to your arsenal and allow you to work with situations that others can't.

M Query Structure

To get started, you'll pull a table into Power Query and then examine the code that is working behind the scenes:

- Open Ch20 Examples\Understanding M.xlsx → select any cell in the Sales table
- Create a new query → From Table
- Delete the Changed Type step

Your query should now look like this:

Figure 255 The initial query is ready to examine.

Query Form

So far, everything you've seen has been driven through the user interface. You've seen Power Query act as a macro recorder, and you have been able to interact with it via the Applied Steps box. You've also had some limited interaction via the formula bar. What you haven't seen yet is the programming language that resides underneath the covers of this incredible tool. It's time to change that.

- Go to Home → Advanced Editor

The Advanced Editor window appears, and it contains the code for the entire query created to date:

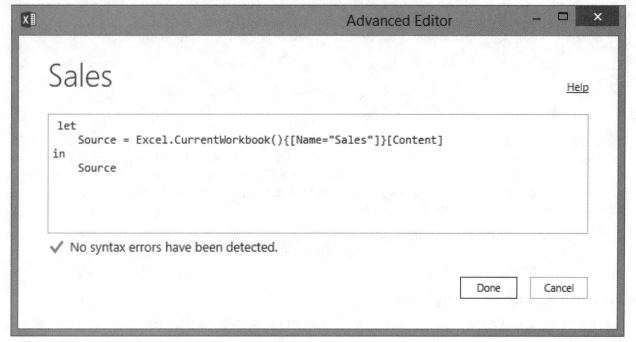

Figure 256 Power Query's Advanced Editor.

You can see that the feature set at this time is very limited. The Advanced Editor is essentially just a text editor with a syntax checker in the bottom-left corner. This area will no doubt see some investment in future, but right now it is essentially just a text box.

> Before you get frustrated trying to resize the editor to make it as small as the image shown above, be aware that you can't. (We shrunk it with photo editing to save page space.) The Advanced Editor can be expanded to make it bigger, but it can't collapse much more than the default size when you first open it.

Take a look at the code inside the window shown above:

```
let
    Source = Excel.CurrentWorkbook(){[Name="Sales"]}[Content]
in
    Source
```

There are some key pieces here that are required to build a successful query, so we'll break this down line by line.

The first line of every query must begin with the word *let*. (This changes for functions, which are covered in Chapter 21.) Nothing else goes on this line at all.

The second line begins with the word Source. This is important, as this is the step name from the Applied Steps box. It's via this step name that you can work out which line of code relates to the step you want to examine. In this case, you can see that when the new query From Table was created, Power Query invoked the Excel. CurrentWorkbook() function. It then appended a list of the records (the Excel table) that it imported. Finally, it drilled into the content records for that table object.

The second-to-last line of every query is the sole word *in*.

The last line is a single word that refers to the step containing the output you'd like to return at the end of the query. This is usually the previous step but doesn't have to be.

Now you can add another step to this query:

- Close the Advanced Editor by clicking Done
- Right-click the Price column → Change Type → Decimal Number
- Go to Home → Advanced Editor

You can see that a new step has been added to the window:

```
let
    Source = Excel.CurrentWorkbook(){[Name="Sales"]}[Content],
    #"Changed Type" = Table.TransformColumnTypes(Source,{{"Price", type number}})
in
    #"Changed Type"
```

Figure 257 A new step has been added to the query.

There are a few things worth noticing here. First, a comma has been added to the end of the Source line. (If you check back to the prior code, you'll see that the comma was not there.) This is incredibly important: Every line between the *let* and *in* lines *must* have a comma at the end *except* the last line before the *in* line, which can *never* have a comma at the end. In this case, the Source line ends with a comma, but the #"Changed Type" line does not, as it is the last line before the *in* statement.

> To put this in Power Query terms, you are providing a list of steps between the *let* and *in* lines. As you know, all items in a list need to be separated from each other via a comma, but you don't put a comma at the end.

The Meaning of #"syntax"

The second thing you should notice in the previous screenshot is that the step reads Changed Type in the Applied Steps box but comes into the code as #"Changed Type".

The challenge here is that the space between Changed and Type causes Power Query to treat the two words as separate terms. To deal with this and treat Changed Type as a single term, Power Query prefixes the term with the # character and then wraps the term in quotes. Sadly, you'll see this kind of thing happening frequently in Power Query, as the default names given to steps usually have spaces in them. This results in a whole lot of hash marks and quotes in longer code blocks.

If you wanted to, you could change this to avoid those characters. You can do this in two different ways:

- Right-click the step name in the Applied Steps box (before entering the Advanced Editor) and renaming the step.
- Replace every instance of #"Changed Type" in the Advanced Editor with a new term like NewType.

Regardless of which method you choose, your code will end up looking like this:

```
let
    Source = Excel.CurrentWorkbook(){[Name="Sales"]}[Content],
    NewType = Table.TransformColumnTypes(Source,{{"Price", type number}})
in
    NewType
```

Figure 258 Updating code to remove the #"awkwardness"

If you make your modifications manually, remember that your new term must be identical in all instances (no case changes), and don't forget to also rename the last step!

Tying the Steps Together

The next thing to understand is how the individual lines link to each other. Notice that in the NewType line, there is a reference to Source:

```
let
    Source = Excel.CurrentWorkbook(){[Name="Sales"]}[Content],
    NewType = Table.TransformColumnTypes(Source,{{"Price", type number}})
in
    NewType
```

Figure 259 The Source step referenced in the NewType line.

It's this referencing that allows Power Query to chain all the commands together. You can basically read the NewType line as follows:

- Give us the output of the Source step
- Transform the column types of that step and set Price to a type of number

Using Line Breaks

Another piece of this equation that is interesting is that the code as shown above is equivalent to this block:

```
let
    Source = Excel.CurrentWorkbook(){[Name="Sales"]}[Content],
    NewType = Table.TransformColumnTypes
                    (Source,{{"Price", type number}})
    in
        NewType
```

But this violates the rule about having a comma at the end of all lines except the line preceding the *in* statement, doesn't it? Not exactly.

When Power Query reads your code, it looks for keywords, including the comma and the *in* keyword. As it reads a line, it ignores any commas that are enclosed within matching parentheses, curly braces, square brackets, or quotes. Once it encounters a lone comma, it recognizes that as the end of the current code line and starts reading the next line of code as an independent step. Alternatively, if it finds the *in* keyword, it now knows that the query is going to end and looks to see which step to return.

Why is this important? It means that you can actually place a line break in the middle. Because Power Query hasn't found either a comma or the *in* keyword at the end of the initial NewType line, it keeps moving on, assuming that the next line is still part of the first. In essence, this means that this code:

```
NewType = Table.TransformColumnTypes(Source,{{"Price", type number}})
```

Is equivalent to this code:

```
NewType = Table.TransformColumnTypes
              (Source,{{"Price", type number}})
```

Or this code:

```
NewType = Table.TransformColumnTypes(
    Source,
    {
        {"Price", type number}
    }
)
```

The key to understand here is that you can't place a hard return in the middle of a function name or word, but breaking at any punctuation mark is okay. Looked at on a grander scale, this query will run perfectly well:

```
let
    Source = Excel.CurrentWorkbook(){[Name="Sales"]}[Content],
    NewType = Table.TransformColumnTypes
        (
         Source,
         {
             {"Price", type number}
         }
        )
in
    NewType
```

Why would you even want to do this?

This technique can be very useful when you're trying to debug things like lists of lists, which have numerous pairs of list items. When making manual tweaks to code, it is very easy to get lost in the braces and not realize that you missed closing one. When you do that, you get unbalanced code that will not compile and that can be *very* difficult to correct, especially with the current lack of good debugging tools in Power Query. By separating the opening and closing curly braces and separating the list item pairs onto individual lines, you have a much better chance of keeping your opening and closing braces in balance. Another bonus of this approach is that it's also very easy to add new columns to the TransformColumnTypes step (at least when you know what data types to assign).

Add the data types for all the columns as follows:

Column(s)	Data Type
Date	Date
Inventory Item	Text
EmployeeID, Quantity	Number

You can recognize from the curly braces after the Source keyword in the NewType step that you need to provide a list of columns and data types in a list format. Since you already know from Chapter 19 that all the list items need to be separated by commas, you know that this should work:

```
let
    Source = Excel.CurrentWorkbook(){[Name="Sales"]}[Content],
    NewType = Table.TransformColumnTypes
        (
         Source,
         {
```

```
                    {"Price", type number},
                    {"Date", type date},
                    {"Inventory Item", type text},
                    {"EmployeeID", type number},
                    {"Quantity", type number}
                }
            )
    in
        NewType
```

If you click Done to commit this code (exactly as written), you see that the query returns your desired results, with each data type converted as you requested:

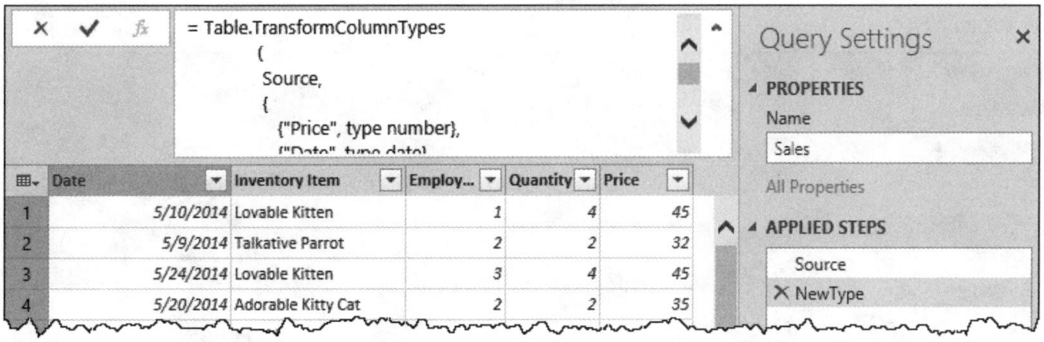

Figure 260 Not only are the dates time-free, but check out the indentation in the formula bar!

Code Comments

The last sets of characters you need to know how to create are those that let you leave comments in code. These can be very useful for leaving notes in code or temporarily disabling a line of code.

To mark a single line of code as a comment, you place two slashes at the beginning of the line, as shown here:

```
let
// Retrieve the Sales table from Excel
    Source = Excel.CurrentWorkbook(){[Name="Sales"]}[Content],
```

Power Query will not read the // Retrieve . . . line, and this line also will not appear in the Applied Steps box, but it is there to remind you of the purpose of the following row.

Sometimes you need longer comments that don't fit on one line. In this case, you place the characters /* prior to the code you don't want executed and the characters */ at the end of the section, like this:

```
/* I broke this code comment across multiple lines
    (by reading M is for Data Monkey)              */
```

Summary of Special Characters

The following table provides a list of the special characters that you will encounter in your Power Query coding journey:

Character	Purpose
(Parameters)	Surrounding function parameters
{List}	Surrounding list items
[Record]	Surrounding records
"Text"	Surrounding text
#"Step Name"	Referring to a step name that contains spaces or other reserved characters
//comment	Commenting a single line of code
/* comment */	Commenting multiple lines of code

Operating on Each Row in a Column

There is one more very important construct to understand in M: how to read and modify code that operates on each row in a column. To get this code, you can take your existing query and add a column to determine the total sales by row:

- Make sure you are out of the Advanced Editor
- Select the Quantity and Price columns → Add Column → Standard → Multiply
- Right-click the Multiply column → Rename → Gross Sales
- Right-click the Inserted Multiplication step → Rename → CalcSales
- Right-click the Renamed Columns step → Rename → Rename

The query will now looks like this:

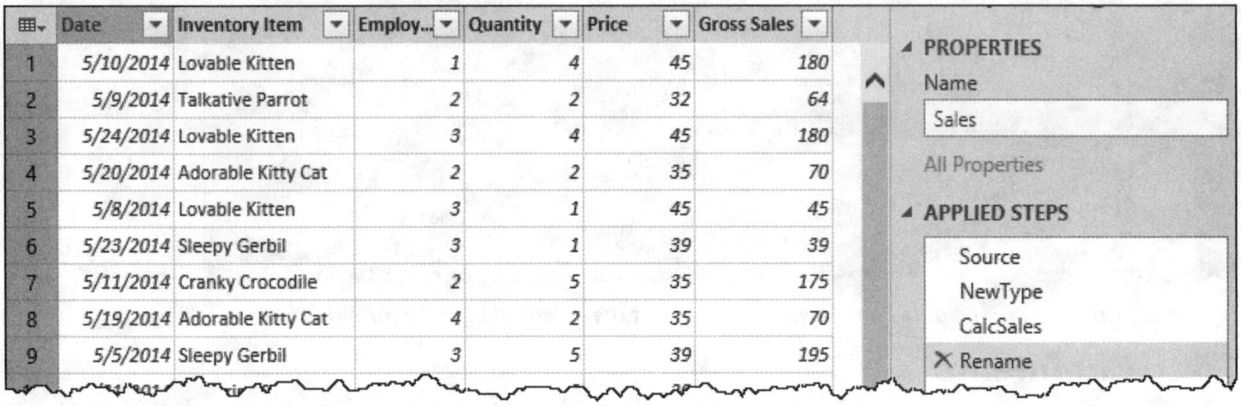

⊞▾	Date	Inventory Item	Employ...	Quantity	Price	Gross Sales
1	5/10/2014	Lovable Kitten	1	4	45	180
2	5/9/2014	Talkative Parrot	2	2	32	64
3	5/24/2014	Lovable Kitten	3	4	45	180
4	5/20/2014	Adorable Kitty Cat	2	2	35	70
5	5/8/2014	Lovable Kitten	3	1	45	45
6	5/23/2014	Sleepy Gerbil	3	1	39	39
7	5/11/2014	Cranky Crocodile	2	5	35	175
8	5/19/2014	Adorable Kitty Cat	4	2	35	70
9	5/5/2014	Sleepy Gerbil	3	5	39	195

PROPERTIES

Name

Sales

All Properties

APPLIED STEPS

Source
NewType
CalcSales
✕ Rename

Figure 261 The query with a Gross Sales column.

Viewing the code in the Advanced Editor yields two new lines of code at the end of the query (wrapped lines have been indented here for ease of identification):

```
CalcSales = Table.AddColumn(NewType, "Multiply", each
        List.Product({[Quantity], [Price]}), type number),
Rename = Table.RenameColumns(CalcSales,{{"Multiply",
        "Gross Sales"}})
```

While you may not necessarily recognize the function used in the Rename step, you can fairly easily recognize that the Table.RenameColumns function refers to the previous step and then provides a list of the previous column names and the new name you'd like them to take. In addition, based on the fact that you see the list open with two {{ characters, you can identify that you could provide a list of lists here and rename multiple columns at once.

The CalcSales line, however, has a new keyword in it that you haven't seen before. The Table.AddColumn function first refers to the NewType step and then provides the value "Multiply". Since Multiply was the name given to the new column, this means that you could probably just change this line to use "Gross Sales" instead of "Multiply", avoiding the step of renaming the column later.

Following the column's name is a new keyword you haven't encountered yet: *each*. The *each* keyword indicates to Power Query that you want this action performed for each row in the query. Following this, you see the List.Product() function, which indicates which columns to multiply against each other and the data type the output should take.

You can now make some modifications to make the code shorter:

- Replace "Multiply" in the CalcSales line with "Gross Sales"
- Remove the comma from the end of the CalcSales line
- Remove the entire Rename line
- Change the last line to read "CalcSales" instead of "Rename"

Your query should now look similar to this:

```
 let
// Retrieve the Sales table from Excel
    Source = Excel.CurrentWorkbook(){[Name="Sales"]}[Content],

/* I broke this code across multiple lines
    (by reading M is for Data Monkey)              */
    NewType = Table.TransformColumnTypes
              (
                Source,
                {
                    {"Price", type number},
                    {"Date", type date},
                    {"Inventory Item", type text},
                    {"EmployeeID", type number},
                    {"Quantity", type number}
                }
              ),
    CalcSales = Table.AddColumn(NewType, "Gross Sales",
                each List.Product({[Quantity], [Price]}), type number)
 in
    CalcSales
```

Figure 262 Modifications made to the query.

 Your line breaks may not appear in the same places—or they may not appear at all. The key pieces to remember are (1) the CalcSales line is being treated as one complete line of code since it was split onto two lines in the middle of the function, and (2) the line does not end with a comma since this line precedes the *in* keyword.

- Click Done

Notice that the Rename step is gone, but the Gross Sales column still exists:

⊞▾	Date	Inventory Item	Employ...▾	Quantity	Price	Gross Sales
1	5/10/2014	Lovable Kitten	1	4	45	180
2	5/9/2014	Talkative Parrot	2	2	32	64
3	5/24/2014	Lovable Kitten	3	4	45	180
4	5/20/2014	Adorable Kitty Cat	2	2	35	70
5	5/8/2014	Lovable Kitten	3	1	45	45
6	5/23/2014	Sleepy Gerbil	3	1	39	39
7	5/11/2014	Cranky Crocodile	2	5	35	175
8	5/19/2014	Adorable Kitty Cat	4	2	35	70
9	5/5/2014	Sleepy Gerbil	3	5	39	195

PROPERTIES

Name

Sales

All Properties

APPLIED STEPS

Source

NewType

✕ CalcSales

Figure 263 The Gross Sales column, generated without needing to be renamed.

The end effect of this code modification is that it now sets the column name up front, avoiding the need to rename the column later. Saving a step makes the code more efficient by preventing processing steps later.

In addition, you now recognize another keyword in the Power Query programming language. When you see the *each* keyword, you now know that the formula after this keyword will be applied to each row in the table.

You can now finalize the query:

- Rename the query GrossSales
- Go to Home → Close & Load

Referring to Steps or Rows

Consider a scenario where you have a text file that contains data like that shown below:

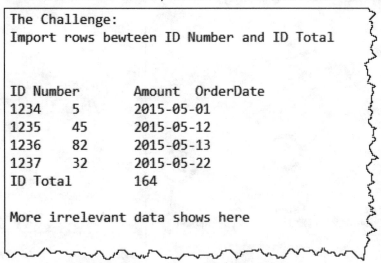

```
The Challenge:
Import rows bewteen ID Number and ID Total



ID Number        Amount  OrderDate
1234     5       2015-05-01
1235     45      2015-05-12
1236     82      2015-05-13
1237     32      2015-05-22
ID Total         164


More irrelevant data shows here
```

Figure 264 Tab-delimited data with a specific requirement.

This data throws a few interesting wrinkles:

- The data is tab delimited, but the first row doesn't contain any tabs. This means you will need to manually trigger the column splits.
- The number of rows prior to ID Number is variable. There could be 5 or 5,000 rows before the row that contains the ID Number text.
- The number of rows between and after the ID Total row is also variable.

Your overall challenge here is that you need to extract rows from the middle of a data set and make it dynamic to deal with however many rows are evident before, in the middle of, and after the needed data.

In addition, as one final wrinkle, you'd like to determine the number of days between each order date compared to the previous order. This task will entail trying to subtract the date on one row from the data on another—something that can't be done via the Power Query user interface.

Connecting to the Data

You need to connect to the data and then figure out which rows you need in order to perform your goals:

- Open a blank workbook
- Create a new query → From File → From Text → Ch20 Examples\Varying Header Rows.txt → OK
- Go to Add Column → Add Index Column → From 0
- Filter Column1 → Text Filters → Begins With
- Set the filter to Begins With ID Number OR Begins With ID Total
- Right-click and rename the Filtered Rows step to RowNumbers

> You could accomplish the same goal by filtering to rows that begin with ID, but you don't know if there are other rows in the data set that begin with ID. By making the terms as tight as possible, you can reduce the chance of errors in the future. (Of course, if another ID Number row enters the data, you will still have to work out how to deal with this.)

The query should now look as follows:

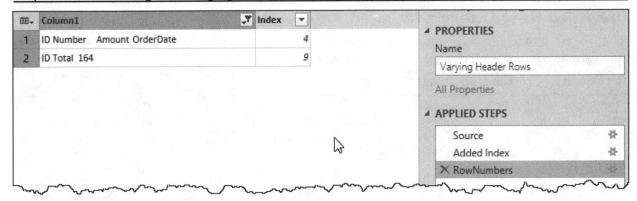

Figure 265 The query shows just the row indexes you need.

You now have a very cut-down view, showing the row numbers for both the ID Number and ID Total rows. Keep in mind that these are fully dynamic, as no matter how many rows precede, follow, or are in the middle of the data, the steps you have taken will still generate the correct rows.

Combining Power Query Steps

Now, could you make this code shorter if you wanted to? You are going to need the Source step again, but the Added Index step isn't something you absolutely need in the Applied Steps box. It is, however, possible to combine these two steps into one. You can look at the code for those two steps by going to Home → Advanced Editor:

```
#"Added Index" = Table.AddIndexColumn(Source, "Index", 0, 1),
RowNumbers = Table.SelectRows(#"Added Index", each Text.StartsWith([-
Column1], "ID Number") or Text.StartsWith([Column1], "ID Total"))
```

Notice how the #"Added Index" step contains the Table.AddIndexColumn function. On the RowNumbers line, you also see that the #"Added Index" step is the first parameter fed into the Table.SelectRows() function. If you want to avoid having a separate #"Added Index" step, all you need to do is substitute the actual code within the #"Added Index" step in place of that term in the next line.

> Remember when substituting code in this way that you want everything between the equals sign and the final comma only.

By substituting the code in place, adding some line breaks, and removing the #"Added Index" line completely, you end up with nested code, as follows:

```
RowNumbers = Table.SelectRows(
        Table.AddIndexColumn(Source, "Index", 0, 1),
        each Text.StartsWith([Column1], "ID Number")
        or Text.StartsWith([Column1], "ID Total"))
```

As you can see, this code still runs flawlessly, but it removes the Added Index step from the Applied Steps box:

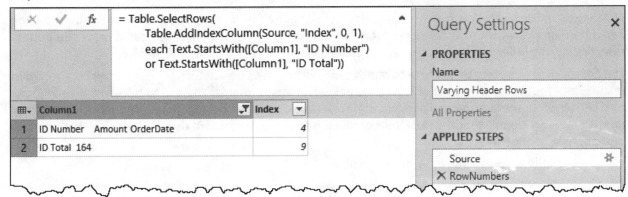

Figure 266 Eliminating the Added Index step while preserving the function.

Creating New Query Steps

Next, you need to be able to use this data in your query, but there is an issue: Power Query works as a sequential macro recorder, which means you've left your original source data behind. So how do you get it back?

The answer is to click the fx button in the formula bar:

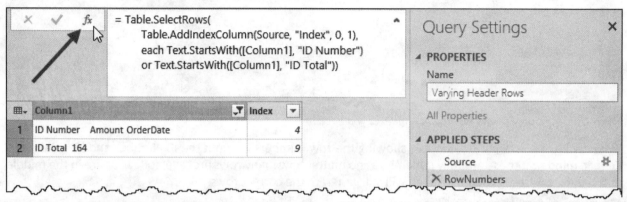

| ✕ | ✓ | fx | = Table.SelectRows(
        Table.AddIndexColumn(Source, "Index", 0, 1),
        each Text.StartsWith([Column1], "ID Number")
        or Text.StartsWith([Column1], "ID Total")) | |

Query Settings ✕

▲ PROPERTIES

Name

Varying Header Rows

All Properties

▲ APPLIED STEPS

▦▾	Column1	▼	Index	▼
1	ID Number Amount OrderDate		4	
2	ID Total 164		9	

Source   ⚙

✕ RowNumbers

Figure 267 Manually creating a new query step.

If you're not paying attention when you click this button, you'd be forgiven for thinking that nothing happened. The data in the preview window doesn't appear at all. You will see, however, that you have a new step in the Applied Steps box called Custom1, and the formula in the formula bar has changed to this:

```
=RowNumbers
```

Clicking the fx button always creates a new query step that refers to the previous step. So how is that useful? Change the formula to this:

```
=Source
```

You now see that you are back looking at the original data.

> If you check the Advanced Editor, you see that you could have typed this in manually by adding a new step right before the *in* keyword, as follows: `Custom1 = Source` Of course, in order to keep the code working, you would also need to add a comma to the preceding line and change the term after the *in* keyword to Custom1 from RowNumbers.

You're now in good shape here, as you can select the RowNumbers step to see the first and last rows you want to find, then step back to Custom1 so that you can start doing exactly that.

Referring to a Previous Applied Step

You now want to restrict your data to just the necessary rows.

To start with, you set up your command via the user interface. The reason for this is that it will give you the syntax for the functionality you're after—instead of looking up the function and doing things manually from the beginning.

The index number for the last row is 9 as the data set currently sits. If you filtered out the rows from the top first, however, this would need to be updated. Rather than complicate things, you can remove the bottom rows first, as the index for the top rows won't change when we remove the bottom rows.

The approach you're going to use here to remove the bottom rows isn't actually driven by the Remove Rows feature, as it requests the number of rows to remove. This means that you'd need to calculate all rows in the data set, work out the last row, and perform some math to determine how many rows to remove. Rather than do that, you can identify that the final row you need is in row 9, so you can use the Keep Top Rows feature instead, to keep the top 9 rows:

- Go to Home → Keep Rows → Keep Top Rows → 9

You now get a table filtered to show only the top 9 rows:

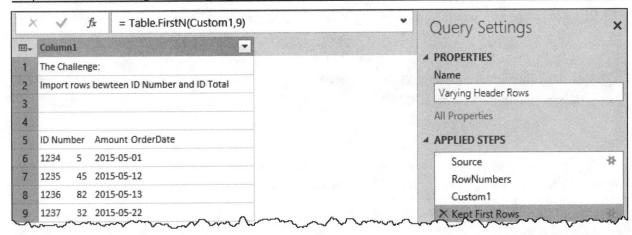

Figure 268 The data now shows the top 9 rows.

Notice that you don't have the row that starts with ID Total. This is to be expected because the ID Total row was actually the tenth row in the file, but you used a base 0 index to count rows. By pulling the ninth row, however, you get the data you're after, without the total row (which you'd just need to filter out anyway).

Now how do you make this dynamic? Look at the code in the formula bar:

```
=Table.FirstN(Custom1,9)
```

In theory, you just need to replace the 9 with a reference to the correct value from the RowNumbers step. This can be done by referring to a previous step and extracting the value from the Index column in that step. To do this, you would use the following code:

```
RowNumbers[Index]{1}
```

As you can see, you refer to the RowNumbers Applied Step, provide the [Index] column, and then drill into the row you need. In this case, you want to use {1}, as this would refer to the second row of the column. (Remember that {0} returns the first value in a base 0 system, {1} returns the second, and so on.)

This means you can rewrite the formula in the formula bar as follows to pull the value dynamically from the table:

```
=Table.FirstN(Custom1,RowNumbers[Index]{1})
```

Can you do even better than this?

If you check back on the code for the Custom1 step, you see that it simply refers to Source. Can you skip using the Custom1 step and just refer to Source in the formula? You bet you can! Update that formula again:

```
=Table.FirstN(Source,RowNumbers[Index]{1})
```

The result still gives you exactly what you need:

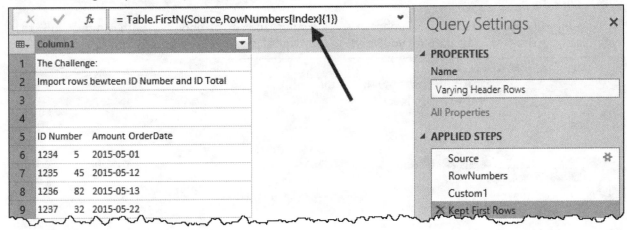

Figure 269 The updated formula still works nicely.

And now, since the formula refers to the Source step, you don't need the Custom1 step any more at all.

- Delete the Custom1 step from the Applied Steps box

With that step cleaned up, you're now down to a three-step query, and you're on your way. Add your dynamic filter to filter out the top rows as well:

- Go to Home → Remove Rows → Remove Top Rows → 4 → OK
- Rename the Removed Top Rows step ExtractRows
- Update the formula bar from this:

```
= Table.Skip(#"Kept First Rows",4)
```

- To this:

```
= Table.Skip(#"Kept First Rows", RowNumbers[Index]{0})
```

The result is a set of rows limited to the header row and the raw data you need:

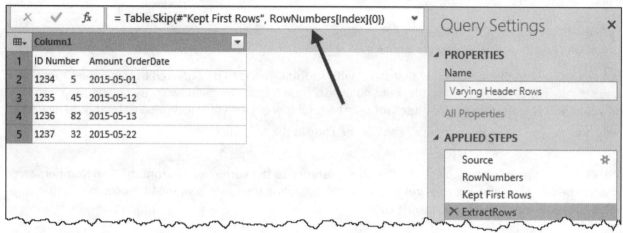

Figure 270 The code is now dynamically pulling in both the starting and ending rows.

You can consolidate the last two steps as well, just to keep the code cleaner to this point:

- Go to Home → Advanced Editor
- Edit the following code:

```
#"Kept First Rows" = Table.FirstN(Source,RowNumbers[Index]{1}),
ExtractRows = Table.Skip(#"Kept First Rows",RowNumbers[Index]{0})
```

- By nesting the #"Kept First Rows" step into the second line as follows:

```
ExtractRows = Table.Skip(
        Table.FirstN(Source,RowNumbers[Index]{1}),
        RowNumbers[Index]{0})
```

- Click Done

Once again, you have shortened the number of applied steps, and you've ended up with compact code that dynamically retrieves the raw data set you need:

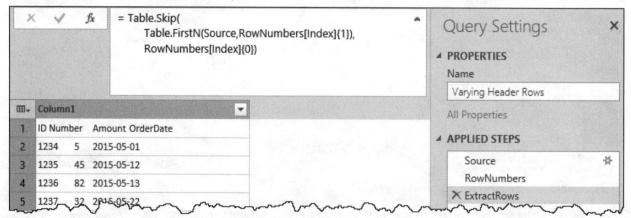

Figure 271 The dynamic data set is ready for cleanup.

The next steps are just run-of-the-mill cleanup steps:

- Go to Transform → Split Column → By Delimiter → Tab → At Each Occurrence → OK
- Delete the automatically created Changed Type step (It sets all columns to text, which won't be accurate in the long term)
- Go to Transform → Use First Row as Headers
- Right-click the ID Number column → Change Type → Whole Number
- Right-click the Amount column → Change Type → Whole Number
- Right-click the OrderDate column → Change Type → Date

The result is a perfectly clean data set:

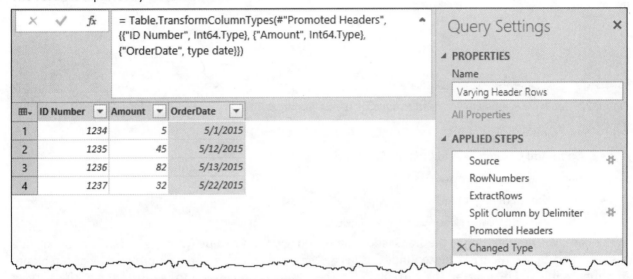

Figure 272 The data set, all cleaned up and ready to use.

So far you have managed to import a set of data and dynamically restrict the rows that you wish to use. At this point, no matter how many rows of data exist before the ID Number row, the query will still start in the right place. In addition, regardless of how many rows exist after the ID Total row, you'll never see them in your output query, and the query will also pull in any number of rows between those two headers.

Compacting the code is an entirely optional step. You are able to keep nesting your code by copying the previous step and substituting it into the next step in place of the previous step name. While this can make your code more compact and efficient, be aware that it can also drastically affect your ability to debug your code in the case that something goes wrong. The trick is to find a happy medium that makes sense to you.

Referring to the Previous Row Dynamically

There is one more task to accomplish with this data set: working out the number of days since the previous order. Unfortunately, while it would be incredible to just click a button to make this happen, you're not so lucky, as Power Query doesn't have this functionality built in. You can still accomplish your goal, but you have to do it manually.

To make this work, you need to figure out a way to create a new column that holds the previous order's date.

You already know how to refer to a previous step, and you even know how to refer to the column within that step. You also know that you can provide a row number between curly braces to pull back a specific row. All you need to do here is extend that logic a little bit and provide a number that is one less than the current row number.

In order to work that out, you need the index number for each row in the data set. As you are going to be using this new step in future calculations, you should also rename it to avoid #" coding awkwardness:

- Go to Add Column → Add Index Column → From 0
- Right-click the Added Index step → Rename → Transactions

You are now set up and ready to build a formula that spans rows:

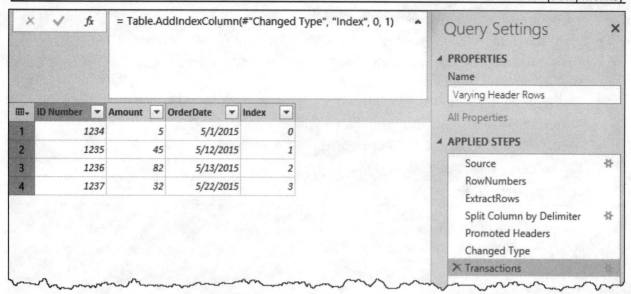

| ✕ ✓ *fx* | = Table.AddIndexColumn(#"Changed Type", "Index", 0, 1) |

⊞▾	ID Number ▾	Amount ▾	OrderDate ▾	Index ▾
1	1234	5	5/1/2015	0
2	1235	45	5/12/2015	1
3	1236	82	5/13/2015	2
4	1237	32	5/22/2015	3

Query Settings   ✕

▲ PROPERTIES
Name
Varying Header Rows
All Properties

▲ APPLIED STEPS
Source   ✳
RowNumbers
ExtractRows
Split Column by Delimiter   ✳
Promoted Headers
Changed Type
✕ Transactions   ✳

Figure 273 You have everything you need to build cross-row formulas.

Add a new column:

- Go to Add Column → Add Custom Column
- Name the Column PreviousOrder
- Enter the following formula:

```
=Transactions[OrderDate]{[Index]-1}
```

In this case, you are referring to the Transactions step, and you want a value from the OrderDate column. It's the next part that is the tricky piece. [Index] is inside the curly braces, and it isn't prefixed by a step name. This means it is still referring to the current step rather than previous step's value. In addition, since it was entered in the Add Custom Column dialog, it will be prefixed by the *each* keyword, operating on each row individually. You simply take the Index value for each row, subtract 1, and that will be the row you return from the Transactions step.

> The [Index] column is generated so that you can tell Power Query which row you want to retrieve from the target data set, but it is not necessary to have the Index column present in that target. You could just as easily use the formula =#"Changed Type" [OrderDate]{[Index]-1}, and it would work, despite the Changed Type step not containing an Index column.

Everything isn't perfect, however, as you'll see when you commit the formula:

⊞▾	ID Number ▾	Amount ▾	OrderDate ▾	Index ▾	PreviousOrder ▾
1	1234	5	5/1/2015	0	Error
2	1235	45	5/12/2015	1	5/1/2015
3	1236	82	5/13/2015	2	5/12/2015
4	1237	32	5/22/2015	3	5/13/2015

Figure 274 Ugh. An error.

The very first record returns an error, even though the rest of the records are working well. Why?

On this row, what is the Index value? It's 0. Subtract 1 from that, and you get -1. Which row would [Order-Date]{-1} return? Since you're working in a base 0 system, the first row is {0}, so you can't start at {-1}. This is the reason for the error.

So what should this value return? If there is no previous record, why not return the OrderDate instead? That way, when you do your calculation, you'll just have 0 days since the previous order.

To fix this, you need to use the try statement, as described in Chapter 18:

- Click the gear icon next to the Added Custom step

- Modify the formula to use the try statement as follows:

```
=try Transactions[OrderDate]{[Index]-1} otherwise [OrderDate]
```

The results make you much happier:

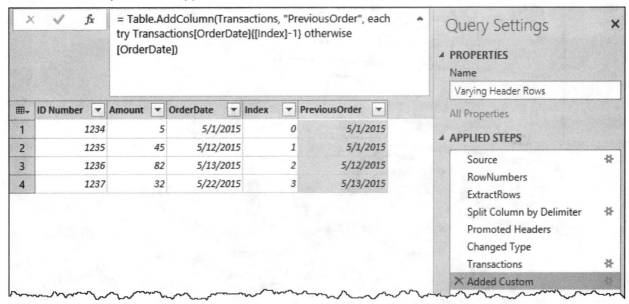

Figure 275 The PreviousOrder column returns the previous order date.

With those dates in place, you can now calculate the number of days between them:

- Select the Order Date column → hold down Ctrl → select the PreviousOrder column
- Go to Add Column → Date → Subtract Days

And you have it:

⊞▾	ID Number ▾	Amount ▾	OrderDate ▾	Index ▾	PreviousOrder ▾	DateDifference ▾
1	1234	5	5/1/2015	0	5/1/2015	0
2	1235	45	5/12/2015	1	5/1/2015	11
3	1236	82	5/13/2015	2	5/12/2015	1
4	1237	32	5/22/2015	3	5/13/2015	9

Figure 276 The date difference has been calculated.

The order in which you select columns here is important. If you select the PreviousOrder column first and then the OrderDate column, your difference will show up as negative.

At this point, the only thing left to do is the final cleanup:

- Right-click the Index column → Remove
- Right-click the PreviousOrder column → Change Type → Date
- Right-click the DateDifference column → Rename → DaysSinceLastOrder
- Go to Home → Close & Load

At this point, you can test the query by opening the Ch20 Examples\Varying Header Rows.txt file and making modifications to the file. Here's what you'll see when you play with the data:

- Rows added before the ID Number row or after the ID Total row will not show up when you refresh the query.
- Rows inserted between the ID Number and ID Total rows will show up, but you need to make sure you enter them in the format ID Number <tab> Amount <tab> Date <Enter>.

Chapter 21 Creating Custom Functions

If you think way back to Chapters 3 and 4, you might remember a couple of issues with the way that Excel pros have historically imported and appended data sets. This was the classic method to consolidate these files:

1. Import and transform file #1.
2. Import and transform file #2.
3. Copy file #2's data and paste it at the end of file #1.
4. Save file #1 as a consolidated file.

And then, as each new month came along, a similar import, clean, copy and paste workflow would follow.

This, of course, led to several dangers in both the transformation steps and the copy and paste. The more complicated the transformations required, the longer the process ran and the more the job turned over into new hands, the more likely something would go wrong. Steps would be missed or performed incorrectly, resulting in a compromised data set.

While you can solve many of these issues by creating append queries, and with enough foresight you can import all files in a folder, what happens in the following situations?

- You built a query with significant transformations against a single file. The boss liked it so much that it turned into the business intelligence system and now needs to be performed on each monthly file and appended.
- You attempted to import all files in a folder, but the files required transformation *before* being appended.

Either of these scenarios creates problems, but each can be solved by creating a custom function. These functions can be used to take an existing set of Power Query code, package it up, and allow it to be executed multiple times. In the case of the first scenario, you can reuse what you've already built and apply it consistently to each new file (reducing the human error factor). In the case of the latter, you can apply the process to each file, landing the result of each preprocessed set of data into a column of tables that can then be combined.

And the best part? It's actually not that difficult!

Building a Custom Function

In order to build a custom function, you basically follow a three-step process:

1. Build a single-use scenario first.
2. Convert the single-use scenario into a function.
3. Call the function from another query.

This sounds easy enough in practice. Let's take a look how to put it all together.

Rather than build a new use scenario, you will fall back on the scenario from Chapter 18 on conditional logic, where you imported the 2015-03-14.txt timesheet file. In that chapter you already built the code to perform the import you needed, targeted at a specific timesheet.

Not surprisingly, you'd now like to apply the same logic to a different file. Rather than just change the source, however, you'd also like to consolidate those files and any others that are later added to the directory. To do this, you can use a custom function.

Building a Single-Use Scenario

You already built the single-use scenario previously, and you can just load it to begin your work here. Open the Ch21 Examples\Custom Functions.xlsx file to get a copy of the routine that you built previously. This file contains code identical to what was built in Chapter 18, with one exception: The file path is pointed to a sub-folder called Source Files, which now contains three separate files (including the original 2015-03-14.txt file).

When you go to Edit Query, you get an error message because the Source step refers to a location that is different from where you have copied the sample files. To resolve this:

1. Click the Go to Error button at the top right of the yellow error message bar. Power Query shows the path that is currently being used.

2. Click the Edit Settings button, and in the dialog box that opens in the middle of your screen, click Browse.

3. Navigate to the folder where you have copied the source files, select 2015-03-14.txt and click OK, and then click OK again.

Remember that the query built loads the records from the text file, extracts the employees into a new column, and fills them down before removing helper column and extraneous rows:

Out	Reg Hrs	OT Hrs	Misc Hrs	Expenses	Employee
6:00:00 PM	8.5	0	0	0	John Thompson
6:00:00 PM	8	0	0	0	John Thompson
6:00:00 PM	8.5	0	0	0	John Thompson
6:00:00 PM	8.5	0	0	0	John Thompson
3:30:00 PM	6.5	0	0	0	John Thompson
6:00:00 PM	8.5	0	0	0	John Thompson
6:00:00 PM	8.5	0	0	0	John Thompson
6:00:00 PM	6	0	0	0	John Thompson
6:00:00 PM	8.5	0	0	0	John Thompson
6:00:00 PM	8.5	0	0	0	John Thompson
6:00:00 PM	9.5	0	0	0	Bob Johnson

PROPERTIES

Name

Timesheet

All Properties

APPLIED STEPS

Source

Changed Type

Removed Top Rows

First Row as Header

Added Custom

Added Custom1

Figure 277 The query to reformat the timesheet.

Converting the Query into a Function

Next, you need to convert the query into a function. This involves three steps:

1. Come up with a name for the variable that will hold the data you wish to replace.

2. Edit the query and place the following text at the beginning:

    ```
    (variable_name)=>
    ```

3. Scan your query for the data you wish to replace and overwrite it with the variable name.

It's a good idea to come up with a variable name that is somewhat descriptive of the data it will hold, as this helps self-document your M code. The goal here is to convert the single-use scenario into a function where you can dynamically update the file path, so you should use something similar to filepath to describe what it holds. (Ultimately, you get to choose the name. Just make sure it doesn't contain any spaces or special characters.)

> Windows File Explorer has a set of rules about which characters are allowed for file names and paths. Power Query uses slightly different rules, however. For example, if you set up a folder such as D:\!!Data Monkey, it can be read by Windows, but Power Query will choke on it, as Power Query will not allow a file path to start with the ! character.

Now that you've determined your variable name, edit the query to turn it into a function:

*   Edit the Timesheet Query → Home → Advanced Editor

*   Place your cursor right in front of the let statement

*   Type the following:

    ```
    (filepath)=>
    ```

*   Press Enter

Your code should now start like this:

```
(filepath)=>          ⬅
let
    Source = Csv.Document(File.Contents("D:\pqTraining\M is for Data Mo
    #"Changed Type" = Table.TransformColumnTypes(Source,{{"Column1", ty
    #"Removed Top Rows" = Table.Skip(#"Changed Type",4),
    #"First Row as Header" = Table.PromoteHeaders(#"Removed Top Rows"
```

Figure 278 The filepath variable is now in place.

At this point, you've already converted your query into a function. Because you haven't subbed the variable name into the code, however, the function won't actually change anything.

The next step is to scan the code, find the existing file path, and replace it (and any quotes that surround it) with the variable name:

- Locate the full file path in the line that starts with Source
- Select the file path, being careful to exclude the quotes on both ends
- Press Ctrl+C to copy the file path (for later use)
- Press the Delete key to clear it and remove the quotes on both ends of your selection
- Enter filepath as the variable name

Your code should now look like this:

```
(filepath)=>
let                                                      ⬅
    Source = Csv.Document(File.Contents(filepath),null,"#(tab)",null,1252),
    #"Changed Type" = Table.TransformColumnTypes(Source,{{"Column1", type text}, {"Column2", ty
    #"Removed Top Rows" = Table.Skip(#"Changed Type",4),
    #"First Row as Header" = Table.PromoteHeaders(#"Removed Top Rows"),
    #"Added Custom" = Table.AddColumn(#"First Row as Header", "Custom", each try Time.From([Out
    #"Added Custom1" = Table.AddColumn(#"Added Custom", "Employee", each if [Custom]=null then
    #"Filled Down" = Table.FillDown(#"Added Custom1",{"Employee"}),
    #"Removed Columns" = Table.RemoveColumns(#"Filled Down",{"Custom"}),
    #"Changed Type1" = Table.TransformColumnTypes(#"Removed Columns",{{"Work Date", type date}
    #"Removed Errors" = Table.RemoveRowsWithErrors(#"Changed Type1", {"Work Date"}),
    #"Changed Type2" = Table.TransformColumnTypes(#"Removed Errors",{{"Out", type time}, {"Reg
in
    #"Changed Type2"
```

Figure 279 The filepath variable subbed into the code in place of the full file path.

When you go to select the file path using the mouse, Power Query selects extra characters as well, including the parentheses. It's a better idea to click in front of the first quote, hold down the Shift key and arrow to the right to select the code you want to replace. Selecting text in this way doesn't automatically grab extra characters.

At this point you can click OK, and your query changes drastically:

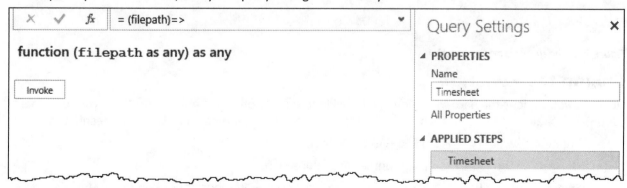

Figure 280 What happened to my query??

These changes are, unfortunately, entirely to be expected. While it's great that it is obviously now a function and not a query, and it plainly states the variable that needs to be input, you'll notice that you've lost all items in the Applied Steps box. Don't worry: They're still all there, but you just can't see them right now.

Testing the Function

It's a good idea to test that everything still works at this point. To do that:

- Click the Invoke button
- Press Ctrl+V to paste the file path you copied earlier

> If you included the quotes when you copied the file path earlier, you need to remove them from both ends of the pasted value, as Power Query can't read the path properly when it's surrounded by quotes.

When you click OK, the query loads the information from the file and runs it through all the steps that you originally wrote:

⊞▾	Work Date ▾	Out ▾	Reg Hrs ▾	OT Hrs ▾	Misc Hrs ▾	Expenses
1	3/3/2015	6:00:00 PM	8.5	0	0	
2	3/4/2015	6:00:00 PM	8	0	0	
3	3/5/2015	6:00:00 PM	8.5	0	0	
4	3/6/2015	6:00:00 PM	8.5	0	0	
5	3/7/2015	3:30:00 PM	6.5	0	0	
6	3/10/2015	6:00:00 PM	8.5	0	0	
7	3/11/2015	6:00:00 PM	8.5	0	0	
8	3/12/2015	6:00:00 PM	6	0	0	

◢ PROPERTIES
Name
Timesheet
All Properties
◢ APPLIED STEPS
    Timesheet
✕ Invoked FunctionTimesheet ⚙

Figure 281 The data loaded from a dynamic file path.

Notice also that you now have a new step in the Applied Steps box. This step shows that you invoked the function. While this is great for testing the function, it essentially breaks the function's ability to be called from anywhere else. Now that you've tested your function, you need to remove this step:

- Remove the Invoked FunctionTimesheet step
- Rename the query fnGetTimesheet
- Go to Home → Close & Load

Notice that the Timesheet table that resided in the Timesheet worksheet disappears. This is because, despite just clicking Close & Load, the query has been changed from a query to a function. Functions, by their very makeup, can only be created in a Connection Only format:

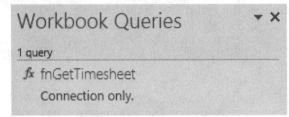

Workbook Queries ▾ ✕

1 query

fx fnGetTimesheet
Connection only.

Figure 282 The query is now a function.

Calling the Function

Now that you've done the hard work, you need to call this query from another function. Since your end goal is to consolidate all the timesheets in a folder, you can kick off a new query to import all the timesheets at once:

- Create a new query → From File → From Folder
- Navigate to the Ch21 Examples\Source Files folder → OK
- Select the Folder Path and Name columns → right-click → Remove Other Columns

Even though you've restricted the data to just the folder path and filename, you have everything you need to add a custom column and call the function. So do exactly that:

- Add Column → Add Custom Column
- Enter the following formula in the Add Custom Column dialog:

```
=fnGetTimesheet([Folder Path]&[Name])
```

- Click OK

The trick here is to remember the name of your function and get the case right. Once you've done that, it's as easy as filling it with the appropriate data. In this case, you simply concatenated the file path and file name together using the & character, just as you can do in an Excel formula. That gave you the full file path, which was then passed into the function. The function then executed all the steps contained in the function and returned a table to the column representing the processed data set for each file, as you can see here:

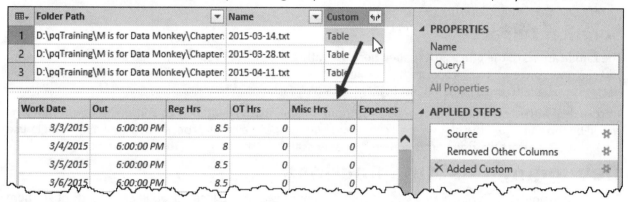

Figure 283 Previewing the new data import.

You can now remove the Folder Path and Name columns and import your data, thereby consolidating the files together:

- Remove the Folder Path and Name columns
- Click the Expand arrow on the Custom column → uncheck the prefix option → OK
- Rename the query Timesheets

There's one last thing to check before you commit this query: the data types. This is a bit of a shame, but even though the original query you built defined the data types, you'll find that none of those settings persisted when you turned it into a function and combined the files in this way:

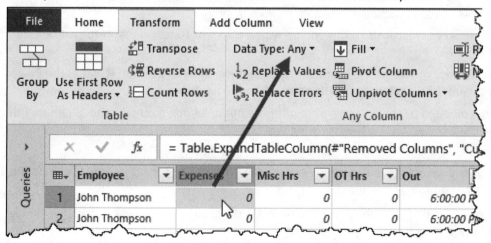

Figure 284 Beware the evil Any datatype!

To safeguard against poor interpretations by Excel or Power Pivot, it's a good idea to set those data types now. Set them as follows:

- Text: Employee
- Decimal Number: Expenses, Misc Hrs, OT Hrs, Reg Hrs
- Time: Out
- Date: Work Date

With that done, you can finally load the query:

- Home → Close & Load To...
- Select Existing Worksheet → Timesheet → A1

Solution Impact

The ramifications of the process described here are rather extensive. Even if you build a single-use scenario, you can now convert it to be consistently applied across multiple files. That is a huge benefit that was previously unavailable to Excel pros, at least in easy-to-deploy fashion.

You can deal with situations where your data footprint expands across multiple files and where transformations would be too complex if the files were all combined into one before being processed. By building a single-use case, you can perfect the transformation on a smaller scale and then append the end results.

Debugging Custom Functions

One of the painful pieces of working with custom functions is that you lose the ability to step through them easily. That makes debugging custom functions a bit of a challenge.

While it's not ideal, there is a way to convert a function back into a query so that you can test it. The unfortunate part of this process is that it is a temporary state because converting the function into a debuggable state converts it out of function mode, breaking any subsequent queries during the debugging process. However, it is the only way to accomplish the goal, so you'll learn about it next.

Restoring Query Steps to the Applied Steps Box

In order to restore the Applied Steps box so that you can debug a function, you actually need to turn it back into a query. To do this you need to do two things:

1. Comment out the line that turns the query into a function
2. Duplicate the variable used in the initial line and assign it a value

Failure to do either of these steps will cause you to end up with a query or function that returns the wrong results at best or errors at worst.

To comment out a line in M code, you insert the characters // at the beginning of the line. This tells the Power Query engine that the remaining characters on the line should not be executed.

To duplicate the variable, you need to set up a new step *after the initial let line* to create and assign a value to the variable. That line must be built using the following syntax:

```
Variable_name = assign_value_here ,
```

The variable name must be the variable that is currently enclosed in the opening parentheses for the function, and the line must end with a comma. Take a look:

- Edit the fnGetTimesheet query → Home → Advanced Editor

Wait . . . something is different than the last time you looked at this code:

```
let
    Timesheet = (filepath)=>
let
    Source = Csv.Document(File.Contents(filepath),nul
    #"Changed Type" = Table.TransformColumnTypes(Sour
    #"Removed Top Rows" = Table.Skip(#"Changed Type",
    #"First Row as Header" = Table.PromoteHeaders(#"Re
    #"Added Custom" = Table.AddColumn(#"First Row as H
    #"Added Custom1" = Table.AddColumn(#"Added Custom
    #"Filled Down" = Table.FillDown(#"Added Custom1",
    #"Removed Columns" = Table.RemoveColumns(#"Filled
    #"Changed Type1" = Table.TransformColumnTypes(#"Re
    #"Removed Errors" = Table.RemoveRowsWithErrors(#"C
    #"Changed Type2" = Table.TransformColumnTypes(#"Re
in
    #"Changed Type2"
in
    Timesheet
```

Figure 285 New lines of code injected into the solution.

Where did those new lines come from?

They were injected when you clicked the Invoke button. They're entirely unnecessary for the function to operate and can just be removed so that the function starts with (filepath) again.

Once you've removed those portions, modify the first three lines to read:

```
// (filepath)=>
let
    filepath = "C:\yourfilepath\Source Files\2015-03-14.txt",
```

Don't forget the final comma at the end of the line, or your code won't work!

When you're done, the code should look similar to this:

```
//(filepath)=>
let
    filepath = "D:\pqTraining\M is for Data Monkey\Chap
    Source = Csv.Document(File.Contents(filepath),null
    #"Changed Type" = Table.TransformColumnTypes(Source
    #"Removed Top Rows" = Table.Skip(#"Changed Type",4)
    #"First Row as Header" = Table.PromoteHeaders(#"Rem
    #"Added Custom" = Table.AddColumn(#"First Row as He
    #"Added Custom1" = Table.AddColumn(#"Added Custom"
    #"Filled Down" = Table.FillDown(#"Added Custom1",{
    #"Removed Columns" = Table.RemoveColumns(#"Filled
    #"Changed Type1" = Table.TransformColumnTypes(#"Rem
    #"Removed Errors" = Table.RemoveRowsWithErrors(#"Ch
    #"Changed Type2" = Table.TransformColumnTypes(#"Rem
in
    #"Changed Type2"
```

Figure 286 The modified code to convert this back into a query.

When you click OK, you can step through and verify what is happening in your query:

⊞▾	Work Date ▾	Out ▾	Reg Hrs ▾	OT Hrs ▾	Misc Hrs ▾	Expenses
1	3/3/2015	6:00:00 PM	8.5	0	0	
2	3/4/2015	6:00:00 PM	8	0	0	
3	3/5/2015	6:00:00 PM	8.5	0	0	
4	3/6/2015	6:00:00 PM	8.5	0	0	
5	3/7/2015	3:30:00 PM	6.5	0	0	
6	3/10/2015	6:00:00 PM	8.5	0	0	
7	3/11/2015	6:00:00 PM	8.5	0	0	
8	3/12/2015	6:00:00 PM	6	0	0	
9	3/13/2015	6:00:00 PM	8.5	0	0	
10	3/14/2015	6:00:00 PM	8.5	0	0	

PROPERTIES

Name

fnGetTimesheet

All Properties

APPLIED STEPS

filepath
Source
Changed Type
Removed Top Rows   ✿
First Row as Header

Figure 287 The steps are back.

The nice thing here is that you can even click the filepath step to see the path you set, and then you can review each step to see how it is reacting. If you find errors in the way your data is handled, you can correct them and then turn your query back into a function again.

> While your function is in debug mode, any subsequent queries that refer to it will not function!

Restoring "Function"ality

To turn the query back into a function, you again need to edit the M code to do two things:

- Remove the // characters from the initial row
- Place the // characters in front of the row that is currently declaring the filepath variable

Once these things are done, your function will resume its normal operation method, and all queries using this function will be able to use it again.

> Forgetting to comment out the temporary variable line will result in that line overwriting any variable passed into the function. You don't want to forget to comment that line!

Chapter 22 Advanced Conditional Logic

Chapter 22 Advanced Conditional Logic

In Chapter 18, you learned how to replicate the functionality of Excel's IF() and IFERROR() functions. Of course, the IF() and IFERROR() functions are not the only functions in Excel that you use to implement conditional outputs or matches.

Unlike the formulas examined previously, replicating other formulas in Excel's conditional logic library involves a bit more complicated techniques, including using lists and custom functions.

Multicolumn Logic

Occasionally, as you are trying to filter down raw data, you may need to filter based on multiple criteria. Consider the following data set, which is included in the Ch22 Examples\Multi-Column Logic.xlsx file:

Date	Day	Inventory Item	Sold By	Cost	Price	Commission
5/10/2014	Sat	Lovable Kitten	Fred	12.00	45.00	1.35
5/9/2014	Fri	Talkative Parrot	John	17.00	32.00	0.96
5/24/2014	Sat	Lovable Kitten	Jane	12.00	45.00	1.35
5/20/2014	Tue	Adorable Kitty Cat	John	25.00	35.00	1.05
5/8/2014	Thu	Lovable Kitten	Jane	12.00	45.00	1.35
5/23/2014	Fri	Sleepy Gerbil	Jane	25.00	39.00	1.17
5/11/2014	Sun	Cranky Crocodile	John	10.00	35.00	1.05
5/19/2014	Mon	Adorable Kitty Cat	Mary	25.00	35.00	1.05
5/5/2014		Sleepy Gerbil		25.00	39.00	1.17

Figure 288 A raw data set.

Replicating Excel's OR() Function

What if your boss asked you to list only data where you sold a Talkative Parrot *or* the item was sold by Fred? If this were an *and* scenario, it would be easy: Just filter the Inventory Item column to Talkative Parrot and then filter the Sold By column to Fred. But that won't work in this case because you'd lose any Talkative Parrots sold by John or Jane, and you'd also lose any other items sold by Fred.

If the data is stored in an Excel table, you could solve this by using Advanced Filter or by adding a column using the following formula and filtering to only results that are listed as true:

```
=OR([@[Inventory Item]]="Talkative Parrot",[@[Sold By]]="Fred")
```

But what if the data doesn't originate in an Excel table? What if it is sourced from a database, a web page, or a text file? Plainly, that won't work.

Pull the data into Power Query to see how you should approach this:

- Select any cell in the table on the May worksheet
- Create a new query → From Table
- Right-click the Date column → Change Type → Date

Since you can't filter your data without losing required records, you're going to need to add a custom column and apply a formula to examine each row:

- Go to Add Column → Add Custom Column
- Name the column Match?

You know that you're going to need to test whether a certain criterion is true or false, using a basic formula framework along the lines of the following:

```
= if logic_test then "Meets Criteria!" else "No Match"
```

The challenge here is coming up with that logic test. Power Query doesn't have an OR() function, so what is the equivalent?

When you're looking for text comparisons, it is helpful to quickly scan the list of list functions contained in the Power Query formula categories.

Remember that you can access the list of Power Query formulas by clicking the Learn About Power Query formulas link at the bottom of the Custom Column dialog and then clicking the Power Query formula categories link partway down the page. You end up at the https://msdn.microsoft.com/en-us/library/mt296612.aspx web page.

Within the list functions, you'll find that there is a List.AnyTrue function, which sounds somewhat promising. Selecting that item in the documentation reveals the following example:

```
List.AnyTrue({2=0, false, 1 < 0 }) equals false
```

Based on this, you can see that the function contains a list of values, as indicated by the curly braces within the parentheses. It also shows that the function will return false if none of the items are true.

Try to nest this formula in place of the logic test:

```
=if List.AnyTrue(
{[Inventory Item]="Talkative Parrot",[Sold By]="Fred"}
)
then "Meets Criteria!"
else "No Match"
```

Remember that you need to separate the criteria with commas and then surround the entire list of criteria with curly braces because the List.AnyTrue() function requires a list as a parameter.

Upon clicking OK, you can see that the formula returns your message in any case where the sales item equals Talkative Parrot *or* the Sold By field holds Fred:

Inventory Item	Sold By	Cost	Price	Commiss...	Match?
Lovable Kitten	Fred	~~12~~	~~45~~	~~1.35~~	Meets Criteria!
Talkative Parrot	John	~~17~~	~~82~~	~~2.46~~	Meets Criteria!
Lovable Kitten	Jane	12	45	1.35	No Match
Adorable Kitty Cat	John	25	35	1.05	No Match
Lovable Kitten	Jane	12	45	1.35	No Match
Sleepy Gerbil	Jane	25	39	1.17	No Match
Cranky Crocodile	John	10	35	1.05	No Match
Adorable Kitty Cat	Mary	25	35	1.05	No Match
Sleepy Gerbil	Jane	25	39	1.17	No Match
Slithering Snake	Fred	~~12~~	~~30~~	~~9~~	Meets Criteria!
Sleepy Gerbil	Mary	25	39	1.17	No Match
Hilarious...	...	31	45	1.3	...

Figure 289 Replicating Excel's OR() function using List.AnyTrue().

Since the function returns true if any of the criteria are true, any instances where Fred sold a Talkative Parrot would also display the result *Meets Criteria!* in the Match? column.

You can now finalize this query by taking the following steps:

- Filter the Match? column to only include only *Meets Criteria!* values
- Change the query name to pqOR
- Go to Home → Close and Load

Power Query returns a table containing a total of 88 rows out of the original 332.

Replicating Excel's AND() Function

While it's true that you can reduce records by filtering a table column-by-column, what if you only want to tag records where a condition exists in multiple columns? For this you need to replicate Excel's AND() function.

The trick to this is essentially the same as the trick with replicating the OR() function with List.AnyTrue(), except that for AND() you need to use the List.AllTrue() function. This function returns a true value only if *every* logical test provided returns a true value—just like Excel's AND() function.

Take a look at how it differs from the previous function:

- Go to the Workbook Queries pane → right-click pqOR → Duplicate
- Rename the query name pqAND
- Select the Added Custom step → click the gear icon (to edit the formula)
- Replace List.AnyTrue with List.AllTrue
- Select the Filtered Rows step

As you can see, the results are quite different than the results you get by using the original List.AnyTrue() function:

Inventory Item	Sold By	Cost	Price	Commission	Match?
Talkative Parrot	Fred	17	32	0.96	Meets Criteria!
Talkative Parrot	Fred	17	32	0.96	Meets Criteria!
Talkative Parrot	Fred	17	32	0.96	Meets Criteria!
Talkative Parrot	Fred	17	32	0.96	Meets Criteria!
Talkative Parrot	Fred	17	32	0.96	Meets Criteria!
Talkative Parrot	Fred	17	32	0.96	Meets Criteria!

Figure 290 Using the List.AllTrue() function to tag records based on multiple-column criteria.

While this example obviously filtered the data based on the results from the formula output, the great thing about this function is that you can easily tag records *without* filtering first. This allows you more flexibility in building more complicated logic while still preserving your original data—something that can't be done if you filter columns to drill into the end values.

Replicating Excel's VLOOKUP() Function

As much as some people try to avoid VLOOKUP(), it is an incredibly useful function for Excel pros. Those who love it will certainly want to replicate its functionality in Power Query at some point. However, depending on which version of VLOOKUP() you need, it can be quite tricky to implement.

VLOOKUP() Using an Exact Match

In truth, you don't need to do anything special to emulate VLOOKUP's exact match, as this functionality can be replicated by simply merging two tables together, as described in Chapter 9.

VLOOKUP() Using an Approximate Match

Replicating VLOOKUP()'s approximate match is a totally different case than the exact match scenario. It requires some logic to emulate those steps because you're not trying to match records against each other but actually trying to find the closest record to our request without going over. While you won't create the function from scratch here, you will see the function and how it works.

To get started, open Ch22 Examples\Emulating VLOOKUP.xlsx. In this file you'll find two tables: BandingLevels and DataTable.

	F	G	H
1	**Banding Levels Table**		
2	Revenue	Band 1	Alt Band
3	1	0-100k	< 100 k
4	100,000	100k-200k	100k > 200k
5	200,000	200-300k	200k > 300k
6	300,000	300 – 500k	300k > 500k
7	500,000	500 – 750k	500k > 750k
8	750,000	750 – 1M	750k > 1M
9	1,000,000	1 – 1,5M	1M > 1.5M
10	1,500,000	1,5 – 2M	1.5M > 2M
11	2,000,000	2 – 3 M	2M > 3M
12	3,000,000	> 3M	> 3M

Figure 291 The BandingLevels table.

	A	B	C	D
1	**VLOOKUP the Excel Way**			
2	Values	VLOOKUP(v,rng,2,true)	VLOOKUP(v,rng,3)	VLOOKUP(v,rng,2,false)
3	99,000	0-100k	< 100 k	#N/A
4	110,000	100k-200k	100k > 200k	#N/A
5	220,000	200-300k	200k > 300k	#N/A
6	300,010	300 – 500k	300k > 500k	#N/A
7	505,000	500 – 750k	500k > 750k	#N/A
8	3,000,050	> 3M	> 3M	#N/A
9	-	#N/A	#N/A	#N/A
10	100,000	100k-200k	100k > 200k	100k-200k

Figure 292 The DataTable table.

If you review the functions in columns B:D of the DataTable table, you'll see that they contain VLOOKUP() functions, as shown in the column headers. Each column is looking up the value shown in column A for that row against the BandingLevels table. Columns B and D are returning the value from column 2 of the BandingLevels table, and column C is returning the value from the Alt Band column of the BandingLevels table.

In addition, notice that columns B and C are returning approximate matches because the fourth parameter has either been set to True or omitted. Column D, however, is asking for an exact match (as the fourth parameter has been set to False), resulting in all records returning #N/A except for the very last one.

You should set up the Power Query function we need now, and then you'll see how it replicates Excel's version of VLOOKUP():

- Using Windows Explorer go to Ch22 Examples\pqVLOOKUP.txt
- Open the file and copy the entire contents of the file
- Return to Excel
- Create a new query → From Other Sources → Blank Query
- Open the Advanced Editor → select all the code in the window
- Paste the contents of the text file (replacing all of the existing code)
- Click Done
- Rename the function pqVLOOKUP
- Go to Home → Close & Load

With the function created, you need a pointer to the BandingLevels table:

- Select any cell in the BandingLevels table → create a new query → From Table
- Go to Home → Close & Load To… → Only Create Connection

We are now ready to see how it works. Pull in the DataTable, and remove all of the Excel versions of the functions.

- Select any cell in the DataTable table → create a new query → From Table
- Right-click the Values column → Remove Other Columns

You are now down to a single column of data:

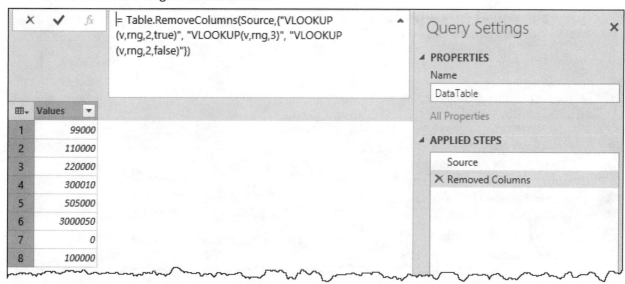

Figure 293 Ready to try the pqVLOOKUP function.

To see if the pqVLOOKUP function works for you, you can try to replicate the following formula:

```
=VLOOKUP([Values],BandingLevels,2,true)
```

To do that, you can take the following steps:

- Go to Add Column → Add Custom Column
- Name the column 2,True
- Use the following formula:

```
=pqVLOOKUP([Values],BandingLevels,2,true)
```

The results are identical to what Excel would show:

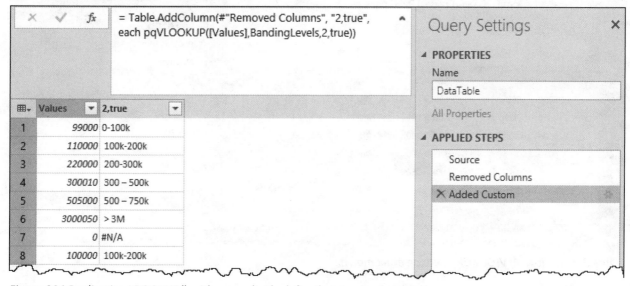

Figure 294 Replicating VLOOKUP() with an explicitly defined approximate match.

This looks good. Now try leaving the ,*true* off the end and returning the third column from the lookup table instead of the second:

- Go to Add Column → Add Custom Column
- Name the column 3,default
- Use the following formula:

    =pqVLOOKUP([Values],BandingLevels,3)

The results are again identical to what Excel would show:

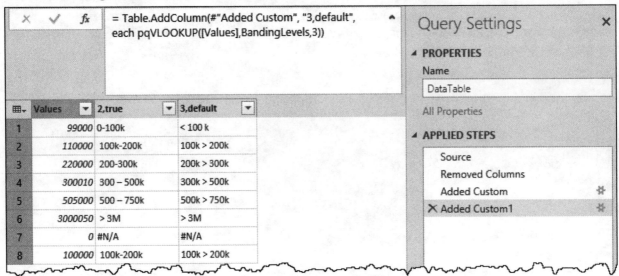

Figure 295 Replicating VLOOKUP() with an implicit approximate match.

Try one more. What if you wanted to define an exact match against the second column of the lookup table? To do this:

- Go to Add Column → Add Custom Column
- Name the column 2,false
- Use the following formula:

    =pqVLOOKUP([Values],BandingLevels,2,false)

Once again, the results are spot on with what Excel delivers:

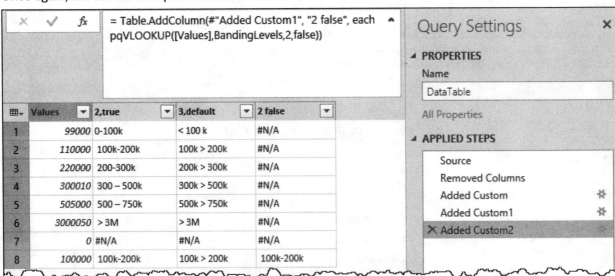

Figure 296 Replicating VLOOKUP() with an exact match.

Even though you can use this function to emulate VLOOKUP()'s exact match, you shouldn't. The reason is that you can accomplish an exact match effect by merging tables together—a method that will be much faster. If you need the approximate match functionality, however, this is a viable method.

Finalize the query:

- Go to Home → Close & Load

At this point, you should be aware of one minor difference between Excel's VLOOKUP() and the pqVLOOKUP function: the #N/A value returned by pqVLOOKUP is actually text, not a true error, as you can see below.

◢	A	B	C	D
1	**VLOOKUP the Excel Way**			
2	Values ▼	VLOOKUP(v,rng,2,true) ▼	VLOOKUP(v,rng,3) ▼	VLOOKUP(v,rng,2,false) ▼
3	99,000	0-100k	< 100 k	#N/A
4	110,000	100k-200k	100k > 200k	#N/A
5	220,000	200-300k	200k > 300k	#N/A
6	300,010	300 − 500k	300k > 500k	#N/A
7	505,000	500 − 750k	500k > 750k	#N/A
8	3,000,050	> 3M	> 3M	#N/A
9	-	#N/A	#N/A	#N/A
10	100,000	100k-200k	100k > 200k	100k-200k
11				
12	**Emulating VLOOKUP in Power Query**			
13	Values ▼	2,true ▼	3,default ▼	2 false ▼
14	99,000	0-100k	< 100 k	#N/A
15	110,000	100k-200k	100k > 200k	#N/A
16	220,000	200-300k	200k > 300k	#N/A
17	300,010	300 − 500k	300k > 500k	#N/A
18	505,000	500 − 750k	500k > 750k	#N/A
19	3,000,050	> 3M	> 3M	#N/A
20	-	#N/A	#N/A	#N/A
21	100,000	100k-200k	100k > 200k	100k-200k
22				

Figure 297 pqVLOOKUP's #N/A "errors" are actually text.

Returning text is as close as you could get when returning error, as there is no way to output a true #N/A error in Power Query.

Understanding the pqVLOOKUP Function

So how does the pqVLOOKUP function work? Take a look at the code:

```
(lookup_value as any, table_array as table, col_index_number as number,
optional approximate_match as logical ) as any =>
  let
      /*Provide optional match if user didn't */
      matchtype =
      if approximate_match = null
      then true
      else approximate_match,

      /*Get name of return column */
      Cols = Table.ColumnNames(table_array),
      ColTable = Table.FromList(Cols, Splitter.SplitByNothing(), null,
          null, ExtraValues.Error),
      ColName_match = Record.Field(ColTable{0},"Column1"),
      ColName_return = Record.Field(ColTable{col_index_number - 1},
          "Column1"),

      /*Find closest match */
      SortData = Table.Sort(table_array,
          {{ColName_match, Order.Descending}}),
      RenameLookupCol =
          Table.RenameColumns(SortData,{{ColName_match, "Lookup"}}),
      RemoveExcess = Table.SelectRows(
          RenameLookupCol, each [Lookup] <= lookup_value),
      ClosestMatch=
          if Table.IsEmpty(RemoveExcess)=true
          then "#N/A"
          else Record.Field(RemoveExcess{0},"Lookup"),

      /*What should be returned in case of approximate match? */
      ClosestReturn=
          if Table.IsEmpty(RemoveExcess)=true
          then "#N/A"
          else Record.Field(RemoveExcess{0},ColName_return),

      /*Modify result if we need an exact match */
      Return =
          if matchtype=true
          then ClosestReturn
          else
              if lookup_value = ClosestMatch
              then ClosestReturn
              else "#N/A"
  in Return
```

The code is fairly long and complex, and it uses a variety of tricks, but the basic methodology is this:

1. Pull in the data table.
2. Sort it descending by the first column.
3. Remove all records greater than the value being searched for.
4. Return the value in the requested column for the first remaining record *unless* an exact match was specified.

5. If an exact match was specified, test to see if the return is a match. If it is, return the value. If it is not, return #N/A.

Note the following in the code:

- Each of the variables in the parameters has an explicit data type declared. This is to prevent the user from accidentally providing a table where a numeric column number is required.

- The *approximate_match* variable is defined as optional, meaning the user can ignore it.

- The *matchtype* variable tests to see if a match type was specified. If a match type was specified, it is assigned to the *matchtype* variable, but if not (*approximate_match* is null), a value of *true* will be assigned.

- The name of the column to be returned is pulled by reviewing the column headers of the table, splitting them into a list of records, and pulling out the record whose index matches the requested column (less 1 to adjust to base 0).

- The data is sorted in descending order, based on the column to be searched. All records greater than the requested value are removed (by selecting all rows where the value is less than or equal to the value being searched for).

- If no rows remain, a #N/A result is then stored, but if there are rows, the first record in the lookup column is stored. This result can later be checked to see if it matches the record being searched for (which is important for the exact match scenario).

- The approximate match value is then (*always*) calculated, even if an exact match was requested. If no rows are present in the data set, a #N/A result is stored; otherwise, the closest value is pulled from the return column.

- The final test checks the type of match requested. If it is an approximate match, then the closest match is always returned (which may be #N/A). If, however, the match type was an exact match, the code will return #N/A instead of the closest match *unless* the lookup column's value matched the value being sought exactly.

It should go without saying that this is not a function you'll knock out in a few minutes. It is long and complicated, and it took several hours of development and debugging in order to get it correct. It is, however, a fairly robust function in the way it works, and it showcases how to build complex functions using Power Query.

Replicating Power Pivot's SWITCH() Function

Power Pivot has a function called SWITCH() that allows you to perform multi-condition logic by declaring a table of index values and results and then passing in a variable index value. The function then looks up the provided index value and returns the matching result. This is easier to maintain than several levels of nested IF() statements, so it sometimes makes sense to replicate the SWITCH() function in Power Query.

The syntax for this function in Power Pivot is as follows:

```
=SWITCH(expression,value_1,result_1,[value_2,result_2],…,[Else])
```

One example of where this can be really useful is when breaking down encoded patterns like customer billing codes, where each character represents something specific. Take a code like the MP010450SP, where the ninth character could be one of the following:

```
E = Employee, S = Yacht Club, N = Non-Taxable, R = Restricted,
I = Inactive, L = Social, M = Medical, U = Regular
```

To break this apart in Excel, you could build a function with many nested IF statements and build a VLOOKUP() based on the letter options. In Power Pivot, though, it's much easier with the SWITCH() function, as follows:

```
=SWITCH([Column],"E","Employee","S","Yacht Club",
"N","Non-Taxable","R","Restricted","I","Inactive",
"L","Social","M","Medical","U","Regular","Undefined")
```

There are several ways to accomplish this goal. You could, for example, extract just the ninth letter and merge the results against a table. The purpose of this section is to give you yet another alternative.

Building a Power Query SWITCH() Function

Building the function isn't overly difficult once you know the basic structure. Here's how you get started:

- Open Ch22 Examples\Emulating SWITCH.xlsx
- Create a new query → From Other Sources → Blank Query
- Name the query fnSWITCH
- Go to Home → Advanced Editor
- Enter the M code shown below:

```
(input) =>
let
    values = {
        {result_1, return_value_1},
        {input, "Undefined"}
    },
    Result = List.First(List.Select(values, each _{0}=input)){1}
in
    Result
```

This code is the basic framework for any SWITCH() function. These are the key parts to recognize here:

- *result_1* is the first of the possibilities that you may pass *to* the function
- *return_value_1* is the value that you'd like to return if the first value is *result_1*
- If you need more values, you just insert another comma after the *{result_1, return_value_1}* section and put in a *{result_2, return_value_2}* section
- You can keep adding as many values as you need
- The input value in the list will return the text *Undefined* if the value you pass isn't in your provided list of options (it's the Else portion of the SWITCH() statement)

Using this structure, you can modify the fnSWITCH function for your scenario as follows:

```
(input) =>
  let
  values = {
     {"E", "Employee"},
     {"S", "SCYC"},
     {"N", "Non-Taxable"},
     {"R", "Restricted"},
     {"I", "Inactive"},
     {"L", "Social"},
     {"M", "Medical"},
     {"U", "Regular"},
     {input, "Undefined"}
     },
  Result = List.First(List.Select(values, each _{0}=input)){1}
  in
     Result
```

The changes you made here were simply to replace *value_1* with *"E"* and *return_value_1* with *"Employee"* and then to add more list pairs of potential inputs and desired values to return. Note that you're not restricted to looking up single characters. You can look up values or longer text strings just as easily; just make sure that your options are always entered in pairs between curly braces and have a comma at the end of the line.

When you're done making the modifications:

- Click Done
- Go to Home –> Close & Load

Using the fnSWITCH Function

Now that the fnSWITCH() function has been created, you can use it to extract the billing type from each customer record in this file.

- Select any cell in the table on the Customers worksheet → create a new query → From Table

The data loads into Power Query as follows:

⊞▾	CustomerCode ▾	Boat Type	BillingCode ▾
1	65121	Grand Banks/Power	MP010450UP
2	65124	Samson/Sail	MA120435UP
3	65125	US 25 (sail)	MA120430SP
4	65126	Sail	MP010325UP
5	65131	Sail	MA120330SP
6	65133	King Fisher-Pwr	MP010440SP
7	65146	ranger 255C-Pwr	MA120330UP
8	65159	Sail	MA120350SP
9	66108	O'Day/Sail	MA120440SP

Figure 298 The raw data table.

The fnSWITCH() function is designed to convert the ninth character from the BillingCode into the corresponding customer type. In order to use it, you need to extract that character:

- Go to Add Column → Add Custom Column
- Name the column Customer Type
- Enter the following formula:

```
=fnSWITCH(Text.Range([BillingCode],8,1))
```

> Remember that you need to start at character 8 in order to get the ninth character because Power Query uses base 0 indexing for this parameter of the Text.Range function, as shown in Chapter 17.

The results are perfect:

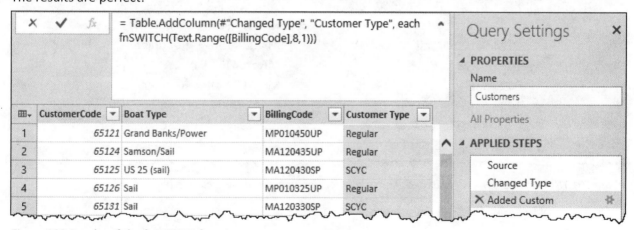

Figure 299 Results of the fnSWITCH function.

You'll find that all the sample codes in the data work just fine and that nothing comes back as undefined. Follow these steps to see how the query reacts to different items:

- Change the query name to Billing
- Go to Home → Close & Load
- Change the second-to-last letter of any billing code to something else

When you refresh the table, it evaluates the new character and returns the appropriate result. Here you can see what happens when the first record's billing code is updated to MP010450**X**P:

▲	A	B	C	D	E
1	CustomerCode ▼	Boat Type ▼	BillingCode ▼	Customer Type ▼	
2	65121	Grand Banks/Power	MP010450XP ➔	Undefined	
3	65124	Samson/Sail	MA120435UP	Regular	
4	65125	US 25 (sail)	MA120430SP	SCYC	
5	65126	Sail	MP010325UP	Regular	
6	65131	Sail	MA120330SP	SCYC	
7	65133	King Fisher-Pwr	MP010440SP	SCYC	
8	65146	ranger 255C-Pwr	MA120330UP	Regular	

Figure 300 X is not a valid character for the billing code.

Note that the function as written above is case sensitive, meaning that the code MP010450**u**P would also return Undefined, even though MP010450UP is a valid code. In the case of the original source of the data, this was entirely expected because valid codes are made up of uppercase letters.

If you wanted to accept either uppercase or lowercase, you would need to modify the Billing query (not the function) and force the results of the Text.Range function to uppercase:

- Right-click the Billing query in the Workboook Queries pane → Edit
- Select the Added Custom step → click the gear icon
- Update the formula to read:

```
=fnSWITCH(Text.Upper(Text.Range([BillingCode],8,1)))
```

- Click OK
- Go to Home → Close & Load

As you can see below, this adjustment allows you to pass lowercase values into the function and still get a positive result:

▲	A	B	C	D	
1	CustomerCode ▼	Boat Type ▼	BillingCode ▼	Customer Type ▼	
2	65121	Grand Banks/Power	MP010450uP	Regular	
3	65124	Samson/Sail	MA120435UP	Regular	
4	65125	US 25 (sail)	MA120430SP	SCYC	
5	65126	Sail	MP010325UP	Regular	
6	65131	Sail	MA120330SP	SCYC	
7	65133	King Fisher-Pwr	MP010440SP	SCYC	
8	65146	ranger 255C-Pwr	MA120330UP	Regular	

Figure 301 The customer type is calculated consistently for uppercase and lowercase letters.

Chapter 23 Dynamic Parameter Tables

In Chapter 21 we explored how custom functions can be used to preprocess data sets prior to merging. While this is a fantastic benefit of custom functions, it is far from the only one.

Consider the example in the last chapter, of pulling timesheets from a folder. Say that you've built the master consolidation file, saved it in H:\Payroll, and for months have been storing the timesheets in the subfolder H:\Payroll\Timesheets. After working hard all year, you finally get a few weeks off and have to pass the solution to someone else to maintain while you're gone. There's a problem, though: Their system has the path to your solution mapped as J:\HR\Payroll. Rather than recode the solution for your replacement and then have to recode it again when you return, you'd really like to make the path relative to where the workbook is located. That way, if the user opens it up from J:\HR\Payroll or H:\Payroll or something else, it shouldn't make a difference.

The real challenge? There is currently no function in the M language that allows you to work out the path to the workbook you're using. Interestingly, an Excel formula can do this work.

Before we embark on the journey of making the file path dynamic, there is something you should know about this technique: Queries where data access happens inside a function and where the data source is dependent on parameters to the function can't currently be refreshed in Power BI. This is because Microsoft performs static analysis of the query to discover the data source, and the static analysis can't yet handle this scenario.

This does not mean that the functionality is not useful, and it doesn't mean that it won't be supported one day. It simply means that you should rely on it only if the solution is going to live in Desktop Excel and not on the web.

Implementing Dynamic Parameter Tables

There are three steps to implementing parameter tables into your solution:

1. Create a parameter table in Excel.
2. Create the function to extract the values from the table.
3. Retrofit your existing queries to call the function.

We will walk through each step of this process using the Ch 23 Examples\Parameter Tables.xlsx file.

Upon opening this file, you'll recognize that it is a continuation of the Timesheets file that you've built over a couple of chapters. The challenge with this file is that currently the paths are all hard coded to your PC, (the author's in the case of the example file,) and now you'd like to deliver the solution so that it works no matter where you store it.

Step 1: Creating a Parameter Table

The first thing you need to do is create a table to hold your parameters. This table should take a specific form, and it needs to have certain components set up correctly.

Create the table shown below in cell A7:B8 of the Info worksheet:

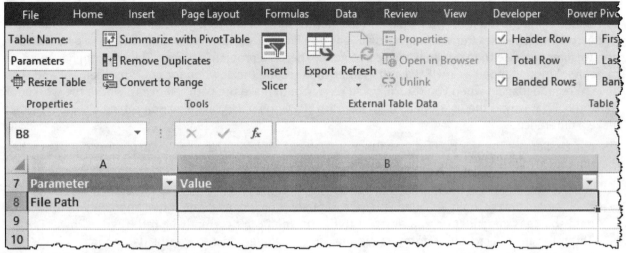

Figure 302 The barebones Parameters table.

Notice several key characteristics of this table:

- The first column's header is: Parameter
- The second column's header is: Value
- The table has a name of: Parameters

Each of these characteristics must be correct if you want to copy and paste a function you've been provided in the download files. If even one of these items is spelled differently, you will need to debug the table or the function.

The table is now set up to hold every piece of data that you want to use as a dynamic variable in your solution. Simply provide the name of the parameter on the left and the value for the parameter in the Values column.

The items in the Values column can be hard coded text or values, they can be driven by data validation lists, or they can use formulas. How you get the correct value in the cell is completely up to you as the solution designer.

Next, you need to determine the file path to the current workbook. Enter the formula below into cell B8:

```
=LEFT(CELL("filename",A1),FIND("[",CELL("filename",A1),1)-1)
```

If you haven't saved your file, this function won't return the path as it can't determine where the workbook lives. Saving the file will fix this issue for you.

Upon doing so, you should see the file path to the workbook listed. The only challenge is that you actually want this file path to point to the Source Files folder, which is where the timesheets are stored. Update the formula as below:

```
=LEFT(CELL("filename",A1),FIND("[",CELL("filename",A1),1)-1)&"Source
Files\"
```

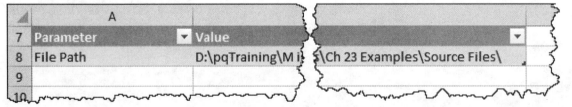

Figure 303 Dynamically returning the file path using an Excel formula.

Step 2: Implementing the fnGetParameter Function

With the parameter table now in a state that can hold any variable you need, you need to give Power Query a method to read those values. This portion can be done by using the following custom function:

```
(ParameterName as text) =>
let
    ParamSource = Excel.CurrentWorkbook()
        {[Name="Parameters"]}[Content],
    ParamRow = Table.SelectRows(ParamSource,
        each ([Parameter]=ParameterName)),
    Value=
        if Table.IsEmpty(ParamRow)=true
        then null
        else  Record.Field(ParamRow{0},"Value")
in
    Value
```

 This function is contained in the fnGetParameter.txt file in the Ch23 Examples folder. In addition to the code, it also contains instructions to use the function, as well as the formula to return the file path from a cell. The file is provided to give you a template you can store and use multiple times.

This code connects to the Parameters table in the workbook and then selects the row of the table where the dynamic parameter's value matches the record in the Parameter column of the Excel table. With that match in place, it then returns what it finds in the Value column. It is because each of these names is hard coded in the function that both the table and column names for the Excel table match what was specified above.

Rather than retype this entire block of code, open the Ch23 Examples\fnGetParameter.txt file and copy all lines inside the file. With those in the paste buffer, it will be deadly simple to implement this function into your solution:

- Create a new query → From Other Sources → From Blank Query
- Go to Home → Advanced Editor
- Highlight all rows of code in the window
- Press Ctrl+V to paste in the content of the text file
- Click Done
- Change the function's name to fnGetParameter

And you're done.

Step 3: Calling the fnGetParameter Function

With the parameter table built, and the function in place, the last step is to retrofit the existing query to actually use it. Doing so will allow you to source the file path from the cell and use that in your query. Because the file path updates when the workbook is recalculated, it will always be accurate, which means the solution will always look for the timesheet files in the subdirectory of where the solution resides.

To retrofit the Timesheets query, you don't even have to leave the Power Query editor. You can just click the little arrow on the left next to the word Queries to expand the Navigator window:

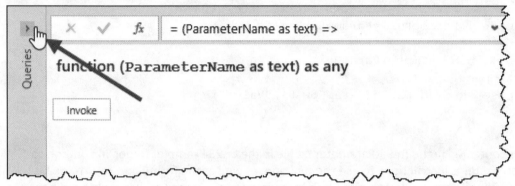

Figure 304 Expanding the Navigator window.

The Navigator allows you to select any of your queries or functions, so you can very quickly flip back and forth, making changes and testing the effects that they have on other queries. Here's what you do now:

- Right-click the Timesheets query → Advanced Editor
- Insert the following line of code immediately after the let line:

```
fullfilepath = fnGetParameter("File Path"),
```

The query should now look like this:

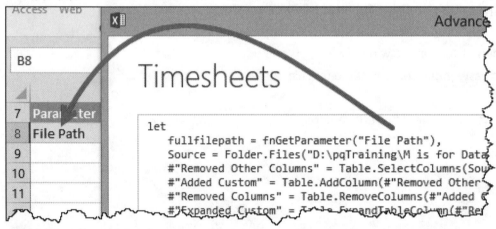

Figure 305 Calling the fnGetParameter function.

You have created a new variable called *fullfilepath* to hold the value from the File Path row of the Excel table.

It is also worth noting here that you are not strictly required to create a new variable in order to use our function. You *could* skip this step and just nest the fnGetParameter call in place of the file path on the next row. By adding this call on a separate line, however, you make the query much easier to debug, as you'll see now:

- Click Done
- Select the fullfilepath step in the Applied Steps box

The full file path to the folder is displayed nicely in the editor, giving you the comfort that you have that part correct:

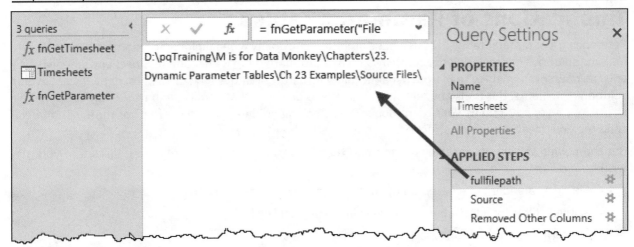

Figure 306 The fullfilepath variable is correctly pulling the file path.

Now that you know that the function is returning the correct path via the Excel formula, you can slipstream the variable in place of the hard-coded file path in the Source step:

- Go to Home → Advanced Editor
- Locate the file path in the Source line
- Select the entire file path (including the quotes) and replace it with *fullfilepath*

The first three lines of the query should now read as follows:

```
let
    fullfilepath = fnGetParameter("File Path"),
    Source = Folder.Files(fullfilepath),
```

You must edit the M code manually to make this work. It can't be accomplished by clicking the gear icon next to the Source step, as fullfilepath is not a valid folder to the Windows operating system.

When you've made the modifications, you can click Done, and you'll see that every step of the query still functions correctly.

	Employee	Expenses	Misc Hrs	OT Hrs	Out
1	John Thompson	0	0	0	6:(
2	John Thompson	0	0	0	6:(
3	John Thompson	0	0	0	6:(
4	John Thompson	0	0	0	6:(
5	John Thompson	0	0	0	3::
6	John Thompson	0	0	0	6:(
7	John Thompson	0	0	0	6:(
8	John Thompson	0	0	0	6:(
9	John Thompson	0	0	0	6:(
10	John Thompson	0	0	0	6:(
11	Bob Johnson	0	0	0	6:(
12	Bob Johnson	0	0	0	6:(

PROPERTIES

Name

Timesheets

All Properties

APPLIED STEPS

fullfilepath

Source

Removed Other Columns

Added Custom

Removed Columns

Expanded Custom

✕ Changed Type

Figure 307 The retrofitted query still works.

Implications of Parameter Tables

Referencing a parameter table gives us a huge amount of flexibility when building solutions. Whether you are building solutions internally in your company and need to share them with team members or other divisions, you can now set them up to read from dynamic folder structures relative to your solution path. If you develop solutions for clients, this is also hugely impactful, as it is doubtful that you'll ever have exactly the same file structure on your system as your client does. The last thing you want to do in either of these situations is send the end user a file with instructions on how to edit the M code.

But the power of parameter tables doesn't end there. Consider each of the following tasks that you may wish to perform:

- Build a calendar table based on the dates in cells in an Excel worksheet
- Drive a filter for a table based on the value in an Excel cell
- Determine which of four Excel tables to load into a solution

By setting up and using a custom function to read from an Excel table, we can accomplish any of these goals. This affords us not only the ability to dynamically drive our content, but also gives us the ability to generate data in an environment more familiar to us, and in some cases do things that Power Query wouldn't otherwise allow us to do.

Again, we need to call out the caveat that **if you are publishing to Power BI, this solution won't work for you, as Power BI doesn't currently support dynamically generating paths to databases and the like**. If you are developing your content in an Excel desktop environment, however, you'll find this to be one of the most useful techniques in this book.

Chapter 24 Dynamic Calendar Tables

When working with Power Pivot in Excel 2010 and 2013, you need to provide your own calendar table for your models. This is really easy in organizations with a cooperative IT department that publishes a calendar for users.

If you don't live in an organization like that, however, things are more difficult. You can reach out to web sources, but those don't work when you're tinkering with your model while sitting in an airplane or on the way out to visit your operations in that mine in Africa. You can also build your calendar in an Excel table, but this leads to challenges when the data keeps expanding, as the date table doesn't automatically expand for you.

For those users, Power Query has come to the rescue. As you'll see, it is super easy to set up a fully dynamic calendar in Excel using Power Query. And building on the techniques from Chapter 23, you can drive the whole thing based on the value in a few Excel cells.

Creating a Dynamic Calendar Table

Creating a full dynamic calendar for your solution requires a total of four steps:

1. Add a parameter table to hold the calendar boundaries.
2. Implement the fnGetParameter function to retrieve the boundaries.
3. Build the basic dynamic calendar framework.
4. Add the required calendar columns.

Building on the methods explored in Chapter 23, in this chapter you'll see that this process is actually quite quick to set up.

Step 1: Adding a Parameter Table

For this example, you'll start from a completely blank workbook, although you could easily retrofit this into an existing model as well. If you happen to already have a Parameter table in your solution, you can simply add new fields to it. If not, you'll have to build the table from scratch.

Remember the key pieces here as you build your table:

- The table must be called Parameters
- There must be a Parameter column and a Value column

You should build the table to hold the start and end dates:

- Start Date   1/1/2014
- End Date   =EOMONTH(TODAY(),0)

When the setup is complete, the table will look as shown below:

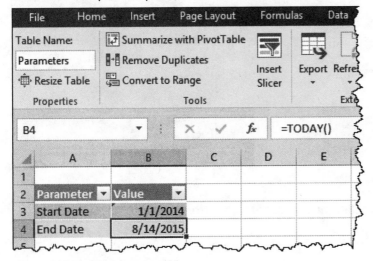

Figure 308 The Parameters table.

The EOMONTH() function has the following syntax:

```
=EOMONTH(start_date,months)
```

If you use 0 for the *months* parameter, the function will return the last day of the given month. If you provide -1, it will be the end of the previous month, and if you use a positive value of 3, the function will give you the end of the month 3 months after the provided date. This function is very useful when driving your calendar table.

Step 2: Implementing the fnGetParameter Function

Once the table is built, you can create the fnGetParameter function:

- Open the Ch24 Examples\fnGetParameter.txt file
- Copy the entire contents of the text file
- Create a new query → From Other Sources → Blank Query
- Go to Home → Advanced Editor
- Highlight all the code in the window → Ctrl+V → Done
- Rename the query fnGetParameter

The fnGetParameter function is now installed as well, ready to be used:

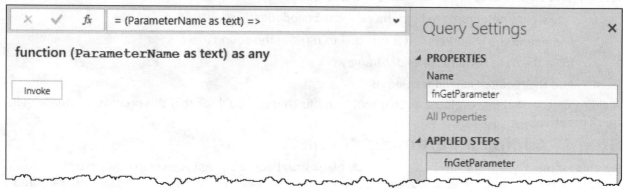

Figure 309 The fnGetParameter function is ready to go.

Step 3: Building the Basic Calendar Framework

With the groundwork quickly laid, you can now get to the real task at hand: building the calendar. Rather than exit the Power Query editor, you can create a new query right inside it:

- Go to Home → New Source → Other Sources → Blank Query
- Rename the query Calendar

You now have a new query with nothing in it at all:

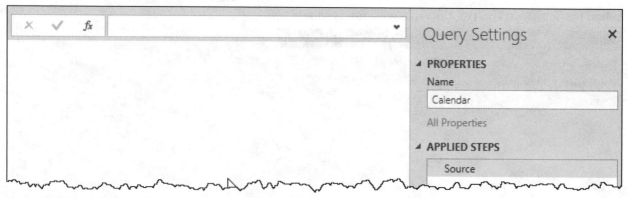

Figure 310 Starting the calendar from a clean slate.

An easier way to start building the calendar, believe it or not, is to start from a simple list. Click inside the formula bar and enter the following formula:

```
={1..10}
```

This creates a list from one to ten:

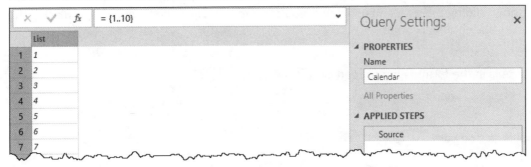

Figure 311 You now have a simple list.

Next, convert this list into a table and see what happens if you change the resulting column into dates:

- Go to List Tools → Transform → To Table
- Leave the default options and click OK
- Right-click Column1 → Change Type → Date
- Right-click Column 1 → Rename → Date

Although it's not exactly the date range you're after, you do actually get the beginning of a calendar table:

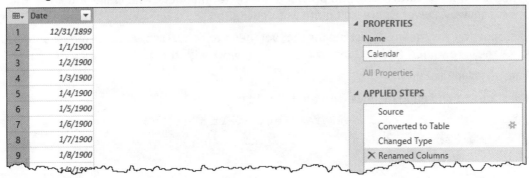

Figure 312 It's a calendar table but a little out of date!

Even though it doesn't necessarily look like it, you're in really good shape here. Remember that parameter table you set up? What if you inserted a couple of steps at the beginning of this query to extract the start and end dates and tried to feed those into the list instead of using 1 to 10? Try it:

- Go to Home → Advanced Editor
- Immediately after the let line, add the following two lines of M code:

```
startdate = fnGetParameter("Start Date"),
enddate = fnGetParameter("End Date"),
```

- Click Done

At this point, it's a good idea to just check both steps and make sure they are actually returning the date that you're expecting them to return.

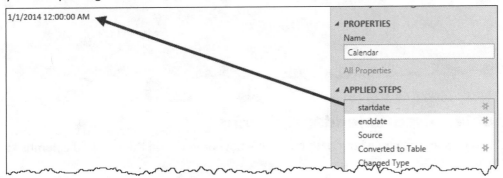

Figure 313 startdate is returning a date as expected.

With the variables now holding the start and end dates, you can sub them into the Source line, replacing the 1 and 10 you put in as placeholders earlier:

- Select the Source step
- Edit the formula in the formula bar to read as shown below:

```
= {startdate..enddate}
```

- Press Enter

Unfortunately, things go sideways:

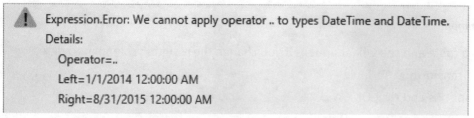

Figure 314 What in the world does this mean?

This error message isn't extremely clear. Better wording would indicate that Power Query can't use the .. operator unless it has numbers on either side. You provided dates, not numbers. And while you know that dates are just numbers anyway, Power Query isn't quite as forgiving.

This is not a show-stopper by any means. It just means that you need to convert these dates into their date serial numbers. Once they are values, Power Query will be able to work with them. Here's what you do:

- Go to Home → Advanced Editor
- Replace the startdate and enddate lines with the following:

```
startdate = Number.From(fnGetParameter("Start Date")),
enddate = Number.From(fnGetParameter("End Date")),
```

- Click Done
- Select the startdate step

startdate is now converted to the date's serial number, 41640. If you step to the end of the query, you can see that you now have a working calendar that runs from January 1, 2014, through the ending date provided by your Excel table:

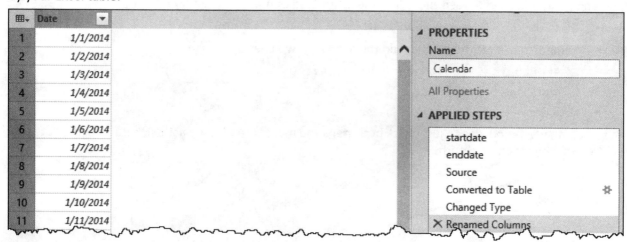

Figure 315 The Calendar table is ready for use.

Step 4: Adding Required Calendar Columns

With the Calendar table set up and covering your date range, it's now time to add the required columns to it. This is actually pretty easy:

- Select the Date column → Add Column → Date → Year → Year
- Select the Date column → Add Column → Date → Month → Month

- Select the Date column → Add Column → Date → Day → Day

As you can see, the Calendar table is really starting to take shape:

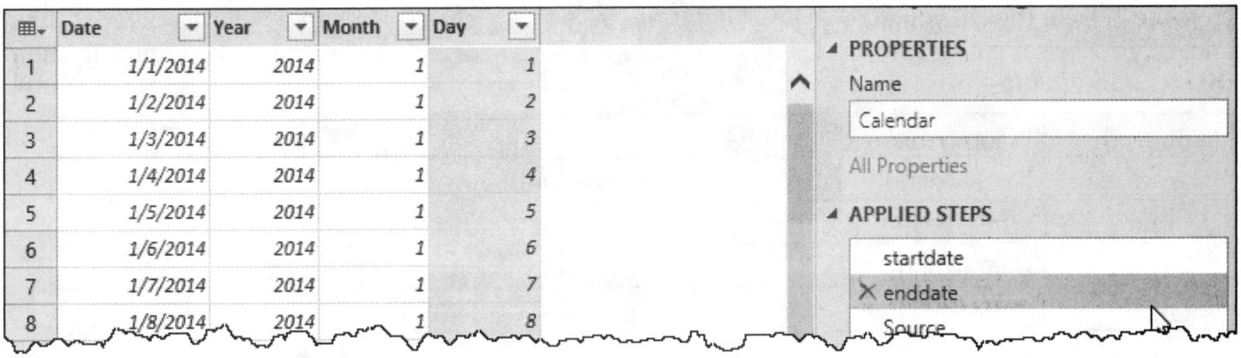

Figure 316 Building out the required columns in the Calendar table.

Power Query has a variety of formats that are very easy to add to the table. However, there are also some formats that don't exist.

Power Query Date Functions

Many of Power Query's date functions are different from Excel's—some subtly and others not so subtly. Therefore, the following pages give you the means to easily work out in Power Query what you already know how to do in Excel.

Excel Date Functions

Excel has a variety of date functions that can be of great benefit when building the Parameters table to drive your calendar. Each of them is explicitly for use in Excel (not Power Query) and can be used to drive either start or end dates to give yourself a range that is scoped nicely to your needs.

To Return	Formula
The current date	TODAY()
End of the current month	EOMONTH(TODAY(),0)
End of last month	EOMONTH(TODAY(),-1)
End of next month	EOMONTH(TODAY(),1)
End of the current year	EOMONTH(TODAY(),12-MONTH(TODAY()))
End of year for date in B25	EOMONTH(B25,12-MONTH(B25))

Date Function Equivalents: Extracting Date Parts

Like Excel, Power Query also has functions specifically targeted at returning parts of dates or offsetting dates. Some key conversions you will want to know are listed here:

Excel Formula	Power Query Version
DAY([Date])	Date.Day([Date])
MONTH([Date])	Date.Month([Date])
YEAR([Date])	Date.Year([Date])
WEEKNUM([Date])	Date.WeekOfYear([Date])
WEEKDAY([Date])	Date.DayOfWeek([Date])
EOMONTH([Date],0)	Date.EndOfMonth([Date])
EOMONTH([Date],-1)+1	Date.StartOfMonth([Date])

Date Function Equivalents: Adding Dates

You're likely to be frustrated if you try to take a valid date or time and just add a value to it in order to increment it. Even though you know that all dates are based on a date serial number, Power Query cannot implicitly convert the data type like Excel can. For this reason, there are a collection of Date.Addx functions to use for this purpose:

Adding x	Excel Formula	Power Query Version
Days	[Date]+x	Date.AddDays([Date],x)
Months	EDATE([Date],x)	Date.AddMonths([Date],x)
Years	EDATE([Date],12*x)	Date.AddYears([Date],x)
Weeks	[Date]+7*x	Date.AddWeeks([Date],x)])

Date Function Equivalents: Returning Text Dates

In order to convert and return dates in a textual format, you would use the TEXT() function in Excel. In Power Query, the equivalent functions are provided by Date.ToText(), but they have an additional wrinkle: Not only is the function case sensitive, but so are the parameters.

To Return	Excel Formula	Power Query Version
Sun	Text([Date],"ddd")	Date.ToText([Date],"ddd")
Sunday	Text([Date],"dddd")	Date.ToText([Date],"dddd")
Aug	Text([Date],"mmm")	Date.ToText([Date],"MMM")
August	Text([Date],"mmmm")	Date.ToText([Date],"MMMM")
Aug 9, 2015	Text([Date],"mmm d, yyyy")	Date.ToText([Date],"MMM d, yyyy")
Aug 09, 2015	Text([Date],"mmm dd, yyyy")	Date.ToText([Date],"MMM dd, yyyy")

Dealing with Date Conversion Errors

Many of the functions listed above require a *date* or *datetime* data type as an input and will return an error if an alternate data type is provided. To guard against this situation, you can wrap the [Date] column input with the Date.From function as shown here:

```
=Date.AddDays(Date.From([DateColumn]),1)
```

Chapter 25 Query Organization

With all the work you've done learning Power Query, you wouldn't expect to suddenly get hit by an error when trying to merge two tables. Unfortunately, this is a real possibility if the tables come from two different data sources.

The Formula.Firewall Error

One of the things that you haven't seen so far in this book is the dreaded Formula.Firewall error, but it can be quite a shock when it hits you. And while there are strategies for avoiding it, it is best if you know up front what causes this nasty error message to appear.

Triggering the Formula.Firewall Error

In the timesheet example that was used through several chapters, recall that you built a fairly robust solution. The solution file is saved in a specific location, and the data files are stored in the Source Files subfolder, which hangs off the solution directory. You've repurposed code to import a single timesheet, turning it into a function and leveraging it to preprocess all the files in the Source Files directory so you can combine them afterward. The data lands nicely in an Excel worksheet (or the Power Pivot Data Model if you were inclined to push it there). What could possibly go wrong?

A scope change. That's what. Suppose your manager tells you that he wants the department for each employee merged in with the data set.

You've got the employee records stored in another Excel file with each employee's name and department. You know you can import from Excel files, and you know how to merge data sets together. How hard can it be? Try it to see:

- Open Ch25 Examples\Query Organization.xlsx
- Create a new query → From File → From Excel Workbook
- Navigate to Ch25 Examples\Departments.xlsx
- Select the EmployeeDepts table

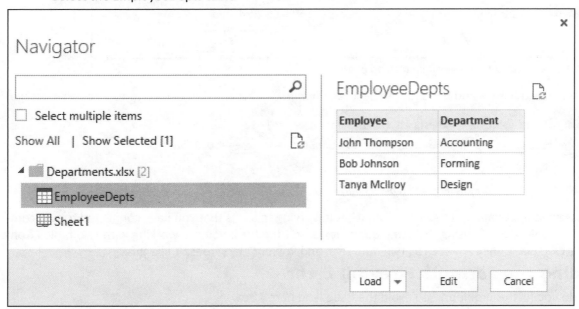

Figure 317 Importing the EmployeeDepts table.

This table looks pretty good. In fact, it looks so good, you try just loading it to a connection right away, as it really doesn't need any modification at all:

- Click the arrow on the Load option → Load To… → Only Create Connection

You get a nice new EmployeeDepts query in your Workbook Queries pane, and all is looking good so far.

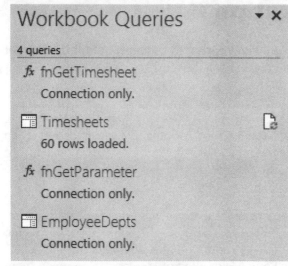

Now merge these tables together:

- Right-click the Timesheets query → Edit
- Go to Home → Merge Queries
- Choose to merge the EmployeeDepts table
- Select the Employee column on each table

Figure 318 Things are looking positive so far.

Oddly, Power Query is unable to determine how many rows will match:

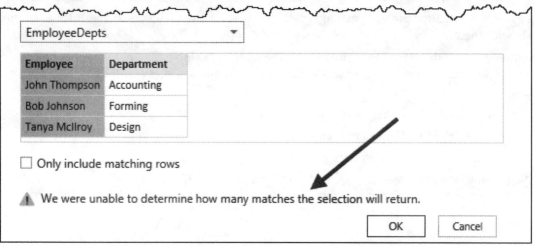

Figure 319 Why is Power Query having matching issues?

Never mind this. Click OK and hope for the best. And *boom*, you get the dreaded Formula.Firewall message:

 Formula.Firewall: Query 'Timesheets' (step 'Merged Queries') references other queries or steps, so it may not directly access a data source. Please rebuild this data combination.

Figure 320 The dreaded Formula.Firewall rears its ugly head.

This message is a bit intimidating. In English, what it is trying to say is that you have connected to two completely different data sets using the same query. It doesn't matter if you are working with two tables from the same workbook; they are seen as two data sets, and Power Query doesn't like this.

Avoiding the Formula.Firewall Error

So how do you fix this problem? You avoid the issue, and here's how:

- Delete the Merged Queries step
- Close the Power Query editor
- Go to the Workbook Queries pane → right-click the Timesheets query → Load To...
- Change the query's load behavior to Only Create Connection
- Confirm that you're okay with Excel removing the table

You now have a connection-only pointer set up to both the Timesheets data and the EmployeeDepts data. Create a new query to merge them:

- Right-click the Timesheets query → Merge
- Choose the EmployeeDepts table
- Select the Employee column on both tables

Notice that this time Power Query identifies the matches:

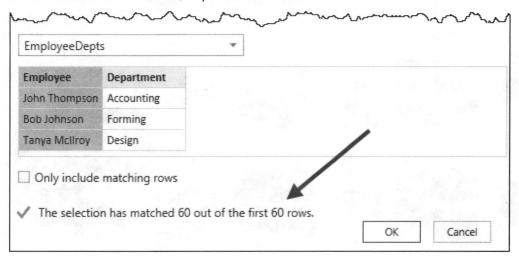

Figure 321 This is much more promising.

With the merges apparently going to happen, you can continue on:

- Click OK
- Rename the query to Consolidated
- Expand NewColumn → no prefix → only the Department column
- Go to Home → Close & Load To... → Existing Worksheet
- Load the data to A1 of the Timesheets worksheet

This time, it works:

	A	B	C	D	E	F	G	H
1	Employee	Expenses	Misc Hrs	OT Hrs	Out	Reg Hrs	Work Date	Department
2	John Thompson	0	0	0	6:00:00 PM	8.5	3/3/2015	Accounting
3	John Thompson	0	0	0	6:00:00 PM	8	3/4/2015	Accounting
4	John Thompson	0	0	0	6:00:00 PM	8.5	3/5/2015	Accounting
5	John Thompson	0	0	0	6:00:00 PM	8.5	3/6/2015	Accounting
6	John Thompson	0	0	0	3:30:00 PM	6.5	3/7/2015	Accounting
7	John Thompson	0	0	0	6:00:00 PM	8.5	3/10/2015	Accounting
8	John Thompson	0	0	0	6:00:00 PM	8.5	3/11/2015	Accounting
9	John Thompson	0	0	0	6:00:00 PM	6	3/12/2015	Accounting
10	John Thompson	0	0	0	6:00:00 PM	8.5	3/13/2015	Accounting
11	John Thompson	0	0	0	6:00:00 PM	8.5	3/14/2015	Accounting
12	Bob Johnson	0	0	0	6:00:00 PM	9.5	3/3/2015	Forming
13	Bob Johnson	0	0	0	6:00:00 PM	8	3/4/2015	Forming

Figure 322 The departments are merged into the data set.

Creating Staging/Loading Queries

The secret to avoiding the Formula.Firewall error is to separate the job of connecting to the database and loading to the end destination. We call these staging queries and loading queries.

You use staging queries to ensure that you create separate queries to extract the initial data from each data source. You then do as many transformations as possible in the staging query in order to get the data into a shape where it can be used by as many other queries as possible. What you never do, however, is try to merge to another data source or load the end result into a worksheet of the Data Model. Both of those tasks are reserved for a loading query.

A loading query is designed to pull data from one or more staging queries and merge or append as required before making any final transformations that are needed. You then set up these queries to load the output to the final destination, whether it's the worksheet or the Data Model.

Visually, the process looks as follows:

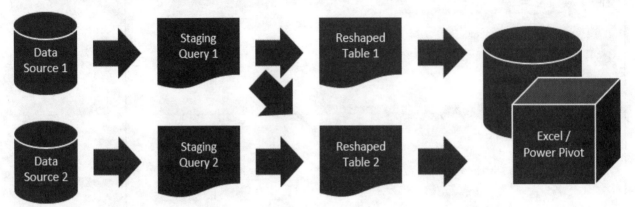

Figure 323 Organizing staging and loading queries.

Technically, combining any two different data sources can cause a Formula.Firewall error to appear; even trying to inject a parameter from an Excel parameter table can trigger the error. If you get a Formula.Firewall error when trying to nest a dynamic parameter call in the middle of a query, try to declare your variable up front rather than avoid the variable declaration and nest the function later in your code. This often resolves that issue.

Caveats

When working with staging and loading queries, you need to be careful in certain cases, especially when the data source you connect to can take advantage of query folding to improve performance. The reason for this is that query folding can be executed only from the primary connection to the data source (the staging query).

When using a staging/loading approach against a database that supports query folding, you should always try to accomplish as many filtering and grouping operations as you can in the staging query. This will allow Power Query to pass the processing job back to the database. *As soon as you move out of your staging query into a secondary staging query or the loading query, no more commands can be passed back to the database to be folded, which means Power Query has to do the processing work.* This can significantly slow down the process. It may also make sense to make several connections to the database to pull individual data sets, allowing the database to do the heavy lifting for you since databases are optimized for the sorting, filtering, and grouping operations.

By contrast, if you are targeting your solution against sources that don't support query folding (such as text or Excel files), it's a good idea to create one staging query to pull in the data and cut it down as much as possible. Then you can create as many secondary staging/loading queries to reshape the data as needed in order to get it into your model. Since there is no ability to take advantage of a more efficient processing engine, you want to bring the data in once and try to make sure each step works with as few records as possible to improve processing time.

You should also be conscious of not trying to set up too many levels of staging queries between your data source and your loading queries. Whereas using one staging query feeding one loading query can be quite easy to follow, things get much more complicated when you start feeding data through five or more intermediate staging queries on the way to the end result. It's a longer trail to process, which could have performance impacts, and most certainly there will be a longer trail to audit should something go wrong. Keeping the query flow tighter will help you when you're trying to debug and maintain your queries.

You should also be aware that Power BI doesn't generally appreciate long trails of queries using the staging and loading query approach. *If you are intending to push your solution to Power BI, it is a good idea to try to keep the approach to a single query if possible and limit the number of steps if not.*

Keeping Queries Organized

As you build more and more Power Query queries, you'll find that things start to get a bit unorganized in the Workbook Queries pane. As it happens, there are a couple ways you can keep a handle on this issue.

Changing Query Display Order

As you start building queries, Power Query will just add them to the bottom of the list, in sequential order. You can, however, change the order in which these queries are presented in the Workbook Queries pane (and Power Query Navigator inside the Power Query editor). To change where a query shows in relation to the others, follow these steps:

- Right-click your query
- Choose Move Up (or Move Down)

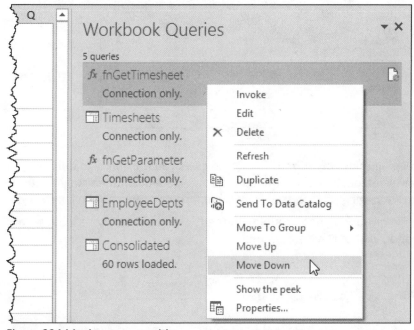

Figure 324 Moving query positions.

Grouping Queries

Ordering is great, but it doesn't help you categorize queries very easily. Especially when using the staging and loading approach, it is very helpful to create groups in which to store each query. Here's how:

- Right-click the fnGetTimesheet query → Move to Group → New Group...
- Call the new group Functions

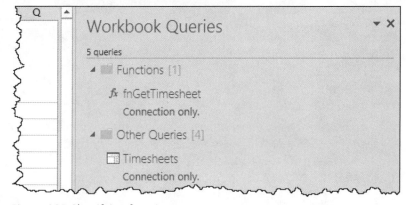

Figure 325 Classifying functions.

You can now move the fnGetParameter into the Functions group as well:

- Right-click fnGetParameter → Move to Group → Functions

It's then just a simple matter of creating new groups for the staging and loading queries as well:

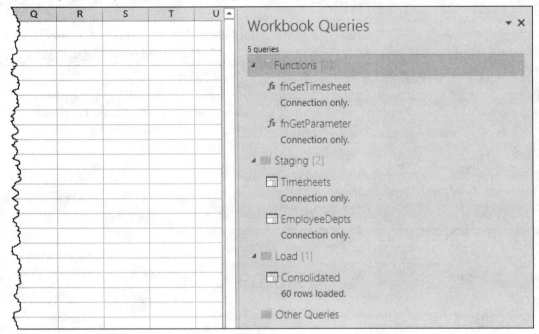

Figure 326 All queries, nicely organized.

This approach works very nicely for keeping things organized, and it also gives you the ability to quickly scan the queries to see if they are set up as expected. If you see the text "x rows loaded" under a staging query, you know it's not actually taking a specific staging role, and you can either fix it or move it to the Load group.

In addition to being able to perform the reordering and grouping in the Excel interface, these features are also supported in the Power Query editor, via the Navigator pane:

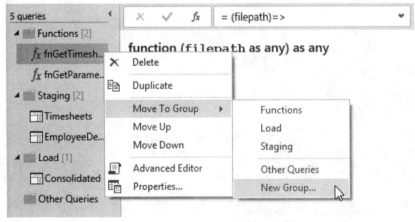

Figure 327 Organizing Power Query queries in the Navigator pane.

Index

A

B

C

D

E

F

G

H

I

K

© 2012
WALTER
MOORE

Continue the Journey

Sharpen your
Power Pivot, Power Map,
Power Map, and Excel
skills with books from
leading authors.

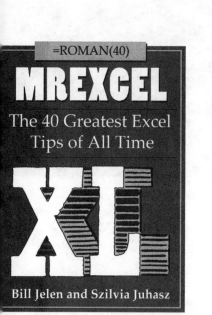

Power Query Workshop

Live Training for You and Your Team

The Workshop Bundle

Live Online Classes

HD Video Recordings

Workshop Labs

FREE eBook

Top Instructors

Q&A Sessions

Scheduling, pricing and our fully detailed course brochure can be found at

http://powerquery.training/course